THE RIPPLE EFFECT
Copyright © 2009 by Sarah Lawson

First Published in the UK by
Paul Mould Publishing

In association with
Lincs Premier Book Productions: zlfdesign@yahoo.co.uk

In association with
Empire Publishing Service www.ppeps.com
P.O. Box 1344, Studio City, CA 91614-0344

A CIP Catalogue record for this book is available either from the British Library or, as below, from the US Library of Congress.

Simultaneously published in
Australia, Canada, Germany, UK, USA

Printed in Great Britain

First Printing 2009

US 13 ISBN 978-1-58690-082-3
UK 13 ISBN 978-1-904959-75-5

Acknowledgements

I have been unable to find the source of the quotation by Zbigniew Herbert on page 1. "Bringing in the Sheaves" on p.18 is a hymn by Knowles Shaw (words) and George A. Minor (music) from ca. 1880. The lines quoted on p.112 are from "The Day is Done" by Henry Wadsworth Longfellow. "Gimme Forty Acres" quoted in chapter 8 is credited to Earl Green and John William Greene. The Erie Canal Song (slightly misquoted) on pp.209-210 is by Thomas S. Allen (1905).

Grateful thanks are due to the following friends who read and commented on the manuscript of *The Ripple Effect* and saved me from many errors of fact, spelling, and geography: Ania Bentkowska, Małgorzata Koraszewska, Magda Lachaut, and Ania Mach. Howard Fritz rendered invaluble help with the map of Poland. Sarah Getty gave me sound advice and saved me from many infelicities. Any remaining errors and infelicities are all my own work.

Prologue

It was 25 years ago that I first set foot in Poland. It was August 1980. I didn't know any Poles nor did I have any Polish connections. I was an American in my 30s married to a Scotsman and living in London. We had given up the car some years before when it flunked its MOT and now cycled everywhere. We rode around London, sailing through the traffic jams on the Old Kent Road. We extended our fondness for our bicycles by taking them with us on summer holidays. We rode down the Cotentin Peninsula and across Brittany; we cycled to York and back through the Fens; we rode up the Loire Valley from Nantes to Blois; we rode across the Afsluitdijk—out of sight of land in both directions—and into Friesland.

I wondered about Poland. It was in the forbidding East, but I was curious to see where so many of my own compatriots had come from. People could travel to eastern Europe now; it was no longer quite the closed prison it had appeared to be in my childhood nor even the exotic adventure it had been in 1963 when I had gone to Prague and East Berlin during a tour of Europe with a group of other American students. During the "Copernicus Year" of 1973 Western tourists had been enticed to Poland with pictures of old buildings and lovely scenery. I had thought about going then, but we decided to visit my mother in Indiana instead. Poland was still waiting, so in the summer of 1980 we got visas and made the cumbersome arrangements about money necessary when visiting countries with "soft" currency.

We had a youth hostel handbook, new orange nylon travel bags for the back of our bikes, and some experience of travelling around northern Europe on the cheap. The roads in Poland were going to be flat and lightly travelled. We were going to cover a lot of ground and see interesting and unusual places.

We rode up to Liverpool Street Station and got on a train to Harwich, where we caught the ferry for the Hook of Holland. We bought a through ticket to the exotic destination of Warsaw. My only associations with Warsaw at that moment were probably an Uprising and a Concerto.

But now, 25 years later, friends in London say, "But how do you know all these people with extraordinary names like Małgorzata and Agnieszka and Andrzej? And who is Ula? And Mirka and Magda and Marysia? And Władek and Witek? And Tomek, Staszek, various Anias, and the others we can't pronounce? How do you come to know all these Poles?"

Looking back, I find it a fairly bizarre story myself.

This trip, one of our many bicycle jaunts, was going to have far-reaching effects on my life. On our other similar travels we had met lots of people—B&B landladies, fellow Youth Hostellers from various places, Australians doing Europe—people to chat with agreeably for an evening, even people to keep in touch with briefly and exchange snapshots with. I could never have predicted how this trip would differ from the others, and because it was to Poland it would be easy to isolate the later "Polish" element in my life. As the years passed the Polish strand—negligible at first—became more and more marked until a place that had been just another foreign country gradually became almost a second home. If we had gone to Inverness or Cologne that summer some other odd chain of events might have resulted, but I doubt it. Poland is a special case.

Poland in 1980 was not quite like any other place we might have visited. It was a very unusual place that summer, but even so, that wasn't the real reason it has had such an effect on me for the past 25 years. The real reason was something so tiny that I completely missed it at the time.

Sarah Lawson
London
Dobrzyń nad Wisłą
2005

Contents

Alastair Pettigrew and Sarah Lawson sometime after the trip to Poland in 1980. My bike here is a folding French Sutter with three derailleur gears. I took my full-size Hercules Balmoral to Poland.

A wooden die can be described only from without. We are therefore condemned to eternal ignorance of its essence. Even if it is quickly cut in two, immediately its inside becomes a wall and there occurs the lightning-swift transformation of a mystery into a skin.

Zbigniew Herbert

Chapter One

The Wooden Die

We crossed the Oder, which changes names in the middle and becomes the Odra. The young man in our compartment didn't want us to miss the significance of it. "Polen!" he said, gesturing toward the train windows. "Polska."

We admired the silver birches of Poland now passing outside the windows. We said "Yes" and "*Ja*". In another week we would learn to say "*Tak*".

The train didn't stop until we got to Kunowice, where we had to change our money vouchers into złoty. The customs inspectors didn't seem interested in our bags but they examined our compartment-mate's suitcase very carefully. I watched him unfasten his suitcase. It contained immaculately folded shirts. It was indescribably neater than my own case and he was at the *end* of his journey. By the end of my journey, my bag would not be fit to be inspected by the fastidious. The man's other suitcase was filled with oranges. In August 1980 when you had the chance to go to West Germany, you brought back oranges.

This time yesterday we were stowing our bikes down in the hold with all the cars and trucks, roping them together with some other bikes. We both, Alastair and I, have bright orange cylindrical bags for this trip; they fit on the back of our bikes but we can carry them by hand, too. Such bags are increasingly fashionable now in the summer of 1980, as though people need to carry rolled-up sleeping bags with them everywhere or segments of yule logs. We carry our orange yule-log cases with us on the upper decks of the ferry, guarding them carefully as though the other passengers, with quite enough of their own impedimenta, are waiting for a chance to appropriate our modest cycling clothes and road maps.

1

It is a sunny day in early August on the intensely blue North Sea. The sea is a deep, deep, blue-green, a breathtakingly rich colour. The foam from our boat is a brilliant white and feathers out into a green and white marbling where the ship disturbs the water. The colours are dazzling as I watch the sea from the rail of the *St. Edmund.* We are merely out of Harwich bound for the Hook of Holland but I stare into the water and wonder where the bottom is and whether there are really ancient tree trunks there from the distant age when it was dry land.

The other passengers seem to be British, German and Dutch. Once before I saw Poles on this crossing, because our ferry connects with a train that goes to Warsaw and ultimately to Moscow but I have not noticed any Poles or Russians on board today. The Poles have been having trouble this summer. We have read about food shortages and only a month ago floods devastated some important farming land. In the newspapers there were indistinct photos of flat grey surfaces where there should have been rolling fields.

The adults on the boat are reading paperbacks, as though we are all on a leisurely study holiday. We are reading Isaac Bashevis Singer because we are going to Poland, and deep in my orange bag I have a small volume of Shakespeare's sonnets. Just as travellers carry condensed or folding versions of the more bulky things they use at home, so I have these sonnets, the most condensed and portable form of English literature. They will comfort me when I have been surrounded by Polish for a week. I will want to look at some English, if only a ketchup label, and what better English to look at than "Let me not to the marriage of true minds / Admit impediments" and so forth?

At the Hook of Holland we find our train and get on one of the two cars going all the way to Warsaw or Warschau or Warszawa. The carriages that go on to Moscow are Russian and carry notices in Russian, French, German, Italian and English. You have to scan through the whole paragraph to find a bit you can read telling you not to lean out of the window or drink the water.

We search for a snack bar ("Surely they've got a samovar or something on the Russian coach," we say to each other) but we find nothing. However, we have a big plastic Safeway shopping bag full of food. We munch our groceries while we have the compartment to ourselves, which is all across Holland and into Germany as far as Hannover and Braunschweig, where more people get in. It is past one in the morning but we speak to them in a friendly way. They are Poles who are returning home to Poznań. We all try to sleep, except in Berlin, when the train stops and it is impossible to sleep. We sit in three different Berlin train stations. At dawn we sit and sit in the Ostbahnhof. Grey-uniformed Vopos guard all the doors of the train. They stand with their legs wide apart and with their backs to the train doors. What exactly are they guarding? Are they afraid that someone will creep into this train station in the early morning while the cleaners are sweeping up crumpled cigarette detritus and sneak onto our eastbound train?

When we move off at last, we see our bicycles still on the platform. In alarm we point at them and call to the conductor. He tells us in a bit of English and a bit of German that everything is quite in *Ordnung*. There is no baggage car between Berlin and Warsaw. Our bicycles, however, will come on a later train. Only an hour later. There is no mistake; this is all perfectly normal. All we have to do is go to Centralna Station in Warsaw and collect the bicycles later in the afternoon after we arrive at Warsaw Gdańska. Presumably the confident, fatherly conductor believes all this but in fact it is not at all true, as we discover during the following week.

Out in the train corridor, where people go to stretch their legs or have a cigarette, a young man is standing looking out of the open window. The wind is blowing his collar-length blond hair back as we pass through the broad plains of western Poland. He is a strong, well-built young man and he is an absolute picture of Socialist Realism. I see him in profile with his square jaw and his

3

fair hair and I think *he* must be the one in Soviet art who is always ploughing fields and operating blast furnaces.

Warsaw is big, modern-looking, very post-war. The scale is a little bewildering. It seems to be designed for a race of giants, not your average 5'6" human being like me. The main streets have three lanes of traffic going each way. Add in the tram tracks and the wide sidewalks, and the distance between the buildings is vast. We like the Old Town better. It was lovingly rebuilt after it was demolished in the War. ("I never go there," says Krysia, a teacher we meet. "Oh, I take students sometimes, but I don't like it at all. I remember the way it used to be before the War. It's not the same now.")

The boy from Gdańsk is brimming over with his good luck to be born Polish. One of President Carter's main advisers is Polish, he says, the prime minister of Austria has a Polish name, and most important of all, the Pope is one of us! Important Poles are everywhere. The boy from Gdańsk doesn't mind when people call his hometown Danzig. Lots of Polish cities have both Polish and German names, he says. It doesn't matter at all whether you call it Gdańsk or Danzig. Wrocław or Breslau, it's the same place, and it's Polish and he loves it.

Nina keeps a large picture-book about Warsaw during the War in her office at the youth hostel. "My father was sent to Auschwitz on the train," she tells me, "but he escaped off the train and came home. Again they sent him to Auschwitz and again he came home. He was fighting in the Uprising of Warszawa. My husband's mother was in Auschwitz. She has the numbers on her arm, here. She still has them now." Nina was born during the Warsaw Uprising and is a year younger than I am. She was lucky to survive babyhood. It would have been very extraordinary if I had *not* survived. The place where I was born has not seen warfare since Tecumseh was defeated at the Battle of Tippecanoe.

Nina shows me pictures of Poles being hanged on their own front door lintels by the Nazis. Buildings were dynamited; Poles were mown down with machine guns. "I hate war," she says simply. "I have two children. I want only peace." I assure her that I feel exactly the same way. But I have only the ordinary reasons for preferring peace to war.

"It should be very simple to find vegetarian dishes in Poland," we had said to friends before we left. We had heard all about the meat shortages and had seen pictures of the queues. In restaurants, however, most dishes contain meat in some guise or other. Salads are not plentiful, and unless we want to live on desserts, we are obliged to order meat in restaurants. We have our own cheese sandwiches for lunch, and until it runs out, Grape-Nuts for breakfast, but the evening meal is a problem. We try at first. In a cafeteria where we can see what we are getting I choose a plate of *barszcz* (beet soup) and something like cylindrical doughnuts or fried bread. The "doughnut" turns out to have a layer of grey fish paste in the middle. At other times the *barszcz* is booby-trapped with dumplings containing sausage meat. At length we begin ordering fish or chicken just to avoid the sausage and fish paste.

A sign saying *Lody* or *Gofry* stops us in our tracks. The former is delicious ice cream and the latter are sweet waffles like French *gauffres*. Neither of them contains fish paste. Although these ice cream stands are easy to find, ordinary restaurants are not. Sometimes we stumble upon them because we happen to look in a window at the right moment or we see a small sign that seems to indicate an eating place. They don't seem to advertise themselves much or care greatly whether you patronise them.

I am not prepared for all the denim. Everyone is wearing jeans. There is even more denim on the streets of Warsaw than in a Western European or American city. What adds a slight surreal touch to it all is that, although no one seems actually to *speak* English, they *wear* English. Here comes a girl wearing a khaki-coloured blouse with "U.S. Army" brightly embroidered on the pocket. Other people wear near-nonsense phrases on their clothes made up of words from pop songs and words like *Love*, *Sport*, *Club*, *American*, or *City*. These are put together in random combinations, yielding, for example, *City Club* or *American Sport*. It all seems unbelievably absurd to me until I remember that I have a cheese dish marked *Caws* although I do not speak Welsh. A Welsh-speaking person might find my cheese dish, or rather my possession of it, ridiculous. The fact is that foreign words, for various reasons, are fascinating. They are fascinating because we know what they mean, and fascinating because we do not know what they mean. *Uwaga* is fascinating because I have learned that it means "Attention!" or "Look out!" and is written on signs where cars may come out of concealed drives or side-roads. *Dwuprzejazdowy* is fascinating because it is on the bus tickets and I haven't the foggiest idea what it means.

The conductor on the train in early-morning Berlin had been right the—bikes arrived at Centralna Station. But that was about 10 days later. One of the bicycle bells had been removed by sticky fingers somewhere between the Ostbahnhof and Centralna. On top of that the young lout at Centralna wanted a tip; a couple of hundred złoty would do nicely, thanks. But in the meantime we are without private wheels. The trams are amazingly cheap—about a penny for a ride of any distance. The trains likewise are only about a penny a kilometre. After seeing the main sights of Warsaw and growing very, very weary of enquiring after our bikes every day at Centralna, we decide to go by train to Wrocław and Kraków, far to the south.

In other Western countries, you buy a ticket and wait for the train to come in. When it does, disembarking passengers step down onto the platform, and then the waiting passengers board the train, find a seat that appeals to them, and stow their minimal luggage or other belongings nearby. In Poland you wait in a queue at a ticket window, which may close before you reach it. If you succeed in getting a ticket, which is at least unbelievably cheap, you go nervously to the platform and work out where you should stand, as one long platform may accommodate several trains. If you are Polish, as opposed to a tourist, you carry with you a big old suitcase with a rope around it, three bulging plastic bags with broken handles, a length of copper tubing, and two cabbages. When your train arrives, you make a mad dash for the door and begin heaving your baggage up the steps of the train. Some people trying to get off climb over your bags, dragging their own bulky collection of oddments with them. If you have a travelling companion it is all much easier. He climbs through a window, stakes a claim on the seats, and helps you wangle your baggage through the same window. You are well ahead of the game a moment later when you throw yourself at the train steps like a salmon desperate to get upstream.

The little boy sitting opposite me in the train carriage has obviously been well brought up. He knows it is impolite to eat in front of people without offering them something. He carefully opens his bag of potato crisps and offers them around. The woman next to him, who seems to be his mother or aunt, takes one, the man across from him politely declines, as do Alastair and I. I have good reason. I don't want to eat food, I don't want to look at food, I don't want to think about food. It must have been something I ate yesterday. Had fish paste been concealed in something? The only thing I can bear to think about is grapefruit juice. Everything else is nauseating.

The child has no sooner finished his potato crisps than he is opening another bag of something salty and offering it around. I try to doze and get as horizontal as I can without tripping people entering or leaving the compartment. As the train passes the half-way point to Wrocław the boy moves on to sweets and biscuits. He always offers them to all of us and I always decline. Alastair thoughtfully finds a can of orange juice in the buffet car. It is distressingly warm, but it is almost the first food I have had all day.

7

Now the boy is offering everyone chocolate and orange biscuits. He is serious in his generosity and seems hurt that I always refuse. "*Proszę,*" he says, with real sadness in his eyes, please take one. I know he won't go away until I take one. I take a Jaffa cake. "Thank you," I say in English. (It is interesting that it doesn't matter what you say in these situations as long as you say something in the right tone of voice.) The boy is genuinely relieved that I have finally accepted one of his biscuits. I am feeling slightly better. I sit up and eat my biscuit as appreciatively as I can. (My stomach tells me quietly, "All right, just this once, but *watch it!*")

He is being such an impeccable little gentleman. He must be about 10 or 11. I must be nice to him. I must say something. I will introduce us to them. I had better give the international version of my husband's Scottish name. I point to Alastair next to me and say clearly, "Alexander". Then pointing to myself, "Sarah". Now with the same exaggerated movement I point to the boy. He looks blank, but the woman next to him understands and explains to him. So we learn that he is called Mariusz and his companion is Maria. Except that she isn't his companion. Maria is going to visit her son at his army base near Wrocław, and Mariusz is going home after spending a month with his grandmother in Warsaw while his mother had a baby. This is his first long trip by himself, and Maria has taken him under her wing. Maria, bless her, speaks some English. It is extraordinary how little of a common language is really necessary to have long, friendly conversations in foreign trains with the right people. The man who left our compartment to have a smoke in the corridor when I had been feeling so blotto (I remember moving my feet for him, or was it him, or were they my feet?) must be surprised to return and find us exclaiming over Maria's family snapshots as though we were old and dear friends. She is an architect and teaches in a technical college. We talk about *Król Lear,* now playing in Warsaw, where they like our celebrated dramatist Szekspir.

Mariusz has taken to peering out of the window and announcing every few minutes that we are approaching Wrocław. What he takes for his hometown later turns out to be an out-of-the-way shunting yard or a village. His homesickness is reaching the acute stage of the not-quite-returned traveller. He is Marco Polo mistaking every coastal island for Venice.

I tear a page out of my notebook and write my name and address on it and give it to Maria. She writes her name and address and telephone number for me and invites us to come and stay when we are in Warsaw again.

Later when we are standing in the forecourt of the Wrocław railway station looking at the town map, we see Mariusz emerge from the station with his father. They are talking with great delight and animation. Suddenly his father stoops down and gives Mariusz a spontaneous and joyful hug. Marco Polo is about to get home and tell of his adventures and meet the new family member.

The Wrocław youth hostel is some distance from the centre of town and on the banks of the Odra, which meanders through Wrocław in several strands. The youth hostel is alive with mosquitoes and other flying insects. It is also alive with graceful house martins swooping in the evening, scooping up the flying insects in acrobatic arcs. There are two nests in the arches of the gateway, and the pairs of martins are raising a second clutch of fledglings in this place where the air is full of unsuspecting snacks.

The next day is Sunday and when we go to look at the churches in the city they are filled with worshippers. It is standing room only everywhere. The people who can't get into the packed main nave sit crowded into side chapels. This church near the University is in the high baroque style, and it already seems crowded with statuary, even without counting the flesh-and-blood people. The statues represent saints and angels, and they stand in the usual places and postures, but also in unexpected crannies, like along a cornice high up over the nave

9

of the church. They perch there as though they, too, had come late and couldn't find a conventional place to sit. They are as inaccessible and as weightless as the nesting martins at the youth hostel on the Odra.

Polish is all around us. We hear it and we see it. The sound is one of *s* and *z* and *sh* sibilants. It looks at first like a bad draw in Scrabble, full of consonants and no vowels. Gradually we crack bits of the code. A *y* is the sign of the plural, and street names seem to be in the genitive. *Woda* means "water", *herbata* means "tea", *kawa* is "coffee", and *piwo* is "beer". Our bicycles are *rowery*. Bread is *chleb* (the same as Russian, Alastair remarks), and "apple" is *jabłko*. These words contain enough vowels, but most words look to us like unpronounceable consonant clusters. They remind me of machine parts locked together with no oil.

One day I get into a conversation with a young woman who speaks a little English. English, she tells me, is such a difficult language, and full of such strange sounds! She shows me how English typically sounds. She opens her mouth wide and makes round vowel noises. "Ooooh, aaaah, wowowo," she says. So that's what English sounds like if you have Polish ears. *Touché.*

In the cellar of the town hall in Wrocław there is a restaurant, but when we look at the menu it might as well be a page from the phone directory. We realize we have no idea what to order. A Polish soldier and his wife sit across the table from us. He must be from the same army base as Maria's son. I ask if they speak English and they do. We ask their advice about the menu. We are still trying to avoid meat, but it is not as easy as we had expected when we read about the meat shortages in Poland. In fact, it is almost impossible to order a meal that does not contain meat in some shape or form. Our soldier knows about vegetarians. He met one once when he was in Syria with his army unit. (Syria?) I say I like *barszcz* and he finds omelettes on the menu, so it all looks very hopeful. When the waitress says there are no omelettes, the soldier comes to our rescue with

10

something else he has found. It is called "steak" but he assures us that it is made with eggs, really. So we ask for the "steak", but when it comes it is made with meat, really. Anyway, the rest of the meal is meatless and very Polish: red cabbage and potatoes and a salad of cucumber slices in thin cream. The salad is called *mizeria* and is always dependably meatless, unlike the borscht, which is sometimes laced with sausage. *Mizeria* sounds unnecessarily sinister; it is simple and good.

The gypsy musicians in the main square in Kraków entertain us with their spirited playing. We have been looking at the famous woodcarvings in the basilica and now we are having a cup of tea at a table in the square. A man in a colourful regional costume moves about among the tables offering himself to be photographed for a small consideration of złoty. A nice way to make your living, being clicked at by a harmless, summer-long firing squad of holiday-makers. A cheap way to travel—in the winter he will be projected onto screens and blank living-room walls all over the world. The gypsy violinist is playing what seems to be an ordinary violin, but it is a moment before I realise that it is really a violin, because he is holding it the wrong way around and bowing it with the wrong hand. He holds the fingerboard close to his chest, and the other end of the fiddle is partly inside his shapeless overcoat. He manages the bow with his left hand in a skilful, if highly individual, way. It is as though he had never seen a violin before but found one in the street and, being naturally musical, figured out how to get sounds out of it. *He* is the one I photograph, not the peacock in the embroidered jacket and the peculiar trousers.

Just before the train to Wieliczka is supposed to come, there is an announcement that causes everyone else on our platform to rush to the end of it, down some steps, and off to some distant platform like a herd of White Rabbits running past Alice. We sit tight and of course miss the train. A young couple stroll up, also having just missed the train. Alastair nods to the young man, whom he recognizes from the Kraków youth hostel last night. We all say little pleasantries in our own languages. Before long we have learned that the next train will be along in a half hour and that our new friends are called Jurek and Bożena and are from Bydgoszcz. We have coffee together in the station buffet and find that he is a policeman and she works in a factory that makes electrical cables. We are all going to see the salt mines at Wieliczka.

We are amazed at the communication that can go on with minimal, or no, language. Every small-talk remark or question becomes an adventure in improvised mime. We laugh delightedly at each other's ingenuity. By the time we get to Wieliczka we are all accomplished mime artists. We have had a bizarre but mutually comprehensible conversation about Russia, birch trees, and the price of petrol. We have a pocket dictionary to resort to in a pinch, and I have a notebook and pen.

At Wieliczka we find a long line of people all waiting to get into the salt mines. We have plenty of time to invent new topics of conversation for our new-found hobby of unconventional communication. We discover a small pool of international words as we go along.

When Jurek discovers that there are two entrance fees for the mines, one for Poles and one for foreigners, he is indignant on our behalf. He and Bożena instantly decide that we must pass ourselves off as Poles and that they will help us. We do not want to cheat the Polish People's Republic out of any revenue, and anyway the surtax for foreigners is not very much. We had to change our British pounds into złoty at the rate of the equivalent of 15 US dollars per day, each. We have been spending nowhere near that much because everything is remarkably cheap—food, travel, overnight accommodation. But we do not want to offend Jurek and Bożena, who want to save us money. Our new system of communication is not quite up to explaining our reservations, so we go along with their plan. We are not really skinflints, but we hate to look like rich foreigners, even when, by all meaningful local comparisons, we are rich foreigners.

Jurek buys all four tickets and, placing Alastair and me between them, he and Bożena keep up a jolly line of repartee that seems, to the casual observer, to include all four of us.

The salt mines are a great tourist attraction. For miles underground, passages extend in all directions and on a dozen levels. The first ones were dug in the 12th century and the mines are still worked today. Over the years things not strictly to do with salt mining have accumulated in the mines. There is an asthma clinic that takes advantage of the excellent air underground; there is what appears to be a basketball floor and a proscenium stage; there are sculptures in rock salt; there are tableaux and chandeliers made of salt; there is a post office and a strange dark lake.

We four go back to Kraków in the early afternoon. In the sign language at which we are now so effortlessly and unselfconsciously expert we compare what we will do in the afternoon. They have certain errands to do; we intend to visit Wawel Castle. I offer my wristwatch and by pointing to the numerals we agree to meet again at 7:30.

With such smoothness that we might all be faultlessly fluent in each other's language, we meet at the appointed hour and go to the restaurant Jurek has in mind. It is a hotel restaurant and Alastair and I, resigned crypto-vegetarians, settle on the baked fish. It is very good, and we have the standard *mizeria* and some excellent beer. Jurek then orders large quantities of vodka for everyone and urges us to bolt it all down at once. I have no flair for bolting firewater, and sip it instead like brandy, but that is not very satisfactory either. I find straight vodka unsatisfactory, period, but after several little glasses of it we have an extravagant and emotional leave-taking, standing in the market square of Kraków in the rain kissing each other good-bye and praising the concepts of friendship and world peace. Jurek and Bożena go off in the direction of the train station to catch the late-night train to Zakopane, and we go in the opposite direction, none too steadily, through the black, glittery streets to the hostel.

In Wawel Castle in Kraków the exquisite marble floors must be protected from tourists' shoes. We select some felt-soled mules to put on over our street shoes and then wander through the fine old rooms of this former royal palace. It is a Renaissance building with French and Venetian furniture. There are Brussels tapestries depicting scenes from Genesis; there are remarkable coffered ceilings and walls covered with Spanish leather. All this, I keep thinking, has been dragged over at least one range of mountains, or else hundreds of miles up the Vistula, to satisfy the demands of royal grandeur. We are charmed. It is not the same as such castles and palaces in Britain and western Europe, but yet all the features have been taken from western Europe.

The next day we leave Kraków by train for Warsaw. We decide to travel first class, because it is cheap and second class has been very crowded. We almost *need* to spend a bit of money, because we are coming out absurdly ahead of the 15-dollar budget that has been forced upon us. Our first-class compartment is roomier than the second-class ones, but all the seats are filled. The walls are thin between our compartment and the next one, and we can hear snatches of a conversation or argument in the next compartment. Alastair, who once took an evening class in Russian, surmises that the language is Russian, but all Slavic languages sound alike to me. The arm rests of our seats are somehow connected to those in the neighbouring compartment, for when the conversation (or argument) grows heated and the man next door pounds his arm rest emphatically, my arm rest also jumps and twitches in an eerie, possessed way. When it happens the other people in my compartment smile and I try to think of a suitable expression to assume. To overhear a voice is one thing, but to have your arm nudged by an unknown and unseen man is more than odd.

Tadeusz lived in England for several years after the War, when he was in the Free Polish Air Force there, but the call of his homeland was too great and he went back to Poland. He is retired and lives in a busy, odd-job leisure in Ostrołęka, north-west of Warsaw on the Narew. His wife, he tells us, was in Auschwitz, and at the end of the war she was sent to Sweden to recover her health and general balance. One day Tadeusz's wife was walking in a public park and found a wallet lying on a bench. She picked it up and took it to a police station, having adjusted to the pervasive honesty in peace-time, civilian Sweden. Instead of praise, however, the Swedish police regarded her gesture with some displeasure. "They said, 'You must take this back to where you found it right away! Someone may come back to look for it and be upset not to find it!'" So she took the wallet back and put it on the park bench.

When we get back to Warsaw and extract our bicycles from the toils of the Centralna train station, we can hardly wait to get on them and hit the road. Much as we have enjoyed public transport, cyclists never like to be separated from their bicycles for very long. We cycle across the Vistula, a startlingly wide river, to the part of Warsaw called Praga. We ride down a wide boulevard named after Jerzy Waszyngton. We cope with tram tracks and cobbles. We have our own wheels again! Now to tackle the real roads!

My bicycle is an old Hercules Balmoral with three hub gears. I bought it in Glasgow in 1967 when I was a student there, and it has been with me in Ireland, France and The Netherlands, besides Scotland and England. I have ridden it all over London. Objectively, it is nothing special. It is unfashionably heavy. It has straight handlebars and only those three hub gears instead of dropped handlebars and eighteen derailleur gears. To complete the amateurish image, I have a wicker basket on the handlebars. I am devoted to this old bike. I tried to get rid of it once but found that I couldn't. I had decided to buy a mixte frame, still

15

with straight handlebars and hub gears, but five instead of three. My preliminary enquiries suggested that this combination did not—could not possibly—exist, but before I went much further I discovered that I could not bring myself to discard the old Hercules anyway. It was one of the first purchases I made when I went to Glasgow to study. It cost £18/19/11 at Halfords. It had been marked down slightly because it was the end of the season (the Michaelmas Term was about to begin) and it was still unsold. And now, in 1980, I am too sentimentally attached to it ever to get rid of it.

Alastair's bicycle looks even more frivolous, if that is possible, for a long trip. It is a Raleigh with 20-inch wheels. It is a replacement for his old yellow Moulton Speed-Six, a sporty little bike with dropped handlebars, 16-inch wheels and six derailleur gears. He was crazy about his Moulton, except on bad road surfaces, and it looked odd enough to cause a lot of gratifying comment in bicycle-conscious Holland when we were there eight years ago. But it became harder and harder to get the narrow tyres for it, and he finally had to get rid of it. This Raleigh is blue, with three gears and straight handlebars. It is speedy enough for our pace, which is generally about 50 to 60 miles a day, and it has the advantage of being more compact than the conventional bike.

We have a good map of Warsaw and a detailed map of the Mazurian region, but only sketchy maps for the roads between. We strike off out of Warsaw one morning in the right direction, but soon find our road getting more and more primitive. Near a junction between our sandy road and a dirt road with grass growing in the middle, we ask directions of four farm workers and get, as near as we can tell, four different opinions about each road. If there is a consensus, it is that each road leads somewhere in both directions if you follow it long enough. We thank them and continue down the slightly better road covered with hard-packed sand. They are still arguing among themselves for as long as we can hear them.

Soon we come to a river, perhaps a tributary of the Narew. The road turns along the side of the river and seems to go in the wrong direction for us, but just as we are beginning to feel perplexed, a little ferry sets off from the opposite side. The ferry holds only three passengers and a little wagon containing empty fruit crates. The passengers are an old woman, a young man, the old man who operates the ferry, and a German shepherd that has seen it all before and is plainly bored with this ferry and the other passengers. We ask them if the large road beyond this river is Road 11. Everyone but the dog pores over the map and offers conflicting opinions. The old woman motions for Alastair to come away with her, then she picks up a stick and draws in the dust how we should proceed to the next town. Meanwhile the young man explains his theory to me in German. We thank them and go across the river, where a man in bathing trunks is fishing. He is rather distinguished looking, even in bathing trunks, and gives us his opinion in German about our route. We thank him and go off down the road and eventually, to our surprise and relief, mixed in equal parts, come to Road 11.

In spite of our resolve to stick to main roads, we find ourselves on a *too* main road with uncomfortably heavy traffic. We watch the uneven road surface and the fast cars shooting past us and agree to turn off on the next side road. We want to cut across to a roughly parallel road that we hope will be good but not too busy.

We were continually hopping off our bicycles to take pictures of the bizarre road signs. The inhabitants of Przasnysz, however, would find our habits more bizarre than the name of their town.

The intervening road is bad news. Some of it is cobbled in much the way the Via Appia must have been in its heyday. Other parts of the road are bad in many, many different ways. Somehow we manage to cover 57 miles on the first day.

It is harvest time in rural Poland, and the whole family is out raking the hay and binding the barley sheaves. Fields are full of people rather than machinery. We meet horse-drawn wagons on the roads. Women in long skirts and kerchiefs work in the fields, as do children of all ages. After a few days of this, I find myself humming the old hymn "Bringing in the sheaves, bringing in the sheaves, we shall come rejoicing bringing in the sheaves". The main reason to rejoice, I now realize, is that the back-breaking labour is finally over. The sheer labour for a loaf of bread! This is the way my ancestors farmed. My grandfather in 1900 in Indiana ploughed with a team of horses and cut the corn by hand. He worked under the hot sun in those cornfields until, hating the undependable horses until tears came to his eyes, he found an excuse to move to town. I don't picture my grandmother working in the fields, though. I imagine her frying chickens and baking pies with the other farm wives and laying out the tables under the trees for all the threshing hands. These fields are like an animated family photograph album in colour instead of sepia, but containing, for all my romanticism, somebody else's family.

At dusk we pass an old woman leading her cow home. She has been out with it all day leading it from one pasturing place to another and tethering it with the long metal stake she carries. She is a picture, but I am not quite such a camera buff that I want to jump off my bike and record her appearance. What would she think of the crazy foreigner, evidently neglecting a barley field or livestock of her own somewhere, with nothing better to do than snap a camera at a person just out bringing the cow home?

While some of the farms are small traditional family businesses, others seem to be the exact opposite. We see farms that are as large-scale and mechanized as the others are small and hand-cultivated. In one field a tank corps of combines works the grain; six or eight of them, staggered in a diagonal line, look like a picture of Kansas. Later another huge field stretches beside our road. After a few minutes I realize that it is *all one field*. We cycle at least a mile before we come to the next fence, and it seems to stretch off away from the road for about another mile or more. If it is a mile square, I think, it is 640 acres. It's the biggest field of grain I've ever seen.

We come back for the night to find the light on in our room, the window open, and our clothes scattered over the beds. Someone has been going through our bags and has fled when they heard our footsteps. The thief has escaped with exactly £1.70 in British coins. Still, perhaps we should report it.

But how do you report a theft when you know about 12 words of the language and none of them pertains to crime? I get out my little English-Polish dictionary and begin looking up relevant words. I arrange these words on a sheet of paper so that, I hope, they will suggest the order of events and cause and effect. "Last night at 9:30," I write (because I intend to give this to someone the next morning) "thief. through window. steal 130 złoty English money". That seems to cover it.

The next morning the young woman in charge of the establishment reads my composition. She is the bursar of what is a college in term time, but in August it is a minimal hotel. She is about 30 and dresses with a flair. A stylish red scarf is clasped at her throat and she wears a crisp summer dress. She is shocked at what she reads. She speaks hurriedly and emphatically with her assistant. What an outrage! And how unfortunate that they are foreigners! You can see what has happened! They don't speak Polish, poor things, but it's clear enough! Have all the window catches checked! I'll call the police!

19

They offer us tea while we wait. I can drink tea in any language you care to name. The bursar holds my notebook page to remind her of the case. When she gets the policeman on the phone, she tells him a lengthy story. It is incredible that my poor little handful of laboriously looked-up and arranged Polish words can be spun out into such expressive fluency. Her voice rises and falls. It is explanatory, indignant, business-like. This shocking event has happened right here in her school, *and* to foreigners on bicycles! "*Tak*, t*ak*, *tak*!" she says, yes, yes, yes. The policeman is a bit dim. "*Tak, tak, tak,*" she says again. Tiresome policeman.

The police promise to send someone to interview us, but first they have to get hold of their interpreter. As soon as they find him, they will be around to get us. While we wait we drink more tea. We make little attempts at conversation, and Alastair gamely tries out some Russian. English is not quite the international language we thought it was, and nobody seems to speak French any more in the land of Chopin and Marie Curie. The silence is broken only by Poles talking to each other in Polish and by English-speakers talking together, but some kind of general conversation seems to be going on, nonetheless. The bursar, as one last preparation for the arrival of the police, takes out a long pair of scissors and snips off the ragged top of my notebook page.

I had hoped that the police might arrive in a car with a siren and *MILICJA* written on the side, but no such luck. We have to walk all the way to the police station, which is far enough away to justify a car, I think, especially as we are wronged foreigners, poor but honest, on bicycles and to all appearances not noticeably capitalists. What are they saving their car for?

When we arrive, we are ushered into the chief's office. The chief is a pleasant young man who is deeply sorry for our misfortune. The elderly interpreter sits at a table. We describe our experience, the interpreter turns it into Polish, and the chief writes it all down. He tells us that even in Poland, there are, unfortunately, criminals, but that if they are caught we can be certain that they will be punished. We say that we are sure that not very many Poles are thieves, really, and that our loss was small. Our interpreter was once in the Free Polish Army and stationed in Scotland. He reminisces with Alastair about smoked haddock and the Cairngorms for long enough to establish the friendliness of international relations regardless of petty pilfering. We recite a more or less recognizably pronounced list of the places we have been and the chief and the interpreter nod approvingly.

After all this we get off to a late start and have to do the whole day's mileage in the afternoon, but it has been a painless way to meet the Polish police and see how theft is regarded.

I am riding alone, almost due west into a sky-filling sunset. I am on my way to Szczytno before sundown to find the youth hostel and then go back to meet Alastair and guide him to it. He is now either repairing his puncture or, having finished, riding a few miles behind me. The farmers have left their barley fields for the day, and the broad golden fields stretch out like a table top on each side of the road. I am the only person in sight. The fields come to an end and I enter a pine forest with a thin silver band of birch trees around the edges. I am in a long, dark-green tunnel with a blazing pink sky at the end. The forest ends and I roll out into more barley fields. I am in top gear on this flat road; I hardly know I'm pedalling. I'm sitting watching the land go by, watching the grey-flecked road unroll under my front tyre. Out of habit my feet revolve on the pedals. I brake slightly and change down for some railway tracks, but in a moment I'm in top gear and back in the old rhythm again.

I have the small Polish-English dictionary in my pocket, a supply of złoty, and a map. I also have an international guileless grin that I hope will see me through any rough spots the other three don't cover.

I muster just enough Polish to ask directions in Szczytno, which is larger than I had thought. I know the words for *where*, *road*, and *town*, and we have learned *bridge* and *forest* on the road. To my amazement the passer-by understands my question, and to my further amazement I understand her answer. I am just able to thank her before I ride off, stunned.

The youth hostel warden speaks German. I tell her that my *Mann* has had an event with his bicycle wheel on the road and that I must go back and seek him. She seems to understand. It is as much telepathy as anything else.

Now I follow the passer-by's directions in reverse, winding up my imaginary Theseus thread that I unroll in strange towns. Alastair is just entering Szczytno. I recognize him and his little Raleigh coming toward me on the other side of the road in the August gloaming. I call his name and do a U-turn. I speak in the language of thought again. I tell him about the German-speaking warden, the sunset, the forests; I hear about his puncture, the forests, the sunset.

East Germans holiday in Poland a lot, or they did in the summer of 1980. At this small resort on one of the many Mazurian Lakes I hear the voice of a young German woman as I lie in the sun on the little pier. Voices get closer and I open one eye. Two women have come down to the lake to wash their hair. I am far enough away not to feel obliged to move or to acknowledge them, but close enough to hear them and smell their shampoo. I go on dozing, on my stomach now, and little silver coins of their shampoo mass in a flotilla under the pier, tarnishing in the shade. They will disappear before they get to the swimming enclosure or to the man in a rowboat that I can see by raising my head slightly. More and more silver coins follow the first ones under the pier, and they all float lazily on out to disappear in this large lake, one of many.

The weather has broken, but good. It has been raining all night, and this morning the sky looks as though the merest nudge would start it all up again. Or all down again. It rains off and on during the day, and our rain capes also go on and off. The wind is an even worse problem. We are heading back to Warsaw now and the wind is coming straight at us from the southwest. It shifts—or our road shifts—so that when the wind is not directly in our faces it is blowing treacherously from the side, causing us to compensate for it constantly. If it suddenly dies down or if a truck passes between us and the wind, we wobble dangerously. Nothing is more irritating to a cyclist than seeing a straight flat road ahead—an obvious top-gear road—and being forced to travel down it in low gear against the wind. The trees that line the road (but not so densely as to be a windbreak) toss the silvery underside of their leaves at us like can-can dancers showing their petticoats. We are a disgruntled audience and plod past the trees at something just faster than a walking pace.

Sometimes the murals on the walls of buildings are just ads for Społem, the ubiquitous co-operative, but very often they are startling *trompe l'oeil* windows or gable ends. One "window" is so extremely realistic that I have to go up to the side of the building and sight up the wall to see if anything really sticks out. Nothing does, but when I step back a few yards and see the window with its sill and architrave, it all looks very convincing again.

In the Old Town, the *Stare Miasto,* of Warsaw, there are a lot of these visual leg-pulls. There is something playful about them, like the baroque churches with their cherubs and saints among the rafters, or like the University of Warsaw, where grimacing stone weight-lifters hold up an ornate balcony, rain or shine. The Old Town is very festive now in August; there are pretty white wooden carts full of bright pots of geraniums, and now and then a horse-drawn carriage clip-clops past with some tourists on board. A good part of the main square is taken up with a sidewalk café that serves delicious ice cream. The speciality of the house is *ambrozja,* a large goblet of chocolate ice cream with nuts and fresh and frozen fruit—walnuts, plums, strawberries, gooseberries, and quarters and halves of fresh peaches. On top of this is chocolate sauce and whipped cream. It is delicious! We can't believe how good it is. There is nothing

23

ersatz here, no sense of shortages or make-do, nothing drably Iron Curtain about this ice cream goblet! Even a hot fudge sundae in Indiana when you're eight years old, remembered years later, is not much better than this.

Something seems to be going on. Last night we waited for a half an hour for a tram and when no tram came, we walked the long way back to the Warsaw youth hostel. Now at breakfast in the basement of the hostel we hear a Canadian boy telling someone that he has just come from Gdańsk, where the shipworkers are organizing daring strikes. Still, except for the tram strike we do not see much evidence of unrest. We are naïve observers, especially without usable newspapers. There is a Polish paper, there is *Pravda*, of which I can read only the title, and an East German paper that seems to be entirely, from front page to back page, about sport. When we first arrived in Warsaw I was surprised to see a copy of *The Guardian*. When I saw a man (who turned out to be Libyan) reading it in a coffee shop, I asked him where I could get a copy, and he directed me to a big new hotel near by. But later that August the supply of British newspapers seemed to dry up and the hotel news kiosk sold only the Polish *Trybuna Ludu*, *Pravda*, and the German sports paper. We never find out what, if anything, is going on until we get back to London a week or ten days later. In retrospect we feel as though we have been to an unfamiliar opera without a programme and have spent most of the time under the seats looking for our gloves.

When we get back to the youth hostel it is closed for the night. When we knock at the door the warden sticks her head out of an upper window and calls testily in German that we must pay her 50 złoty to be let in. We pay, but it is unclear whether this is a fine or a surcharge, a tip, or indeed a bribe. Anyway, the 50 złoty seems to make all the difference, and she is very nice to us after Alastair hands her the banknote.

We are walking along in Warsaw on one of our last days in Poland. A building is under construction and a temporary covered walk-way has been built for pedestrians. The top is supported by a row of wooden uprights. Suddenly I pull out my little camera and try to figure out where to stand to take my picture. The pedestrians, like the citizens of any large city, walk past with no more than a glance at the foreign tourist. Alastair is a little puzzled because there is nothing scenic about this pedestrian detour. Now I am standing on the tram tracks and watching out for trams as I try to compose the picture in my viewfinder.

"You want a picture of *this?*" Alastair asks, motioning toward the ugly temporary walk-way with tattered posters stuck on the hoarding.

"No, those round posts there, all along that side," I say, giggling a little because we have been in Poland for almost three weeks and we must leave soon and it is making me a bit punchy.

"I'm going to show people this picture and I'm going to say, 'When we were in Warsaw we saw a bunch of poles.'" I take the picture and hope it won't be blurred with my chuckles, so that I am caught permanently laughing at my own silly joke. The real Poles keep walking past, as blasé as Londoners would be. Who knows whether some foreign tourists in London, taking pictures in front of this or that nondescript building, have their silly reasons, too.

The Centralna train station in Warsaw is a sleek, glassy place. There is an immense marble-looking concourse, escalators to the train platforms, rows of ticket windows. The place has been skilfully designed by some young Turk of an architect. Outside, the busiest streets in Warsaw bustle with trams and cars, three lanes at a time. We hate the Centralna train station. We detest everything about it, but it is not the fault of the architect or the train drivers or the ticket sellers.

We have spent entirely too much time here against our will. We came every morning for a week to find out whether our bicycles had arrived, but they had not. When they appeared at last we thankfully left with them and managed not to set foot inside beastly Centralna for ten whole days. But then we had to send our bikes back to London.

We take our bikes to the customs office at the station as though we are taking the family dog to the vet to be put to sleep. When might they arrive in London, we wonder, and which bits of them may be missing this time? But after we had all that trouble disentangling our bikes from the bureaucracy, *now* the same finicky bureaucrats won't take them back. We have arrived on a Saturday morning to consign the bikes to the baggage handlers before our passenger train leaves on Sunday. At midnight on Sunday our visas expire. On this Saturday the customs office is closed; it will reopen on Monday. "Come back on Monday," says the lady at the counter, who has nothing to do with Customs but deals with internal baggage.

"But we won't be here on Monday," I say. "We are leaving on Sunday. Tomorrow. Isn't there some way we can leave our bicycles here?"

No, the office is closed. Any system for holding our bicycles until the office reopens does not exist and is beyond the imagination of anyone at Centralna Station.

An alarming difference in attitude and mental fix suddenly arises. We see our situation as a problem to which there is a solution. We can find this solution with the help of the personnel at Centralna. The personnel at Centralna, however, see our situation in a different light altogether. These foreigners have bicycles that they want to check in at the Customs office. The Customs office is closed, so they can't do it. Where is the problem?

"Why does it say 'information' over your desk?" I hiss at the young woman near the ticket office. "You don't seem to have much information!" I am as nasty as possible. I am furious at the blank smiles and the alternating answers: "The office is closed,"and "Come back on Monday."

"But our train *leaves* on Sunday!" I shout, red in the face. "It leaves *tomorrow*!" I have been trapped in a sinister film of a

Kafka novel being shot by Fellini. Somewhere the cameras are rolling and all this is fiction. How can they be so thick? Where is the minimal imagination and *nous* necessary for one of these employees to say, "For a certain number of złoty, I personally will see your bicycles through the Customs formalities when the office reopens on Monday"? Why should it even depend on an improvised measure in the first place? Why isn't there some normal mechanism to deal with our problem, which must be common?

We retreat to the posh lobby of a near-by hotel, full of Arabs and rich Germans. We must think of some plan, as the effort of doing so was beyond the staff at Centralna. I explain our problem to the woman at the travel information desk in the hotel lobby. By this time I have condensed the explanation into one sentence. The problem is simple—it is the solution to it that has buffaloed everyone.

The travel woman is calm; my story does not surprise or baffle her. It is indeed a simple problem. "I advise you to take your bicycles to the train on Sunday. You can give the conductor some little moneys. I am sure he will find an accommodation for them."

Before I even understand what she is saying I know that she must be giving me the solution to our problem. She is not saying that the office is closed or that we must come back on Monday; she is tackling the problem from another angle. She is tackling the problem, period. And of course she has the answer. Of course! Bribery! The people at the train station must have wondered where *our* minimal imagination and *nous* were. In some countries, when you get painted into the corner by the rules, the door out of the unpainted corner is bribery. What ought to be administratively possible is only financially possible.

"Be sure to give him a little moneys," she reminds me. I ask her what sort of little moneys she thinks would be appropriate.

"Perhaps two hundred złoty," she says. She shrugs, because bribery is an inexact science. "Maybe three hundred." She is doing an unknown countryman a favour to the tune of a hundred złoty.

Things are getting critical. We have made a discreet count of our remaining złoty and find we have 6000 of them. Most of the stores in Warsaw are closed today because it is a "free Saturday" and tomorrow we leave. Any left-over złoty will be confiscated at the border because it is illegal to take them out of the country. Six thousand złoty, as well as we can figure, is about two or three weeks' wages for the average Pole. We walk in the shadow of the immense Palace of Culture and Science, a white elephant the Russians presented to Warsaw during the Stalinist era. It looks like the top thirty storeys of the Empire State Building and hulks over central Warsaw. Blocky sculptures of the workers of both nations embrace in brotherhood in an endless frieze around the base. We buy tickets for a movie in a cinema hidden in one of the mousehole-like orifices around the bottom of the Palace. But the tickets, like so many other things, are cheap. What do we do with the remaining thousands of złoty?

We cross the wide and busy thoroughfare between the Palace of Culture and Science and the loathsome Centralna station. We wander into the parking lot of the station, still discussing ideas for divesting ourselves of the unwanted money. We don't have many ideas on this Saturday afternoon with most of the shops in the city closed.

Suddenly our joint pondering is interrupted by a policeman who is asking Alastair for his passport. He and a colleague are sitting in their police car with MILICJA on the side in this parking lot; we have wandered straight up to them. Jaywalking, which is legal, if unwise, in the rest of Europe, is absolutely not allowed in Poland, or anyway not in front of these particular policemen today. The fine for this offence is 200 złoty, payable on demand. We suddenly have 200 złoty less to worry about, and although we feel wronged—fined and not even warned the first time—we are beyond caring. We have landed on a square and drawn a card which says, "Policeman fines you for jaywalking. Forfeit 200 złoty". We walk away wondering if we are unconsciously rolling more dice and what the next square will say.

28

Even allowing for bribes and jaywalking fines and other necessary expenses, most of the 6000 złoty remains to be spent. It is dinnertime, elegant hotels surround us in central Warsaw, and we have money to burn. We will have a grand blow-out! We will have a Dorchester-Ritz-Hilton dinner with all the trimmings!

Ordinary Poles may stand in line for hours for a lump of scrag end, but foreigners with hard currency, or złoty bought with hard currency, can have any delicacy their hearts desire. One of the ironies of the system is that frugal tourists like us may have this dissipation forced upon us. The enforced prodigality amuses us while it irritates us on behalf of the hard-working and deserving Poles who can't share this food with us right in their own capital. We eat a meal that we do not particularly want and that at home in London we would neither want nor be able to afford.

We study the menu. We try to find the most expensive combination of specialities. I order venison and Alastair has wild boar. We both have asparagus. Imported French burgundy is pricey, so we have that. We choose extravagant salads and vegetables to go with our main course. Finally we have superb ice cream desserts and the best coffee.

Our bill comes to 1000 złoty, exactly ten times what we usually spend for dinner.

Still there is money left over. On the way to the train station on our last day I drop an envelope in a mailbox. I have copied Maria Wnuk's address from my notebook. She is a fine person and was a pleasant companion on the train to Wrocław. She deserves a few thousand złoty. Perhaps she can buy some little luxury—a new coat or something for her house. It's a relief not to have the stuff any more.

I have made up a little speech in German, as that language seems the best bet, given that English is practically unknown except for random words on people's clothes. It is a moving story concerning the closure of the customs office at Centralna and our wish to travel with our bicycles. I hold three 100 złoty notes in my hands, easily visible but not obvious. The train conductor understands the situation immediately and is happy to arrange for the bicycles to go on the train. It will be no problem, not the least problem.

I am so pleased to get us and the bikes on a train going west that I do not care where the conductor puts the bicycles, but he might have been more creative. We find them later blocking the door into the buffet car. We climb over them with everyone else and cultivate a blank expression when we hear the inevitable harsh words about them. Our solution to bureaucracy has become everyone else's problem of access to the buffet. Perhaps the conductor is waiting for a bribe from someone else to move our bikes. If so, no one thinks of it, and the bikes remain piled up in the doorway of the buffet car until we move them at the border and block another doorway with them. Finally, when we stop in West Germany at Helmstedt we whisk them down the platform to the new baggage car and load them safely in. Our original well-paid conductor stayed in Poland and we have had two other conductors since then—conductors who have not been paid off and must wonder why the bicycles are blocking the doors of a passenger train. Or perhaps they know perfectly well why the bikes are on a weekend train from Warsaw with no baggage car.

We wind up our long Theseus thread all across Poland. It is nine hours from Warsaw to Kunowice at the border; we spend all afternoon and evening crossing the plains of central and western Poland. The officious East German customs inspectors get in. They give the impression of hoping against hope that there may be something irregular on our train. They check everything meticulously; they even unscrew the ventilator covers on the ceiling of the corridor outside our compartment. The passengers all look at each other with expressions varying from amusement to contempt, and it is very clear what the passengers, mostly Poles, think of East German efficiency. Then we cross the Odra River on the high train bridge and it changes to the Oder in midstream and we are out of Poland.

Chapter Two

The Amber Brooch

We returned home, oiled our bikes, had the pictures developed, and heard about the postcards that continued to arrive at friends' homes. A month went by, and our semi-cycle tour of Poland was put away with the summer clothes.

Then the phone rang and a strange man asked for me by name. He had a mature voice and a foreign accent. He explained that he was Andrzej Mazaraki, and that his wife was a friend of Maria Wnuk's. His wife, Hanna, had been visiting Maria when the envelope with money came, and Maria wanted to buy me an amber brooch with the money. However, it was illegal to remove any amber from Poland, and so she had sent it to London with her friend Hanna. Mr. Mazaraki now had this brooch and was inviting me to lunch near his office so that he could deliver it to me. At the time it seemed a strangely cloak-and-dagger way to go about things, but I came to learn that for Poles it was an entirely ordinary method of arranging their affairs.

I went to our rendezvous at the Pizza on the Park at Hyde Park Corner full of curiosity to meet Mr. Mazaraki, hear about Maria Wnuk, and receive this brooch. We soon identified each other and shook hands. He had the appearance and bearing of a central European aristocrat. (Years later I found his family name on a memorial plaque in the Święty Krzyż Church in Warsaw; his ancestors had distinguished themselves in service to their country.) Now he explained that his wife was an old friend of Mrs. Wnuk's and often went to Poland to visit her.

Andrzej Mazaraki and his wife had been living in London since soon after the War, and he has done well in his business almost from the start. Like many other Poles I would meet later, he had

31

lived through episodes that I could barely imagine. As those episodes were far in the past now and he had described them many times before to other people, he didn't bother to tell me much about them. He was doing his duty to his wife, who was doing a favour (which may well have been a returned favour) for Maria Wnuk, who wanted to recompense us for the favour we had done her. And we? We had just had some, soon-to-be-worthless money to get rid of before we left Warsaw.

Andrzej Mazaraki had been in a military academy in Warsaw when war broke out in September 1939. He and many other cadets did what they could in the underground army. "You know about the Warsaw Uprising?" he asked me (because you can't take anything for granted among a younger, non-Polish generation). "Well, I was in that show." He had various ups and down which he now dismissed with a small wave of his hand. Instead of describing any of his own adventures, he tells me about his wife Hanna, who spent two years in Auschwitz. Over lunch in the Pizza Express he told me about her rations in the concentration camp. Some days it would be only one slice of bread to last the whole day. I looked down at my large, spicy pizza and tried to think of it as a slice of bread to last the whole day. As surely as that double-decker bus was lumbering down Knightsbridge outside those big clean windows I would have another very adequate meal that evening. One slice of bread would have got lost in it.

"When they got their slice of bread," he said, "some of the prisoners would try to eat it one tiny morsel at a time, to make it last as long as possible. But you can hardly taste anything if you eat it in tiny amounts. My wife decided to eat it all at once, so that she would at least enjoy what she had, even if she was hungry later. It's an interesting problem, isn't it? You have to make a decision. Of course, you can understand either decision, but I think my wife was right."

The brooch was very distinctive: a piece of polished irregular amber set in a silver art-nouveau frame. It was so unexpected— this brooch suddenly appearing out of nowhere! I thanked Mr.

Mazaraki for lunch and for delivering the brooch and went away to write a thank-you note to Maria Wnuk. Before long a second gift arrived, not for me but for Alastair. It seemed that Maria still had some of our 6000 złoty left over after she had bought the brooch. The brooch, being a piece of jewellery, was obviously for me, and she felt that she should not forget Alastair with what was, after all, our own largesse. Therefore Alastair received a large, profusely illustrated, coffee-table book about Pope John Paul II, the favourite countryman of practically every Pole. It arrived in the normal way, via the postman.

Before long Maria's letter arrived. I had explained our predicament in Warsaw with the jocular expression, "forcible prodigality", and she picked it up in her letter to me:

> Really, I was astonished when I obtained your letter, dated "Warsaw"! I don't like the waste of money, and your "forcible prodigality" troubled me very much!
>
> It isn't easy to understand economical and political system in our country, peculiar by foreigners! Pole live in difficult conditions and therefore he is resourceful. You can't spend the Polish money, but I can buy something for you, and I bought the brooch! In August arrived to Poland the friend of my sister, and I gave her your address and this brooch. For the rest of the money I bought for you and your husband this book. Excuse me, that this book is about Catholic Pope, but the fate of this man resemble the fate of other Poles.
>
> I waite for latter from you.
> Yours sincerely,
> Maria WNUK

Only a completely preoccupied, desperately harried, uncommunicative person could have avoided getting into a correspondence with Maria Wnuk now, and I was none of those things. We exchanged letters during the winter of 1980-81.

As she was taking a class in French and as I was translating some French at the time, she sometimes wrote in French, which was somewhat better than her English. However, she explained that as my language was English she wanted me to write in that, and then she could brush up on both languages. In October she wrote that she was born on 8 December 1925; she was interested in architecture and literature; her first ambition had been to be a journalist, but she had been steered into architecture by her architect father. She and her husband, Włodek, had two grown children, Staszek and Agnieszka; he was a young electrical engineer and she was studying medicine. Maria's husband Włodek was an architect who specialized in hospitals.

I told her about the rest of our trip in Poland after we had met her on the train to Wrocław. She said we were welcome to visit her any time. I thanked her, but doubted that it would ever happen.

Our letters ranged over both the subjects in which we found a common interest and the subjects that we wanted to share but knew would seem odd to the other. We discussed literature at many levels. ("The literature of criminals give best knowledge of cotidien life. I am ashamed, but I must you confess that I like English criminals! Especially Agatha Christie! I learned English by reading 'A Child's Garden of Verses' by R.L. Stevenson. I like even now to read childish books!") She more than once expressed tactful regret that I was so ignorant about Polish literature: the great works of Sienkiewicz, Prus, and Zeromski. She often referred to *Anne of Green Gables* and urged me to read it.

Alastair and I and my mother were in Spain and Portugal at the end of 1980. Maria wrote that Spain and France both fascinated her, but that they were really too expensive to go to without some scheme of work to offset the costs. It was easy enough to travel in the socialist countries, she wrote. ("Oh, excuse me, now to DDR and USSR there are some troubles—we are a little infectious!")

My mother died suddenly when we were in Lisbon, so Maria didn't hear from me for a while, but she continued to write. In February 1981 she and Włodek and the dog Fizia were in Tuczno having a winter break. I came to hear about these breaks in other parts of Poland, even in the forests around Warsaw, which were times of renewal and rest from the difficult life in the capital. Now from Tuczno she wrote, "I was very tired with our economic and political situation. Especially the political problems lay as the stone on my heart and disturb very much! We make here beautiful excursions every day, and only evening I return to these problems."

Now and then she passed on a joke that was making the rounds, and that winter one of them ran: "Why is this winter not as cold as usual? Because there are so many warm Russian jackets all along the border." Whatever the Poles may have thought about their Soviet neighbours at the time, there was great concern in the West that the Soviet Union might invade, as it had so often done before when its satellites were not docile enough to suit it. But the Poles, if Maria was representative of them, weren't too worried about pushing their luck. In April she wrote: "I send you the best Easter wishes. In my private life all is all right. Every Sunday we are going to the forest (my husband my dog and some other friends). We make 15 km in search of spring. Especially beautiful are the meadows with yellow flowers. Our public life is difficult, but we are full of hope. The empty shops, it isn't the most important problem. I send you the wishes full of the spring and the hope."

To my shame, it wasn't until the summer that I finally wrote to Maria again. I had been preoccupied with my mother's death, the funeral in Indiana, questions of property and probate, and numerous other concerns. I now explained this and sent along some postcards and other enclosures. She was kind and sympathetic and understood my problems at once. On August 21 she wrote, "With great joy I obtained your two letters (with photos, postcards, etc.) Now I understand you taciture. I experienced this trouble 10 years ago." She told me about her recent holiday with Włodek: a two-week kayak trip with their club. It was an "escape from reality," she said. She invited us to come on the trip with them the next year: "Next year (if you will) I invite you and Alastair. My tourist club organises that enterprise every summer." It was a nice idea, but probably unworkable. The rest of her month off had been devoted (and that is the right word) to a pilgrimage to Częstochowa, for there was no Pole more devout than Maria.

But she liked a good joke and now they were getting steadily darker: "If you like Polish joke, I tell you one. In hell Lucifer sits on his throne. A devil comes, very anxious: 'Chief! I don't know what to do with that new group from Poland. They are wild with happiness and can't understand that they aren't in Paradise!'"

As the year wore on I heard more about daily life in Warsaw. It amazed me that inconveniences that hadn't existed in Britain since the 1940s were a constant problem in Poland. In November Maria described the life that those kayak trips and Sundays in the forest were an escape from:

> Once a week I get up early, at 6 o'clock and I stay in the queue. Of course I have some interesting book, but sometimes the life and discussions are more interesting, for example, how many persons obtain the meat? We have ration stamps for cigarettes and alcohol too. These stamps I can change into chocolate, coffee and sweets. In my family nobody smoke and drink (...a little). Therefore I am potentate of sweetness! Or I can change with my friends the cigarettes into the toothpaste or margarine. Plenty of possibility!
>
> The way to buy the industrial objects is very interesting one. Before the industrial shop, there is the long queue—the shop is empty. The people organize the list. We name that list "social list". The people choose "the chairman", and go home. And now, every day they meet together, for example, at 11 o'clock. The chairman

36

verifies the list and the absent ones are struck off. One day, the industrial objects are provided. The first persons from the list obtain desired articles. And next day all begin at the beginnings! I never stay in that queue—I like more my free time!

Once when I mentioned the current hot topic of the arms race, the placing of nuclear missiles at sites in Britain, she found it somewhat academic. She considered their everyday reality more serious: "Worse than the nuclear power, for me, it is the political system founded on the lie."

By December 1981 Poland was constantly in the news. It had been building up all year. The Solidarity trade-union movement had great popular support, and the government under General Wojciech Jaruzelski felt threatened. Furthermore, anyone over 30 remembered the brutal Russian invasion of Czechoslovakia 13 years before when a popular movement there made the Soviet Union feel threatened. Anyone over 40 remembered the brutal Soviet invasion of Hungary 12 years before that, when the Soviets had also apparently felt very threatened. Anyone still older could easily remember the Soviet invasion of half a dozen other countries. The Soviet Union had a record of feeling threatened by the neighbours of its neighbours' neighbours, and Poland's chances didn't look good in late 1981. I could easily imagine Soviet tanks in those wide Warsaw streets where you weren't supposed to jaywalk. Soviet tanks had been in so many foreign main streets. I felt the Poles were pushing their luck.

General Jaruzelski's solution, which nevertheless did not endear him to the mass of Poles, was to declare martial law. One Sunday morning in Warsaw there were suddenly tanks in the street, no phone service, and nothing but noncommital classical music on the radio. Numerous repressive measures were put into force, effective immediately. In London there were demonstrations in Portland Place in front of the Polish embassy. On New Year's Eve there was a large demonstration, and second and third-generation Polish Londoners turned out and sang traditional patriotic songs. Someone passed through the crowd selling little plastic *Solidarność* badges and I bought one.

The shortages that quickly developed affected everyone. (The shortages apparently developed because the black and grey markets that kept things going under the impossible Communist regulations now disappeared out of a fear of the military.) The most common things were either in short supply or completely unobtainable in Poland. Maria and I continued to correspond, but now our letters were cut open, stapled back together, and stamped with *OCENZUROWANO*, which meant "Censored". Her letters to me were never tampered with otherwise—no passages were cut out or blacked over—but still, someone had cared about what this middle-aged teacher in Warsaw was writing to her friend, a cyclist in London. They presumably read the news about her family, her sister Janina and the dog, Fysia. What kind of people kept tabs like that on their fellow citizens in peacetime?

She thought of me at Christmastime and remembered that I had lost my mother the year before. "I can imagine that this Christmas was especially close with your mother memory," she wrote. "My mother is dead 10 years ago, but when we set for Christmas Eve, I must think about her. The free place at the table is sad. This year it was many free places, not happy in my family."

Our censored letters now were taking a month to arrive, but when mine finally got to Maria she was charmingly delighted. "Your letters for me like the dessert! I read after the dinner with cup of tea!"

I sent her a copy of the text of Christina Rosetti's "In the Bleak Midwinter", which she liked. She had never heard of Rosetti before, but:

> "In the Bleak Midwinter" pleased me much. Every Sunday I am going with some friends in the forest (by bus, near my house) I take tea, some sandwiches and *in*

this moment, I am happy. I obtained the letter from my club, who (incorrigible dreamer!) organise "flow down" by kayak (26 July-7 August). Wonderful route! (through the lakes and forest!) I repeat our invitation to you and Alastair. I am incorrigible dreamer also! But it must be better.

I thought I might send something to Maria. I heard of Dar-Pol, a shipping company in London that specialized in sending parcels to Poland. I telephoned Mr. Mazaraki to ask what sort of things were in short supply and might be appreciated by Maria Wnuk and her family.

"Everything!" he said. And then he enumerated several common items. Cleaning materials, tea and coffee, soap, shampoo, butter, meat, and sugar were the most notable.

I got a medium-sized cardboard box and began filling it with some of the items Mr. Mazaraki had mentioned. Every time I went to my local Safeway I picked up a few things for Maria. I found canned Danish ham and butter. When I came home from shopping I put Maria's things aside in the designated cardboard box. Before long it was pretty full, but I rearranged things to make some more space. Finally I really couldn't get anything else in, but there were a few small crevices and pockets of dead space. These I filled with the little individual sugar packets that I was always picking up in cafés and restaurants. I shook and jiggled the box to make the little packets fall into the cracks between other things, then I slotted more sugar packets into the new spaces. Finally I taped it up and took it to the shipping company in Dalston.

They were used to people coming to their seedy little office with parcels for friends and relatives in Poland. A truck went once a week, if not more often. The company had been in existence for a while, perhaps as long as Poland had been having shortages in peacetime, which is to say since 1945. I had not had much experience with parcel services that were not part of the post office. I had great faith in the International Postal Union,

39

but not so much in this haulage firm in Dalston. I would not have been astonished if my parcel had disappeared somewhere between London and Warsaw, going the way of Alastair's bicycle bell. But it did not disappear.

In the middle of May I had a letter from Maria, written on April 2, about receiving the box in late March.

I remember when I was schoolgirl we had often the exercise: "Story of my pen" (garments, shoes, etc.). Now I describe you "story of the box from my English friends". 25 March, I found in my letter box little advice about some dispatch. 26 March I went to the post office—but without enthusiasm—once this "dispatch", it was the letter from my house administration. Now it was something concrete—advice about the box from England—from you! You can imagine my joy! But I dared to go to the transport bureau. This day it was too late (bureau is closed after 14 o'clock). Third day morning. I went to this office—very excite! The custom-house officer verify the contents and at last I stood the proprietor of the box!

At home, my daughter (student of medicine), my sister (she is retired now), friend of my daughter—waited me. We unpacked the box together with "oh! ah!" etc. My daughter grabbed instantly the shampoo, my sister—coffee, and I enjoyed all ingredients. Sarah! You have splendid imagination, indeed! All things are necessary!

When we had a glance at the box, we sat at the table, we drank English tea (*very* good) and we taste some chocolate. We put all items in the box again, that my son (he finished his study now—he is electronic) and my husband will have pleasure to open the box.

I was so touched by this account that I quickly began collecting things for another box. Between the amber brooch and the food parcels, our friendship was sealed. It was inconceivable that we should ever stop writing to each other or stop being involved in each other's lives. Now and then we reminded each other that it was all because of that little boy on the train to Wrocław, polite little Mariusz in 1980 with all his biscuits and candy.

I often sent Maria postcards, especially of interesting buildings. That spring three friends and I went to Shropshire and I sent her a picture of Ironbridge and also a snapshot of three of us half-way up the Long Mynd. It turned out pretty well, considering we were all wearing bulky coats and wellies. I was also still wearing the *Solidarność* badge I had acquired at the midnight rally out in front of the Polish embassy the previous New Year's Eve. I had forgotten it was still pinned to this coat. When I sent the photo to Maria, the letter was checked by the censors like all the others, but no one noticed the badge on my coat in the photo. In the picture it was only a little pale blob and was hardly noticeable. Maria didn't notice it, either, until the sharp-eyed Agnieszka pointed it out to her six months later. She peered closely at the photo (perhaps getting a magnifying glass out of a drawer; look, do you see this red lettering? Look, here, at the tip of my pencil) and announced that this was indeed a *Solidarność* badge on my coat! Now they all examined it and saw that it was true.

It would not have been safe to mention it by name in a letter or to ask how I had acquired it. With the picture tucked away safely, she mentioned—and who could possibly find fault with this?—that she had noticed the "brooch" I was wearing on my coat. As it happened, she said, she had one just like it. (And what, to anyone else, could be remotely interesting, let alone censorable, about such a remark?) Now we knew where the other stood: I knew that she was a sympathizer, perhaps a member, of the now outlawed *Solidarność* union; she knew that I knew something about the situation in Poland and was sympathetic to this movement. As time went on Maria occasionally mentioned my brooch—not the amber one but the one on my coat. "The brooch on your coat," she would say, and then there would be an oblique reference to the outlawed organization, but to any casual reader of her letter she was apparently talking about ladies' jewellery.

But in the meantime, before the photo had been so carefully examined, she just wrote to thank me: "Your last letter, dated 11 April, gave me inspiration. I like Shropshire very much. It is so romantic town! The first iron bridge isn't unknown to me! I teach (you know) in Building School History of Architecture, and when I am finish XX century, I tell always about Industrial Revolution and about the first iron bridge, but I hadn't so beautiful card. Therefore, I thank you for that card very much."

Sometimes we wrote about our earlier life, childhood memories, family history, and such personal matters. I always liked getting these glimpses into her life: who she was and where she had come from. She wrote in *czerwiec* [June] of 1982: "Before the first war my parents lived in Russia and there man drink tea from samovar. Samovar contains average 5 l. = 20 cups of tea. The parents drank one samovar together every evening. This samovar stood in parents' living room till war 1939 and it went lost."

The censorship annoyed me. The nerve of some faceless person reading ordinary mail! Ordinary letters between two friends who had once met on a train! (At one time in the Soviet Union or other places in Eastern Europe such a "chance meeting" might not have been accidental at all, but carefully planned. Maybe it was still possible in 1980, but what I saw of Polish efficiency then and later suggested that any such planning would have been completely beyond any officials. If they had attempted such a plot, we would have certainly ended up on different trains going in opposite directions.)

Maria was a devout Catholic and belonged to a group called the New Catechumens. They seemed to be a sort of study group who went on retreats together and held discussions and prayer meetings. She sometimes described their meetings and discussion topics, often a passage in the New Testament. I looked in a Bible concordance for words like "support" or "friendship" or perhaps "resist" and "oppression" and then piously recommended to her certain verses in, say, St. Paul's Epistle to the Romans or Thessalonians that would contain a veiled message for her. These messages from London to Warsaw by way of Paul of Tarsus were not a perfect means of communication, but they did convey certain ideas, and furthermore, they gave us the invaluable sense of colluding together against a System. We were Us, it was Them.

I couldn't imagine any Polish mail-censor bothering to look up Biblical quotations. Now that we know more about what happened in East Germany, I wouldn't be amazed to learn that they did have a special office concerned with looking up quotations from the Bible if and when they turned up in correspondence. But still, that sounds more like the Stasi than the Polish secret service. ("What do you do for a living?" "It's very hush-hush. Actually, I vet Bible quotations." "You do what?" "'Ask not troublesome questions, neither zealously solicit answers of another man.' Proverbs six..." "Oh, shut up!")

I loved the way Maria could see the funny side of life, even when she was faced with the multitudinous calamities of daily life in Warsaw under martial law. There was the Affair of the Lavatory Pan and the problem of the position of the waste pipe.

We have broken water-closet dish. Staszek himself plastered W.C. The brush dropped and broke the dish! And we can't find a new dish! Now I know that the dishes have left, right and direct twirl. Our dish has right twirl. In the magazine [i.e. department store] there are right and direct twirl. All family begin to have some sort of aberration. We observe carefully W.C. in all places. Is it left? right? direct?

But a month later all these problems were temporarily forgotten when Maria went off to the countryside for a holiday. "I am writing on the lake side. I am listening to the silence of nature and I am almost happy... We are being amazed by the beauty of the lakes and rivers of Szwajcaria Kaszubska. People of this part of Poland are famous for being able to make beautiful tapestry and wood-works."

Looking back on the summer holiday from the vantage point of September, Maria wrote again about her love of the out-of-doors, and coincidentally about the solution to the W.C. problem.

> I had a delightful holiday on the river. When we went back to Warsaw, I observed that I spend all day in the kitchen, Włodek in his hobby room, therefore I said: that will do (we had two weeks of holidays still) and we went in mountain, to the little town near the Czechoslovakia frontier. Every day we spend 7 hours in mountains. What a magnific trip! Complete liberty! We had the physical pleasure of conquer the height, and then to admire the nature in complete peace. We met one, two persons only! When we were hungry, we ate raspberry, when we were thirsty, we drank stream water!
>
> Our closet affair ended at last. Again the proverb: "better to have 100 friends than 100 dollars". One of my friends who lives in other town find lavatory pan (right!) and sent to me by car!

When Maria wasn't urging me to read *Anne of Green Gables* or describing walks in the mountains, she told me about the saints that were important to her. In October 1982 Maximilian Kolbe was canonised. ("10 October we attained new saint, Maximilian Kolbe. Don't be angry with me, at my frequent writing about saints, but in our world we must have examples, as the sailor has the lighthouse.") She had already told me how St. Anthony was

44

a great help when she had lost anything. If she prayed to him and pledged 100 zł, she usually found the lost item. Occasionally that didn't work, because St. Anthony knew how to drive a hard bargain: "But he is a businessman—often 100 zł is not enough. Then I say, 'Oh, St. Anthoni, I shall give you 200 zł for your poor people and...I find my lost object. And all the world is happy: I, St. Anthoni, and the poor peoples who obtained 200 zł, too."

Alastair's father died in October 1982, and Maria expressed her sympathy to us and Alastair's mother and forgave my absence in Scotland and the lack of letters. ("You had a sad sojourn in Scotland. But it was better for Christina and Alastair that you stand with them. One can't be alone in this circumstance.")

Now it was Christmas time again, and Maria wrote me about their tree, but with a veiled allusion to Solidarity. "Our Christmas tree is full of light. I sit and write to you. The lights on Christmas tree isn't according to our tradition—we like better candles, but I can't buy. After all, our tree is gay: we have on it some plaquettes (the same you had on the photo)."

She told me about family illness: everyone else had been ill in turn, and Agnieszka had been running a low-grade fever for a month. But in the New Year Maria went on a retreat with her New Catechumens group and loved it. They prayed and discussed passages in the Bible and ate meals together. It was a wrench to go back to the daily grind in Warsaw, although there was the pleasure of celebrating Włodek's January birthday. "Our visitors drank one glass of wodka (I prepared myself: grapefruit juice and wodka) in your honour! when we ate English ham."

Just as we had discussed Shakespeare in our train conversation in 1980, so he seemed to crop up now and then in our correspondence. She wrote that *Koriolan* was on in Warsaw that season and that "every great actor want to be ('or not to be') Hamlet." She wrote that in Russian literature her favourite author was Tolstoy but that she didn't care for Dostoyevsky. She liked Tolstoy's outlook but found Dostoyevsky strange and uncongenial. (So she did have more serious tastes than *Anne of Green Gables*. But one's taste in a difficult foreign language is not always the same as in something more familiar.)

Now and then the subjects were closer to the political situation in Eastern Europe. "I am enemy of emigration," she wrote. "It must be absolutely important circumstance, when men leave his country. But to leave the country, and to wait for some change, it is wrong attitude. Happy, my children have the same idea. But to travel—it is wonderful thing." I think she would have forgiven all the Poles in Pittsburgh and Chicago (and their ancestors), but she would have had harsh words for the ones who left until things got better through the efforts of others.

Lightening the tone a bit, I told her about my favourite comedy, Wilde's *The Importance of Being Earnest*. At first she didn't recognize it, but then the penny dropped. "Of course I read *The Importance of Being Earnest*. But our Polish title, it is *Lord in a Handbag*. I saw this play three times. It was extremely funny for me. Magnificent comic actors played in this piece."

In June of 1983 the Pope paid a visit to Poland, and Maria was ecstatic. All the parishes in Warsaw were assigned individual sections of the Pope's route through the city to decorate, and Maria's parish in northern Warsaw was in charge of Nowy Świat, a once elegant street with tram tracks down the middle. In addition, people put decorations in their windows at home. Maria was involved with all that, and she was preparing food for the three days so that she wouldn't have to cook during the exciting days of the papal visit.

In July when the dust had settled she wrote me a description: how they had gathered in Nowy Świat and sung psalms, how they had had a radio with them and listened to the Pope's first words on arriving in the country; how she had "obtained" tickets for the Mass in a stadium, and how she and Włodek had gone early on foot and how pilgrims had poured in from all over, and the ones from Gdańsk were given a special welcome. I knew by now that the Poles' reverence for their pope was unlike anything else. No rock star or popular politician came anywhere near it.

46

And then it was time to escape from reality again, and Maria wrote about the kayak trip and sent me a little series of drawings to illustrate typical scenes from the fortnight. This was a bumper year with the annual kayak trip *and* the Pope. In September, we had made a trip, too. Alastair and his widowed mother and I had gone on a tour of the Hebrides, partly to take her mind off the anniversary of her husband's death. I sent Maria a few cards to show the exotic scenery and the vernacular but and bens, for which she thanked me warmly. She and Włodek had spent the second half of their holidays at an architects' resort in the mountains. This sort of *maison de repos* (she was writing me in French again) was supposed to be the success of their system, but it was still expensive, costing the equivalent of Włodek's salary for a month. She loved the spectacular October colours in the mountains and she loved climbing up to the summit of a mountain and the sensation of having conquered it. Now she was inviting Alastair and me to join them in the mountains, too!

December brought a telling little anecdote about Agnieszka's purchase of a winter coat to replace her old shabby ("*très fatigué*") one. She and her friend Małgosia, who also wanted to buy a winter coat, had got up early and gone to the department store before it was open. But in spite of their plans and their early start, there was only one coat in their size in the store. They bought it anyway, and later there was a meeting of the two families at the Wnuks' flat to decide who was to have the coat. They were guided, she said jocularly, by Marx (whose need was greatest?) and the Ten Commandments, and they eventually came to the decision that Agnieszka should be awarded the coat. But the story had a happy ending for all concerned, because only two weeks later Małgosia's mother found another coat, and now both girls had new coats and both were happy! A purchase that would have been an everyday chore in London took on the quality of a big-game hunt in Warsaw.

Maria Wnuk and her family. front: her son Staszek and his wife Mirka with the dog, Fyzia; middle: Maria's sister Janina and Maria; back: Maria's daughter Agnieszka and husband Włodek.

Maria wrote about her new job. She was working on curriculum development in building and architecture, and there was the chance that she would get to travel in the coming year, perhaps to Hungary, to compare the curricula and education problems in other places. The salary wasn't much, but she loved the job and there was always that chance to travel. Mrs. Mazaraki had visited them earlier and now sent a photo she had taken then, and Maria sent it on to me. It was a picture of the family group, including her sister Janina and the dog, Fysia. They were all sitting in some room, apparently in the aftermath of a little joke, and there was some minor problem about who exactly was holding the dog. It was a lively, funny picture of a close-knit family. There was Agnieszka (she of the triumphant coat) and her brother Staszek (the "electronic") and his wife Mirka. Włodek was a solid, heavy set man with a thatch of greying hair.

The following April Agnieszka was married. Wojtek had come, following the respectable custom, to ask for her hand in marriage, and Maria, touched by his earnestness and sincerity, had agreed at once. But then the young couple went to live in another part of the city and Maria saw her daughter only a couple of times a week, if that. Maria wrote me, she said, sitting in her room with her heart *"un peu melancholique"*. But in July there was a serious request.

48

"Sarah!" she wrote, "I have one request: the daughter of my friend has been in London for two years. She study in Wrocław English literature, she had some troubles with the speech, and therefore she went to London. She has good job. She help an ill Polish doctor." But nothing had been heard from the young woman for two months, and her mother was beginning to worry; would I try to contact her and find out if she was all right? Maria was her godmother and felt concern of her own, as well as some responsibility to act. The doctor's address was in Hampstead. I dutifully phoned the place and spoke to young Ania, who must have been startled to hear from me—as startled as I had been four years before to find Andrzej Mazaraki on the other end of the line. It seemed that the "ill doctor" had recently died, and Ania was having to move and change jobs, and she hadn't got around to writing her mother. I had become part of Maria's admirable network, which was one of many such Polish networks, which could discover the whereabouts of a goddaughter, export amber jewellery, get hold of a toilet bowl of strange design, or arrange for ringside seats when the Pope came to town.

In the autumn of 1984 there were two momentous events for Maria: a public one and a private one. Her son became a father when Mirka gave birth to a daughter, and her priest was murdered. The news of the death of Father Jerzy Popiełusko came to Maria during Mass. "His works were great source of hope. His every word was the best nourishment. When his fate was unknown, we prayed every evening in the church. We get to know about his death during the mass. The first time in my life, I heard and participated in great cry—thousands people cried loudly! And then we kneeled down and prayed, '...forgive us our debts as we forgive our debtors'—very hard words!"

Later it all came out how he had been beaten up and his body dumped in a lake downriver where there is a dammed section of the Wisła. In short order his grave on the lawn beside his church of St. Stanisław Kostka near the Plac Wilsona became a site of vigils and pilgrimages. By the next February Maria was telling me about her activities at the church. "This year winter is very frosty. It gives us some [problems], especially when we stand some hours outside. For example every 19th of month. It is the date of death Priest George [i.e. Jerzy Popiełuszko] and we participate in mass. The church is overfull and thousands [of people] stand outside (two hours in the frost!) The second date—it is the last Sunday on the month. We participate in the mass. Intention: our country. And again the long sejour in the frost. And third date: every Wednesday I am on duty near priest George grave. I give informations to the pilgrims and foreigners, too."

Her granddaughter, Małgorzata (a name she always translated for me as "Margaret"), was baptised in February and Maria gave her a religious medallion to wear, one that Maria herself had worn at her own christening. Afterwards they celebrated with a dinner and some wine that Staszek and Mirka had brought back from a bicycle trip to Hungary three years before.

The baptism over, the child was always called by the usual diminutive, Małgosia. Maria had told me when her daughter-in-law was first expecting a baby that the child would be named after either Margaret Thatcher or Ronald Reagan, so Margaret, or Małgorzata, it was.

The next summer the Mazarakis were back in Warsaw visiting Maria. "We were very exciting," she wrote me, "we met them in airport (I like it very much), then we gave them some souvenirs, they made the same too." But now she noticed that her London friends didn't quite grasp the situation she lived with. The 19th of every month had become sacred to her (and countless other Poles) because Jerzy Popiełusko had been killed on October 19. Monthly vigils were held at his grave on the church grounds. "But I observed that they become more strangers for us now. We are in the first line of battle and they are the observers only! They wanted distractions and nothing sorrowful. For example 19 June was for them indifferent date. They wanted to visit the grave of Priest George tomorrow without the crowd—and for us the crowd—it is very important too—the feeling of solidarity."

But all was not well with her little granddaughter. There had been health problems from the start; there were stays in hospitals. Gradually it appeared that beyond a doubt the child had cystic fibrosis. I knew only that this was a very serious congenital condition affecting the lungs and that children with this condition lived for only a few years. I found that there was a British Cystic Fibrosis Society and phoned them to ask for information. They sent quite a helpful information pack, which I read and sent on to Maria. Anytime there was an article in the paper about a new breakthrough in the treatment of CF I cut it out and sent it to her. My information about cystic fibrosis had been badly out of date; I learned that now CF children could hope to live well into adulthood.

One day in early 1986 I had a phone call from a Dutch friend who had heard me speak of Maria and her family. Her daughter's school had made a collection of clothing to send to Poland and the consignment had duly been sent off, but now more things were still arriving at the school. In particular, they had received some very nice baby and children's clothing: would my friend Maria like some of this for her granddaughter? I said she probably would, and dictated the address over the phone.

Some time later I was visiting this same Dutch friend, Annemieke, when the phone rang and she asked me to answer it. When I did, I found that Staszek Wnuk was on the other end speaking English and wanting to thank her for the children's clothing. He was very grateful for the wonderful garments; they were just what Małgosia needed!

In the following summer I was at Annemieke's in Holland and found that she was expecting Staszek to come for a visit. He and Mirka were keen cyclists, I knew, and now he was going to ride his bicycle from Warsaw to coastal Holland—across those broad plains of Poland that had taken us hours on the train, then across East Germany with whatever documents, demands, bribes, and pilfering that might entail; then through the Ruhr with its network of motorways, and finally into Holland and across the valleys of the Maas and Rijn to the islands of the Delta. He was going to do all this so that he could get a summer job and make some hard currency so that he could take it back to Poland and buy a car. Buying a car was a very complicated undertaking. Much depended on whether you were going to pay for it in Polish złoty or hard cash from the West. Foreign currency would expedite the process by years.

After all these years of corresponding with Maria now I was going to meet her son. Staszek was a tall, dark-haired, young man with a quick smile and a friendly manner. He spoke English reasonably well and we could communicate easily in it. He was ambitious, but he lived in a place where there were few outlets for honest ambition. We wanted to help him all we could. In the Polish manner, he had brought all his own food, mostly in tins. Annemieke took one look at the nondescript cans with their plain labels and judged the food inside. "Of course, I will feed him. He can't eat this stuff."

The day after he arrived he wanted to start to work, and Annemieke had found him a farmer who needed a man to pull onions for him. I went with Staszek to see the farmer and do some translating and soon found I was being mistaken for Staszek's wife. After that misapprehension was put right we continued with the matter of the onions. Staszek was offered a certain amount of money and issued with heavy gloves. He was an excellent puller of onions, evidently, and he came home reeking of them. As he was only needed for one day in the onion field, Annemieke phoned around to find him another job. The local Chinese restaurant could use a dishwasher, she discovered, so Staszek and I went to the town square to discuss terms with the restaurant owner. In the end, Staszek was taken on to wash dishes for so much an hour, with a meal included.

It seemed that Staszek now had a regular job for the summer. Annemieke and I wondered privately how a telephone engineer could leave his work for months at a time. Perhaps he had been fired or something, she suggested, but we might have known that this wasn't likely to happen in Poland. There was "full employment" according to the socialist ideal, but that didn't mean that there was necessarily enough work for the "fully employed". Staszek had probably just taken an unpaid leave of absence and allowed his co-workers to cover for him in having little to do.

I went back to London and then heard that there had been a glitch with Staszek's full employment at the Chinese restaurant. The young Polish cyclist had an appetite that shocked the portly, middle-aged Chinese restaurant owner. Staszek was eating too much and therefore soon had to look for another job. Now Annemieke produced a couple of friends of hers, Lejo and Laura. They were teachers during the winter and berry farmers during the growing season, and like Staszek and Mirka, were the parents of young children. They needed help with their berry harvest and took to Staszek at once. Lejo and Staszek soon became great personal friends and found that they had much in common. At the end of the summer the Dutch couple cordially invited him back the next summer, this time with his wife and daughter.

The next year Staszek was again working with Laura and Lejo to harvest their berries, and Mirka and Małgosia enjoyed the entire summer by the seaside in Holland. They had now driven in Staszek's new car, a little Polski Fiat, across the terrain that Staszek had cycled over the previous summer. Maria wrote me that they were all having a wonderful time: Staszek was earning money again—sound Dutch guilders—and enjoying the company of his new friends and enabling his wife and daughter to have a splendid vacation. Furthermore, Małgosia was thriving on the sunlight and exercise. Children with cystic fibrosis need all the exercise they can get to develop their lungs and help them withstand the inevitable infections the condition encourages. Fortunately Małgosia was an active child and enjoyed running and swimming.

There was even travel in the opposite direction, because now Laura and Lejo were such firm friends of Staszek and his family's that in 1987 they drove to Poland at Christmas time. They filled their car with gifts for the Wnuks and were introduced to the extended family, including Mirka's parents. Maria told me that they all toasted me *in absentia* because it was through me, ultimately, that they were all assembled in the Wnuk flat in Warsaw. By now, this extending net of friendships was beginning to get a bit eerie. Not long after Christmas Mirka's father died (a man I had never met) and they were grateful that he had met Lejo and Laura (a couple I didn't know) before he died, and it was all thanks to me.

At some time in the mid-80s I began corresponding with Yvette Roux, a retired English teacher who lived in Besançon. We had quite a cordial correspondence, and when Maria Wnuk lamented that she didn't have any way to practice her French, I put her in touch with Yvette. They then struck up a cordial correspondence of their own. One summer Maria and Włodek and another couple got a caravan and made a tour of several western European countries. They of course went to Besançon and visited Yvette, whom I knew through correspondence, but had never been to visit. Already the ramifications of that casual conversation on the train seemed to me remarkable, but I didn't know the half of it.

Chapter Three

Kayak Trip

As the summer of 1988 approached, Maria invited us yet again to go on her annual kayak and camping trip. That year Alastair was going to go to China with a group of university administrators in September, and so I decided that I would go on the Polish kayak trip in July by myself. Maria was pleased finally to get an acceptance, even half an acceptance, to her invitation, and I was glad to be meeting my faithful correspondent again.

I had never been kayaking, unless you count an evening class in Peckham I took a few years before. It was every Wednesday evening, and every Thursday I had acute sinus congestion. I was not a great success at kayaking in the evening-class swimming pool. We learned how to hold the paddle and get in and out of the kayak. The next step seemed to be the hardest possible step: the Eskimo Roll. I was always assured afterwards in the dressing room that, actually, once you got the hang of it, it was quite easy, really. I never got the hang of it. I rolled over in the kayak and then attempted—remembered all the directions and accumulated advice—to roll back up to the surface, but time and time again I had to pull off my splash deck and slide out of the overturned kayak. Sometimes I almost succeeded in the Roll. I would give a terrific wrench and pull the paddle violently, but I never got up enough impetus to right the kayak. After one term of spending much of Wednesday evening suspended upside down in a capsized kayak and all of Thursday mopping at my nose, I gave up. Eskimo Roll ought to be an ice cream dessert anyway.

But now I was going to go on a real kayak expedition, kayaking during the day and camping under canvas at night. Maria and I would share a two-man kayak; she had done it for years with Włodek and knew all the ropes; I should bring a sleeping bag and warm pyjamas and she would bring everything else. I felt that the Eskimo Roll would probably not be necessary. I suspected that Maria couldn't do it either. It all sounded rather strenuous, in a way, but Maria was 18 years older than I was, so how strenuous could it really be? Maybe it was like those camping sites I had heard about, especially in France, that are decidedly luxurious as outdoor living goes, with hot showers and a laundromat and a restaurant next door: *le camping*. I hadn't been in a canvas tent since I was a Girl Scout, but the previous winter I had done some mild training and swum 5 kilometres in a sponsored "Swimathon" to raise money for Great Ormond Street Children's Hospital. In the past I had acquired life-saving certificates from both the American Red Cross and the Royal Life-Saving Society and a qualification to teach swimming. I felt confident about any really hand-to-hand encounters with the waterways of Poland, and I hoped the kayaking part would somehow take care of itself.

I flew to Warsaw on a British Midland flight in July. Okęcie Airport was like a provincial bus station. It was a haphazard place with ramshackle queues for passports and an ill-defined system for being reunited with your baggage. There was a form, evidently printed on thin paper towels, for listing all the kinds of money you had with you. There were people standing at a little counter trying to count their money as inconspicuously as possible. I had a Visa credit card, although few retail outlets in Poland would have known what to do with one. I had some traveller's cheques, but of course no Polish złoty because, just as in 1980, it was impossible to obtain any legally outside Poland. I had vouchers for złoty, based on the length of my visa. I had also brought some US dollars, because I was going to have to pay a fee to the kayak club, and dollars were the second, unofficial, currency of Poland. I counted everything up and entered the sums in the right boxes on the little paper-towel form and handed it in. It was stamped and put back in my passport, where I had to keep it until it was time to leave the country again. When I cashed my voucher, my $15-per-day-requirement-for-a-visa certificate, I was solemnly handed 157,419 złoty in a pile of paper notes and a few coins.

Now I was ready to go out and look for Maria Wnuk, whom I had last seen eight years before. I found her easily. She was standing with Staszek and Mirka out in the public part of the airport waiting for me. We had an affectionate reunion and Maria handed me a small bouquet of azaleas. I wasn't sure quite what I was supposed to do with it, but it is such a Polish impulse (as I learned later) to give people bouquets of flowers for any reason, that it would have been difficult for her to go to an airport to meet me without taking some flowers along. Staszek took me and my luggage proudly out to his new Polski Fiat, financed with his manual labour for Dutch guilders. We climbed into it and went off to Maria's flat on the other side of Warsaw.

The airport was south of Warsaw and Maria lived in Żoliborz on the north side of the city. This was the first time I had been in a car on the wide streets in the centre of Warsaw, whisking along in a Polski Fiat with real Poles in attendance, answering my questions and making me feel at home even before we got out of the car. The bouquet was beginning to wilt a bit, but I held it carefully and willed it not to wilt any more. (Wilt not, want not. "Wilt thou take this bouquet...")

Yes, I tell Maria, I have a sleeping bag and pyjamas, but she wants to inspect them when we get home. They are going to give me Staszek's old room. This is a particular privilege, I understand, and I thank them both for their generosity. Staszek and Mirka are now living with Mirka's widowed mother in the outlying town of Celestinów. The subject of Małgosia is still a fraught one; her health is a constant concern of the whole family. She is mentioned in hushed voices. In two weeks Staszek and Mirka and Małgosia are going to Holland to stay with Laura and Lejo and look into the possibility of treatments for the girl there. Włodek is also absent. He has heart trouble and is now in a sanatorium where people recover from serious illnesses. Their daughter Agnieszka, now married to Wojtek, is the mother of three small boys, and they, too, are living in an outlying district in a house they have just built. Just as Maria, Staszek and I are finishing off a snack and having some Dutch coffee that Staszek has proudly made from his store of Douwe-Egberts supplied by Laura and Lejo, in walk Agnieszka and Wojtek and little Kuba. They have come to meet the exotic stranger who caused the Dutch connection: the coffee, the Polski Fiat, the holidays in Zeeland. They all try out their English on me with Staszek acting as a safety net.

Maria Wnuk in her kitchen.

When they leave, Maria and I are alone in the flat. It consists of a small kitchen at one end of a hallway, off which open the doors to the living room, the toilet, the bathroom-cum-utility-room, and, clustered at the other end, three small bedrooms. The centre one is Włodek's study, and through a half-opened door I see his architect's drawing board at a desk. Staszek's old room is a pleasant little bedroom looking out onto the grass and trees behind the big concrete block of flats. The building is only about four storeys high and the Wnuk flat is on the first landing, up a curving concrete staircase. The younger members of the Wnuk family are apparently a sporty lot: there seem to be skis stacked up behind all the doors. A clump of them is behind Staszek's bedroom door and I narrowly avert a crash of large pick-up sticks on his floor. I am just getting my bearings and stowing my things when Maria wants to see my sleeping bag and pyjamas. The sleeping bag is all right, but the pyjamas won't do. They are far too thin. I am going to need something much heavier to sleep out of doors in. Very much heavier, she says. We will have to shop for it tomorrow. She takes my wilting bouquet of azaleas away to put in water.

In the evening Staszek and Mirka (short for Mirosława), on their way home to Celestinów, drop Maria and me off at the Church of St. Stanisław Kostka, where Jerzy Popiełuszko is buried. He was the popular young priest who got seriously up the nose of the government and was duly murdered by some appointed heavies in 1985. Lower level thugs were arrested and tried for the crime, but everyone knew that it was officially sanctioned. We find a Mass ending and the crowd comes out and stands in front of the grave singing, many of the singers holding their fingers up in a V for Victory salute. Maria tells me that this is because today is July 19, and as he was killed on October 19, every 19th of the month is specially observed. ("The nineteenth of every mouse," says Maria until I finally correct her.) The grave is under a huge black granite cross. Arranged around it are irregular boulders joined by massive chain links to represent a vast rosary. The outline of the chain-linked boulders is the shape of Poland. I find it a very imaginative and very moving memorial. (Staszek has told me that miracles are already being documented toward Father Popiełuszko's canonisation. For example, someone was dramatically healed on the day he was buried.)

Maria and I walk home by a circuitous route through side streets and across parks and housing estates. I couldn't find my way again if my life depended on it, but Maria knows Warsaw and especially Żoliborz like the back of her hand. She has lived here since the immediate post-war years; she has spent her adult life here, studying, teaching, raising a family, and seeing Warsaw rise from the rubble. Perhaps she learned it one street at a time as the city came back to life.

Back home, we talk and have the light evening meal, *kolacja*. Maria's English is laden with mistakes and strange pronunciations, but I am grateful to her for speaking it at all, as our whole relationship has depended on it since that first conversation on the train to Wrocław. In Poland now, knowledge of English seems quite a rare skill, and ordinary communication in public places would be difficult for me without Maria's help. Somehow she has learned an adequate amount of it and Staszek and Mirka, young professional people, have picked up a working knowledge of it. For Staszek it has been valuable as his means of communication with his Dutch friends, Laura and Lejo, and therefore his means of acquiring a Polski Fiat and seaside holidays for Mirka and Małgosia. Non-English speakers covet our language not just because they are charmed by our irregular verbs and esoteric pronunciation of "bough" and "cough".

Maria is a natural-born mother hen, and if she says we will have to shop for pyjamas, then there is no point suggesting otherwise. Actually, she's right: my yellow pjs are decidedly thin, indoor garments. Perhaps they are not the best ones for camping in Poland, even in July. The next day we take a bus down to central Warsaw to the Wars and Sawa department store. This is sort of two stores and sort of one, with two different names. This is so obviously puzzling and irrational that I don't even think about it, because you can't stop to think about everything that is puzzling or irrational in Warsaw or you would never get through breakfast.

We go straight to the right department. The salesclerk has disappeared and several would-be customers are murmuring. Maria goes behind the counter and knocks on doors but can't raise anyone. In a few minutes a girl turns up with a cup of hot water. The customers all pounce with their requests and demands. Maria does not hang back and I see her go into her mode for dealing with anything official—with anyone who is behind a counter having some kind of jurisdiction over others. She stands with her feet apart and her hands on her hips. She tells the saleswoman that we require a tracksuit to try on. Other customers are hard on our heels, after the same privilege. Soon we have the suit, although it is not the size we were looking for.

This *dress*, which seems to be the word for a tracksuit, doesn't look remotely like a pair of pyjamas; it is thick cotton, grey with red piping, and is made in China for people with small builds. Now I must pay for it before I can try it on, and so I give the salesclerk 300 zł and she writes out a receipt for me. Sure enough, I need a larger size; medium will never work. We go back out, I carefully clutching my tracksuit which doesn't fit but which I have paid to try on. The size that was unobtainable a few minutes ago now seems to exist after all, and Maria gets possession of it. I pay some more money to try it on. I look as though I am on the track team at some second-rate college for mature students, but Maria approves of this outfit as just the thing for our trip. We'll take it! We go back to the counter and hand in the rejected suit and get my 300 zł deposit back, and we leave in triumph.

"In London it is very ordinary, but here it is occasion for joy," says Maria.

So why does it not seem to occur to most British or American shoppers to steal the things they are trying on? It undoubtedly occurs to a few of them, and they do steal things and are then usually caught by the store detective or, nowadays, by the CCTV camera. Is all this extra business of paying for everything and getting receipts and then handing it back and being reimbursed justified? Do they feel that this is the only way to prevent wholesale theft (or rather, retail theft)? Without this system would the customers in fact walk off with anything they could? Or is all the busy-work yet another wheeze to create "full employment"? I puzzle about this on the way home on the bus.

Maria has bought a bus ticket for me. You have to buy them at a kiosk, and these kiosks are all over the place in the city. They sell all kinds of toiletries and cosmetics, books, newspapers, toys, knick-knacks and notions, and also bus and tram tickets. When you get on the bus you cancel the ticket yourself at a little gadget attached to one of the upright chrome posts by inserting the ticket and then punching it yourself. Passengers are trusted to do this themselves—the same customers who might have stolen merchandise from the department store. Perhaps it is easier to be honest—or deemed to be so—in one area but not another. The bus fare is a lot cheaper than a tracksuit. Or maybe the transport authority and the merchandise outlet have no contact with each other and are run by entirely different entities. I must stop expecting things to make sense. It's a bad habit I've picked up somewhere.

We have a couple of more days before we have to leave on the kayak trip, and it gives me a chance to talk to Maria and Staszek and to go shopping. Maria is keen for me to buy some things, like amber jewellery and leather handbags. We go to Nowy Świat, the Bond Street of Warsaw, and the Old Town, where there are shops selling very nice items, probably mainly for the tourist trade. I get a shoulder bag for 12,500 złoty and a silver brooch for 11,250 złoty. Maria wants me to spend money, not for her benefit or to improve the national economy, but because it is best to get rid of the stuff. I do have quite a wodge of złoty, considering I am going to spend most of my time here in pine forests and on waterways. Maybe she is thinking of what happened the last time: how we were so inefficient at getting rid of our cash that I had to send her an envelope bulging with it. I would like to buy her something but she adamantly refuses any sort of gift. I eventually weaken her resolve by saying I would really like to get her a new rosary ring, as the one she is wearing seems to be made of copper and plastic. I can see she is considering it and in the end I have a provisional assent on it.

I am interested in understanding how the system here in Poland works. Staszek tells me that when he was in school, they were taught that when the final stage of communism was in place, the need for money would wither away. Not having grown up hearing about this, I find it a really mad idea. I think money is a brilliant concept. According to Marco Polo, paper money was used in China in the 13th century, long before it appeared in Europe. It was another of those ingenious and practical Chinese inventions, like stirrups or the wheelbarrow. You acquire these all-purpose IOUs that work anywhere, regardless of your relation to the person you are trading with. They are like storage batteries of labour or earning power.

Far from anything "withering away", there seems to be a positive obsession about money here. They have to know exactly what is coming into the country and no złoty are allowed out. Numerous things, like Staszek's car, are unobtainable with the local currency and must be bought with foreign money—Dutch guilders, in this case, which behave like all-purpose IOUs so that dish-washing and berry-picking can be converted into a Polski Fiat. People know the price of things in both złoty and dollars and can quickly convert a price in one currency to the other. I can't see how anything is likely to "wither away" at this rate.

The state is also supposed to "wither away", and that seems an equally mad idea. Is this supposed to happen gradually, so that a totalitarian dictatorship somehow tapers off to nothing? Do the members of the Central Committee decide one day that they are no longer needed and society will now somehow roll along by itself without institutions of law or government? Perhaps the theory is that it is like a splint on a broken bone, and once the bone has set you can take the splint away. The whole notion seems so ridiculous that, not for the first time, I wonder how anyone could have ever imagined that it would work. Even if it seemed barely plausible in 1917, how could anybody have kept the faith (because it is obviously a variety of religion rather than statecraft) after the numerous demonstrations since then of its idiocy? Communism is to political science what the flat-earth theory is to geography, and the hapless Poles have to go through the motions of pretending to believe something that everyone knows is false. They are like adults keeping up the pretense of Santa Claus for the sake of the children, or in this case, by order of their government.

It is time to leave for the kayak trip! We get our things together. I have a duffel bag and my sleeping bag; Maria has that and much more, including a camping stove, a folding stool, and the tent. Staszek takes us in his Polski Fiat to Centralna train station and helps us with our impedimenta. When we get to platform 2, we find a small contingent of kayakers already there, all surrounded with their own bags, tents, camping stoves, folding furniture, and large amounts of miscellany.

I am introduced to several of Maria's friends, and the men all kiss my hand gravely. It is an absolutely charming custom. Here we are, standing on this train platform surrounded by all our camping equipment; people are wearing shorts and old clothes, and these men are kissing my hand as though we were standing in an Austro-Hungarian drawing room! The only problem is that when I unthinkingly offer my hand to be shaken, I am taken by surprise to find it going off in another direction from the one I intended. There is an awkward moment when I am not sure where my hand is going, but then it is reverently kissed by a new acquaintance being a courtly gentleman in these incongruous surroundings. With each other the men shake hands formally with a little bow.

Our train arrives and we get everything on board in a fairly decorous way. Boarding a Polish train is not always a decorous business. It is every man for himself and the devil take the hindmost. But we clamber on board without maiming anyone and arrange ourselves in several adjacent compartments. Maria and I share a compartment with Tomek Mach and his wife Ula and their little daughter, Ania. Tomek (short for Tomasz) is a big broad-shouldered man and easily stows all the big bags on the high racks. There are five bunks in the compartment and later a sixth is lowered.

We set off in the direction of Szczecin far to the west-northwest. This will be a long, leisurely journey, and later we will sleep for part of the night. Maria and the others have quite a reunion, because most of them have not seen each other since the previous year.

This kayak club has to be officially incorporated to have an existence under the Polish state, but it is a very odd organization.

These kayakers are only part of the larger club. There are branches in Szczecin and Wrocław. All the members are architects in the state bureau that designs hospitals. The club started several years ago when one of the employees in Wrocław, an Olympic kayaker, wanted to start a club at his workplace. The people at the other branches of the state concern were invited in, and the kayak club grew to include a hundred or more members. Not everyone went every summer, but the potential is for a sizable number when you add in the families and guests of the members. The chief of the club, the *Komandor*, is a certain Zygmunt from the Wrocław branch.

We eat sandwiches, and finally at about 8 p.m. it's time to take off our shoes, make up the bunks with sheets and blankets, and get some sleep. We doze as the train continues its way north and west. It begins to rain. We are awakened at about 3 a.m. to get ready to disembark during the brief stop at Szczecinek, where it is still raining. Now we all pile out of the train with our possessions onto the dark rainy platform and quickly take everything to the covered part, where to my surprise there is a buffet doing a thriving trade at this hour. We have an hour and twenty minutes to wait for our train, and Teresa, a lively friend of Maria's who is wide awake now, a chemist who seems to be a member of the architect kayaking club anyway, recommends the goulash. Several of the kayakers order plates of goulash and I am offered some, too. It is nice goulash, but I can't say I have a great appetite for it at 3 in the morning.

Teresa is friendly and vivacious, but lacks English. She makes up for this by greeting me with the one English phrase she does know, which is "To be or not to be." In various circumstances it serves the purpose of "Good morning" or "Hello, how are you?" or "How pleasant to see you again." In time she uses it for all these functions and more. Now it means "Have a plate of this goulash and see if you like it."

We have all finished our goulash and stand around for a little while, and then the train for Czaplinek arrives and we board it for the rest of the journey. In a few hours the sun comes up and we at last arrive at the little country station marked "Czaplinek". There is nothing at all within sight of it, except a country road and green fields and some scattered trees.

At length Zygmunt pulls up in a white van. This van will not accommodate everyone and all the baggage, so about half the arriving Warsaw group get in and half wait for the second trip. Our campsite is on Lake Komorze some distance away. During the year before a kayak trip Zygmunt travels around the country choosing a route and all the campsites. Something about this sounds less and less like *le camping* with showers and laundry. I walk up and down the train platform to have something to do.

A half dozen or more of us hang around the Czaplinek train halt for a couple of hours before Zygmunt reappears in his van and we finally get in and move off. Now we are finally on the road, and it is a pleasant drive through country lanes with little other traffic except now and then a farmer's horse and wagon. We come to Lake Komorze, a large lake with wooded banks. Where the road passes near it there is a small beach. We turn to the right, away from the lake and up a rough track through the pine woods and come to some tents. There is no resemblance whatsoever to *le camping*. It is more like Outward Bound.

Zygmunt continues uphill to the edge of the camp, where there is space for more tents. The Szczecin and Wrocław groups have arrived a day or two before and have already set up their tents. They are already enjoying the swimming on this hot sunny day, and children are playing together and being discreetly overseen by their parents. Maria shows me how to set up our old canvas tent and we move into our new quarters. She is a strong and energetic woman and loves the homemaking element of pitching a tent and arranging things, especially her cooking equipment. She is going to do all the cooking for us.

We meet the neighbours. On one side are a man and his young son, Marcin, who is learning English. He can say, "How are you?" but is petrified into silence when the answer comes. I have better luck on the other side of the tent. These neighbours are the people I already know from the train trip: Tomek and Urszula (or Ula) Mach, a couple in their mid-30s, and their 10-year-old daughter Ania. Tomek is an architect in this state-run hospital-designing business and his wife is a gynaecologist at a hospital. Ania is a shy, pretty child, blonde like her mother. Tomek and Ula make valiant stabs at English for my benefit, and I appreciate their efforts. They are a remarkably striking couple, Tomek and Ula. He is tall and muscular with dark curly hair and the profile of a Greek statue; she is small-boned, blonde and blue-eyed and very pretty. One or the other would make heads turn, but together they are a strikingly handsome pair.

We get ourselves organized and go off for a swim. Maria can't swim, but she comes down to the lake shore in her bathing suit anyway. The lake water is cool on this scorching day. There is a sandy beach with shallow, lapping water and a very gradually sloping lake bottom. The bottom is rocky and then at about waist depth there are a lot of weeds, but beyond that the lake bed falls away and the lake is a placid expanse of slightly muddy water. The visibility underwater is poor, but I swim a few crawl strokes away from the shore just to enjoy being in all this water, muddy or not. Anyway, it is certainly no muddier than the Serpentine in Hyde Park, where I have often swum. It is wonderfully refreshing on this hot day after the strange night on a train with a goulash break and then all the hanging around at Czaplinek.

This is definately not *le camping*, and the only running water is in the lake. The forest is a self-catering boardinghouse with as many bathrooms as occupants. I quickly see what the system is and go off to find a private place in the woods. The problem with a pine forest is that there is very little understorey. In a broadleaf forest there are masses of things growing below the canopy—all sorts of bushes and saplings—but in a pine forest you can see for great distances among the trees and there is little cover for any private activities. I walk on up the forest track and then veer off it, noticing a large stone as a landmark. The ground rises for a while, and I come to some fallen pine branches. I pull some of these together, making a little bower for myself. This is quite a satisfactory arrangement. I can't be easily seen and it is much more hygienic than any public toilet I have yet seen in Poland. The enduring mystery is that, although the campers amount to a group of at least 60 we never seem to see each other in our little wanderings through the woods for these personal purposes. Maria devises a shorthand term for these trips to the forest: she says she is going "to a lonely place", and it quickly becomes our code phrase. We seem adept at coded references, even when there are no postal censors about.

The kayak trip is held during the same fortnight every summer, and so the same name days are always celebrated. Tomorrow is Krzysztof's name day. Krzysztof and Basia are friends in another tent. Maria and I gather some wild flowers and, frankly, weeds, but they make a pretty little ad-hoc bouquet, and naturally a bouquet of some description is absolutely necessary. The next morning a little group of well-wishers sing *Sto lat* to him—"May you live a hundred years"—and I step forward with the bouquet and present it to him, saying "*Proszę*", just as Mariusz, the boy on the Wrocław train, kept saying as he offered everyone his biscuits.

Happy campers: L to R Teresa, Maria, Basia; Ula and Tomek Mach, Andrzej (seated) and Krzsztof (standing). Tomek has been fishing and Ula indicates the size of the one that got away.

It is Sunday morning and already hot at 8 a.m. I go down the track for a swim in the lake before breakfast and then come back to our tent for a breakfast of tea, cucumbers, eggs, and mushrooms. The Machs ask if I would like to go with them in a kayak to get some fresh drinking water and of course I agree. Ula and I get into one kayak and Tomek and Ania are in another. We paddle out into the lake, Tomek taking a water canister with him. We stop in a little bay and ask for water, but there is no running water there, so we go on. Another 2 kilometers down the lake there is a pier and a house where he stops and eventually returns with the water. In the meantime Ula and I wait in our kayak and construct a halting conversation out of some scraps of English, as you might put together a rough garment from some rags and remnants: nothing worth keeping but something slapped together to serve the purpose of the moment. I point out some grebes going past, and we build a few remarks around them.

We go back to our end of the lake in a stiff wind, but it is still so hot that I have another quick swim before lunch. Maria and I then walk with a little straggling group of other campers the 2 kilometers to the village of Rabowo to hear Mass. There is no regular church in the village, but a priest comes from Czaplinek at 3 p.m. on Sundays to say Mass at what looks like a converted village hall. There is a little stage at one end and slatted benches. The floorboards are bare and the walls are faded. Maria likes the front row in churches, and so I too become a somewhat unenthusiastic front-row sitter.

The priest is a Graham Greene character, plump and sweating, who mops his forehead and repeated cleans his glasses on his cuffs. He has four local acolytes, schoolboys who wear old trainers and jeans under their diaphanous, full-sleeved acolyte smocks. Maria knows that I am unfamiliar with Masses, and so she whispers tersely, "Credo", or "Benedictus" to me as we go along, on the assumption that I will be able to follow the Polish Mass from such clues. I stand, sit, or kneel as Maria does.

After Mass, a contingent of us go to a woman in the village who sells milk and cucumbers. Today she has a bucket of fresh blackcurrants, too. We all buy some of her produce. She has some ancient scales on a table in the farmyard and a sack of flour or sugar to measure a kilo. She brings a bucket of milk and pours it from a tin cup into our milk bottle. I have a city-dweller's distrust of unpasteurised milk, but Maria likes this country milk, even when it's warm, because it is purer than milk bought in Warsaw, which must, by law, be boiled by the consumer. (Oh? I think of the unboiled milk Alastair and I drank when we were cycling here 8 years ago. I have a flash of retrospective alarm.) The milk containers, Maria tells me, are contaminated with DDT. Furthermore, the big dairies get milk from farmers over a wide area, and the health of these cows may be dubious. Bovine tuberculosis is a problem in Poland. The woman at Rabowo assures Maria that the milk does not need to be boiled. I think naturally she would say that and I wonder how we can be sure. I wonder how we can be sure of anything in this country, but Maria seems confident. She has spent her lifetime learning how things work here, and I seem to have spent my lifetime learning how to misunderstand things here.

On an evening stroll through the forest to the village of Osada Lesna (0.8 km on the road sign) Maria and I discover a farm where *carroty* are sold. They also have some milk that is slightly more expensive than at Robowo, but the road to Osada Lesna is prettier and shorter, so it is worth it. The path through the pines is sandy and the evening light makes long shadows in front of us. Off to one side three deer suddenly bound through the sparse undergrowth. When we come to a cottage with a garden, the cottager is in front of her little house and Maria greets her and strikes up a conversation. The woman offers us a bunch of carrots from her garden, and Maria accepts them graciously.

"Don't we pay her?" I ask as we are leaving. We paid for the milk and other things in Rabowo.

"No, is gift," Maria says. "Custom is to give the travellers food for the journey."

We go on with the carrots, and Maria talks about the situation in Poland, a topic that is always on Polish minds to one degree or another. The problem, she tells me, is "that plague in the East", by which she means the Soviet Union, imposing or propping up the dictatorship in Poland. She warms to her subject. "The *only* American president who understand Russia is President Reagan!"

Not long before this, Reagan had given his notorious "Evil Empire" speech, which made many Americans cringe and most Western Europeans sneer. It seemed so over the top. What good would this rhetorical name-calling do? And after all these years of the Cold War and trying to be conciliatory and understanding, Reagan calls the Soviet Union an "Evil Empire" and publicly introduces this note of confrontation into whatever delicate diplomacy is going on somewhere behind closed doors. Leftist Europeans found this a dangerous, wild-eyed, extravagant mouthing-off and regretted what they saw as the general American tendency to elect lunatics for presidents. After all the negative opinions about the US from the leftish media in Britain, here was an entirely new one from someone living near the epicentre of world leftism.

"Reagan *know* about Soviet Union! He say exactly right! It is Evil Empire! No other president say this. He is first one!" Maria speaks with considerable passion on this subject. What so many people outside Eastern Europe thought was embarrassing hyperbole she sees as the simple truth.

We have come over a small rise in the pine forest and beside the path there seems to be a circle of stones. I am looking at it when Maria says, "Perhaps is grave." I look at her questioningly, and she adds, "Grave of somebody. In war." She shrugs to show that she has no more information about it.

We are to be issued with our kayaks. Zygmunt has brought them in a huge rack towed behind his van. A few of the members have their own, but most of us use the club's kayaks. Each kayak is numbered and we draw lots for them. Maria and I ominously draw number 13, but I am not at all superstitious. The problem is that I have had no experience with a two-man kayak or any other kind on a lake or river. Maria hears about a man, a member of the Wrocław contingent named Henryk, who can teach me the rudiments of kayaking. Moreover, he can speak English. He will take me out for a trial run and then I will be all prepared for the trip, which will begin in a day or two. We are spending four or five days in this camp because the weather and the site are so pleasant, but at some point we must get started on the trip proper.

Chapter Four

Hello, Central, Give Me Dr Jazz

Henryk appears and we are introduced. He will be happy to show me how to manoeuvre a kayak. Henryk is not a good-looking man. He is fat and bald and has crooked teeth and a cast in one eye. Still, he can't help it, and I am not going to hold his appearance against him. He lives in Wrocław and is an electronics engineer, but also seems to run some sort of business, or perhaps hobby, with jazz recordings. He corresponds with people in other countries and they exchange recordings of jazz.

"Ah," I say, "Louis Armstrong."

"No, modern."

"Miles Davis. Dave Brubeck!"

"Dave Brubeck!" he repeats. "John Coltrane."

"I like Dixieland."

"Dixieland too simple."

"Scott Joplin."

"Yes, Scott Joplin. André Previn and Itzak Perlman play Scott Joplin!"

"Stefan Grappelli," I suggest. "Django Rinehart. Hot Club..."

"Of France!" Henryk exclaims.

This was the most coherent and grammatical conversation we ever had.

Several people are going to go to another lake on the other side of Czaplinek with kayaks on what seems to be a kind of wet dry run. Henryk and I are going to go so that he can teach me the fine points of kayaking. Maria reminds me that I am to take it easy; Henryk will attend to everything, and if I get tired I should just stop paddling. We go in a car and the minibus, but Henryk is coming later with another group. Teresa and I wait for Henryk

73

and Andrzej, as we four are going to kayak together. Even when they appear, it becomes clear that we are short by one kayak— our number 13. The others expertly stow their things in their kayaks and soon they have moved off and are disappearing into the distance of this large lake. Zygmunt goes off in the truck to get our kayak, still back at the campsite many miles away. Finally in the early afternoon we four finally get under way. The lake is choppy with a stiff wind. We take the furrows in the lake neatly at right angles, but the headwind slows us down. After about an hour and a half we reach a sheltered river connecting the lakes, but it is obstructed with low tree branches, fallen trees, submerged logs, overhanging bushes, and numerous other things. It is a real obstacle course, but rather beautiful in a swampy sort of way.

Henryk sits behind me and it soon becomes clear that his entire command of English consists of names of jazz musicians. He really doesn't speak the language at all and we have very little means of communication. Henryk not only can't speak English, as advertised, but can't actually steer a kayak either. We run into most of the available obstacles. Teresa and Andrzej are waiting for us at the end where the river opens out into another lake. This pattern is repeated during the long afternoon: Teresa and Andrzej skilfully speed off and wait for us while we poke along, running into things.

Maria's advice to me has passed Henryk by, because when I stop paddling he does, too. We move only if I make us move. At one point later in the day we come even with some friends of his and he calls out to them "*Perestroika!*" Mikhail Gorbachev has recently come to power in Russia and one of his key words is *perestroika*, which means "restructuring". Henryk means that he is taking it easy while I do all the paddling; this is his witty idea of "restructuring". I like Henryk less and less as the day wears on. He is a useless bully. He doesn't dare really bully me, the stranger and guest, but his bullying takes the form of this dominance game. His posturing would be more convincing if he weren't so stupid. By the end of the day we have lost our way two or three times and run into every solid object in the river, and I am exhausted. We finally arrive at the designated spot at about 9 p.m., not near our campsite, but Zygmunt and his son and their dachshund are waiting for us in the white van. I am too tired to stand up at first. I could kill Henryk if only I had the energy. Henryk pokes me familiarly in the breastbone and says, "Do you have heart trouble?" I say "No," as curtly as possible. Henryk is the most objectionable person I have met for a long time. If I never see him again it will be too soon.

It is growing dark when I finally reach the campsite, and Maria and Ula meet me on the track that runs uphill near our tent. Maria embraces me warmly. "I was anxious about you!" she exclaims. I have a bowl of asparagus soup and some bread but am too exhausted to eat more. I tell her a bit about Henryk. Then she tells Tomek and Ula next door (or next tent flap), and before long Henryk is a laughingstock in our little neighbourhood. I fall into my sleeping bag in my clothes and wake up the next morning still wearing my passport around my neck in the waterproof purse.

The next day we hear that Henryk has told a boy that he has cancer. The boy had a sore back, obviously from the backrest in his kayak, and now Henryk, the know-it-all, has frightened him with this absurd diagnosis of his. The man is an all-round menace, and his reputation, partly foolish and partly dangerous, spreads through the camp.

Our *Komandor*, Zygmunt, is a distant, austere presence. It is he who decides what happens next. He has not only chosen the campsites and the route of the trip (or *spływ*), but he now chooses when exactly we will move from one camp to the other. I don't know whether he has really planned it all in advance or decides from day to day on a whim. The impression he gives is the latter. He scents the air, communes with himself, ponders and cogitates, and then issues his decision for the day: we stay put or we break camp. Maria tells me that he is a Communist, a member of the Party. I think it is strange that such a fact should be remarkable in a Communist country, but she explains that he is the only one in the whole club who is. He has done it for some petty motive of advancement, she implies, but he can't be completely committed, she adds, because he is sending his son to catechism classes. So we Polish kayakers are a bunch of non-Party members working for a State bureau and led by a half-hearted pseudo-Communist with Catholic leanings. There are subtleties in this country, I sense, that are going to be beyond me.

"Communism is poverty!" Maria exclaims. "Look at this paper!" She holds out the squares of toilet paper that she has been using to mop her forehead and shakes them at me. "We can't get paper."

"Why is there such a shortage of toilet paper?" I ask her.

"All the paper is used to publish the works of V.I. Lenin!" she says with a slight exaggeration, but she is only half joking. "The epidemic from the East! The red epidemic," she explains, and again, the language may be a bit jokey, but she is entirely serious. Later she sums it all up succinctly for me: "It is all built on lies. We don't believe our government and we hate the Russian government." No wonder she is fond of Ronald Reagan and had been looking forward to having a grandson named after him.

Maria and a good many of her friends are active supporters of *Solidarność*, but I don't know how much they discuss it openly. She tells me, in the confidence of the pine forest, that she once kept a box of contraband literature in her flat for a friend who was expecting to be raided by the police. She hid it away and didn't mention it to Włodek or Staszek. Polish women of her generation have learned how to be circumspect; they have learned who to trust and who not to, and they have seen that there are things that even close family members don't need to know. "One thing I learned during the War, don't tell anybody anything," she tells me.

Maria describes her life during the War years for me. She was a teenager then. Under the German occupation academic studies were illegal. Maria was enrolled in a school of tailoring, which her mother thought would be a useful occupation, and it was suitably unacademic. All over Poland there were clandestine schools, and they were extremely dangerous. The penalty for studying history, physics, or Polish literature could be summary execution or only imprisonment, depending on the mood of the local *Kommandant*. Maria and her friends, Misia and Krystyna, went at certain appointed times with their textbooks hidden under their sweaters to their teachers' houses and gradually acquired a decent secondary education. After the War all the secret records of the schools, with the assumed names of the pupils, were somehow sorted out and certificates were awarded. I get the feeling that there is nothing wrong with Polish administrative ability; it is all to do with motivation.

Maria tells me about her father, Zygmunt Trojanowski. He lived through the Russian Revolution and did his architecture studies in Petersburg. Later when he built his house in Puławy he made a secret wall safe in one room and put things in it for a "black hour" (much more sinister that a "rainy day"): sugar, candles, matches, and salt.

Maria suddenly decides she had better take me to *Komandor* Zygmunt to have my visa stamped. "By Zygmunt?" I ask. "Why by Zygmunt?"

"Zygmunt has stamp," she says.

"But why does he have to stamp my visa?" I persist. I really don't see the connection. Nobody stamped anything when we were in Poland in 1980.

"Zygmunt has stamp. It must be stamped to show where you are. To be on safe side."

So if I leave the address shown on my entry document I need to be able to show where I have been. Maybe this is a new regulation left over from martial law. Zygmunt produces his stamp, which sure enough he is carrying around with him, and stamps my document with it. It gives the name of the club and its official registration number. Along with his tent and camping stove and all the rest of it, Zygmunt has to remember to take his stamp everywhere.

One day Maria and I are walking along the road with Teresa and a few other women when a Russian convoy goes past. We are at the edge of the "Russian Polygon" and now and then a jet flies low over Lake Komorze and creates a terrific roar. The larger area where we are is Pojezierze Pomorskie, formerly Pomerania, once part of Germany and before that, Prussia. Now it is a beautiful nature reserve and also a practice area for Soviet army and air force manoeuvres. "And what are they doing in our country? Russian soldiers in the middle of Europe!" Maria snaps. Teresa points out the Cyrillic letters on the license plates. "USSR," she spells out for me disapprovingly.

I could get used to this camping. I swim in the lake every day. The weather is deliciously warm and the surrounding pine forest is delightful. Sometimes we walk to the town of Rabowo for supplies. One day after my swim and breakfast Maria and I walk to Rabowo for bread and a few other things. There are no eggs in the village shop, but we are directed to the home of a woman who works in the shop to buy eggs privately from her daughter. We get eight of them and pack them carefully in Maria's old rucksack. In the evening I have another swim in the lake as the sun is setting at the far end. The lake is orange with the sunset, and the water is disturbed only by the strokes I make in it. Later I change clothes in the tent and emerge for the evening festivities.

At the tent next door Ula is making open sandwiches for the celebration of Ania's name day. We celebrated Krzysztof's name day yesterday, and now it is Ania's turn. I help Ula make some sandwiches. As we are doing this, a boy comes along and hands us "tickets" for a cabaret performance that the children are mounting, using the empty kayak truck as a stage. Later at around 10:00 we are reminded that the performance is about to begin, so we take our flashlights and troop down to the big truck. We sit on stools and kapok lifejackets and watch the various acts and skits. A little girl sings to a soft guitar accompaniment floating up from the orchestra pit by the truck wheels.

Afterwards we go back to our tent neighbourhood and Basia and Krzysztof plus Teresa and Andrzej go to Tomek and Ula's tent forecourt for Ania's name day celebration. Unlike Krzysztof's celebration the night before, there is no vodka, not so many toasts, but they sing "*Sto lat*" to her.

Sarah and the rack of kayaks.

Finally Zygmunt decides that we should strike camp and get on our way. We pack our things and take our tent down and give everything to Zygmunt, who will transport our bags and equipment to the next campsite and meet us there. Our campsites are always marked with a big colourful cloth banner saying *spływ Kajakowy*, and this will be erected at the place by the river where we are to stop. Maria and I have little bags with some food and water and anything else we will need for the day, and we stow them in the space under the deck of the kayak. We are not wearing splashdecks, presumably because they don't exist and also because we will have to lie down flat on our backs to get under some of the low bridges along the way, and splashdecks would be an encumbrance. Somewhat more worryingly, there aren't enough kapok life vests to go around and, anyway, people use them as cushions to sit on. I give Maria our one life vest, because she is bound to need it more than I will. There are no helmets, but after all, this is not going to be white-water stuff. I am to sit in the back of our kayak number 13 and work the rudder, because Maria's legs won't reach. This rudder is attached by cords to a wooden foot plate that can be pressed with the left or right foot to steer the kayak. I can't do worse than Henryk at this, whatever mistakes I may make. The kayaks are all very old and heavy; they are elderly fibreglass craft and not the light plastic kind like the one I used so unsuccessfully in the swimming pool in Peckham. (I could truthfully say that I used to hang out in Peckham.)

We push off from the shallow water and are on our way. The whole flotilla is strung out in this big lake and before long the front ones are out of sight. We paddle along, stroking in unison, aiming for the far end of the lake. It is another warm, sunny day with little wind, and the lake is calm. The pine forest comes right down to the lakeshore and there is rarely any sign of human habitation. Teresa and her partner draw near us and she calls out, "To be or not to be!" which means "Hi! Have a pleasant time on the water!" Her paddling partner, Andrzej, is a small, round, cheerful man who is very helpful a bit later when we can't find our way out of the lake.

The Piława River flows out of the lake somewhere, if we can only find it. There are reed beds that obscure the topography. The reeds are several feet high and we skirt along a small forest of them trying to see an outlet. Andrzej scouts around, peering through the tall reeds and finally announces that he sees the way through. We follow him and Teresa and find that he has indeed found the river. We thank them gratefully and now enter a pleasant stream bordered by overhanging broadleaf trees with the occasional field or pasture. The green-shaded water is dappled with fleeting patches of sunlight. When there is an obstacle in the river, like an overhanging bush or a pile of tree branches, we carefully skirt around it, and I find that the rudder isn't hard to operate, after all. Once in a while we mistakenly run into the riverbank and have to push ourselves away from it. The current is not very fast. Sometimes there is a more serious obstacle blocking the whole river and we have to get out of the kayak, pick it up, and portage around the obstacle. Some of the more experienced kayakers and the stronger men hang behind at these places to help others with the portaging. These obstacles seem a bit man-made somehow, and Maria says that people have put them there to discourage motorboats.

There are some low foot and road bridges that barely allow a kayak to pass. We hold our paddles parallel with the kayak and lie back as flat as we can while the joists supporting the bed of the bridge pass a few inches above our noses. When we are not manoeuvring the craft around bends in the river or dealing with obstacles, we can paddle along admiring the view. Our attitude to the current differs. I want to keep paddling, because if you do not go faster than the current you are not really in control of the kayak, but Maria likes the idea of coasting on the current like a leaf without paddling when the river is straight and clear. I am not too worried about the life vests, because this river is actually quite shallow. It has a stony bottom and the water is very clear. It looks about waist-deep at the most.

I am not disappointed when we reach our campsite and can get out of the kayaks. There is a low but steep bank here and we have to clamber out of the kayaks and up the rough bank to a flat meadow that will now be home for a day or two until Zygmunt gives us the sign to get back on the Piława. We set to work putting up our tent again and preparing the evening meal. Maria has brought some provisions from our last trip to the village near the first campsite.

I am in our tent putting my shoes on when Ula and Maria call for me to come quickly. I hobble out, one shoe in my hand, to find them pointing at a train line in the distance where, against the pink evening sky, flat cars rumble along carrying army tanks. Just across our river is Russian military territory. It is unmarked, but it is absolutely off limits. I gather they are indignant and contemptuous of the Russian presence, and they want me to witness these tanks, as one might point out to a visitor one's neighbours creating a public nuisance. ("Look what we have to put up with! Didn't we say our neighbours were an uncouth lot?")

We eat and afterwards join some of the others at a folding table. Tomek offers me some vodka and pours out a tumbler of it. But what would they do if I innocently quaffed it all down as though it were a weaker drink? Would they stop me before I got acute alcoholic poisoning? I thank them and raise it to my lips and imbibe about two molecules of it. I hear Maria politely turning down the vodka offered to her, saying that she is almost completely *abstinent.* After another molecular sip or two I am excused further vodka.

The children, encouraged by their recent critical acclaim, put on another "cabaret" in the back of the truck, but the audience is somewhat less charmed by the novelty, except for the parents. Parents, at least, can be counted on for applause.

We are camped in a cow pasture. The next morning there is cold dew on the ground and a few cows cropping the grass near our tent flap. We find a "lonely place" (not so easy in a cow pasture, but there is the forest at a short distance) and eat breakfast. We have a free day in camp after the paddling yesterday, and Maria and I, together with Teresa and Basia, walk to the nearest town, Liszkowy, to look for groceries and generally see the sights. We continue on to Łubowo, a slightly bigger town. There really are a lot of Soviet soldiers around, and they make Maria and Basia nervous on my behalf. They quickly decide that it would be good if my nationality was concealed from these soldiers. I must not speak any English in their hearing. Basia is plainly very concerned about the possibility of an international incident. My instinct is that anyone can go anywhere, but I also know that my instinct can't be trusted here and is almost always going to be wrong. If Maria and Basia say I must lie low, then I must. "Don't say anything in English," they command me. They are really serious about it.

The Russian soldiers are boyish-looking and wear somewhat comical big army hats. The circular crown stands out like a khaki halo behind their heads. They look a bit lonely and nobody speaks to them. They are recruited to come here from parts of the Soviet Union distant from Poland or Lithuania so that they will be less likely to fraternise with the locals.

We make our way to a café and decide to have some tea and cakes. Maria and I sit at a table and save a seat for Basia, who is going to queue up for our tea and cakes. It is a long, slow-moving queue, and after about 20 minutes she succeeds in getting the tea and some dry little cakes for us. I express (quietly, for there are Russian soldiers here, too) sympathy for her long wait in the queue, but it makes her chuckle. Poles have spent their lives waiting in queues for hours, sometimes days, and 20 minutes is like the blink of an eye in comparison. They smile at me indulgently. What do I know about waiting in queues?

I am getting the hang of kayaking, and the Piława River is extremely picturesque. We paddle along the meandering river, now past green fields, now through a wooded patch. The days are warm but the nights are very chilly and I need that heavy tracksuit Maria made me buy in Warsaw. It is not an ounce too heavy on these cold nights.

Among all the equipment Maria has brought for us are earplugs. A group of the other kayakers sit around the campfire and sing until all hours. They start at about the time we are getting into our sleeping bags. No one tells them to pipe down; they just bring earplugs. They sing a melancholy-jaunty song called *"Pierwsza Brygada"* about the "First Brigade" commanded by Josef Piłsudski during World War I. Someone strums a guitar. They launch into another song, apparently an old stand-by. I ask Maria what it is about, and she answers sleepily that it is a ridiculous song. It is all about someone who has lost the key to the privy. That is the entire content of the song, she says. They are always singing it. She pushes the earplugs into her ears and I do the same.

83

One of the Wrocław kayakers has brought a young guest with him, a teen-age girl who chuckles one day when she overhears me asking a question about collective farms. (Collective farms never really caught on in Poland, in spite of an early attempt to form them. The term must sound old-fashioned to her, and perhaps foreign and comical and altogether un-Polish.) She seems to understand some English, but I am surrounded by Maria and her Warsaw friends and I don't see much of the girl from Wrocław. One day, however, when we are off the river and in camp, I am sitting in the shade reading when she comes up to me. She has heard that I know French, and she wonders if I know what this word means, and she shows me a page of a classic French novel she is reading. Her English is quite good, and I translate the word into English for her and she thanks me. It is not a very difficult word, but just unusual enough to serve as a pretext for conversation. We begin talking and get acquainted. Magda has another year or two of high school to do in Wrocław and then wants to go on to the University of Wrocław to study art history or possibly something else. She is undecided about the details. She is bright and has a good sense of humour. I am glad to meet her and pleased to find someone with a confident command of English.

Maria meets and approves of her. She explains to me that as Magda is about 16, she calls her "*panna* Magda", using the honorific title for adult unmarried women. Magda is a young lady now, she says, and will appreciate this acknowledgement of the fact. Magda tells me that her family name, Lachaut, was originally French and that the family story is that their French ancestor was with Napoleon on the march back from Russia and stayed in Lvov, where the Lachauts lived before the Second World War. When the eastern part of Poland was awarded to the Soviet Union, the Lachauts moved, like so many other people from Lvov, to Wrocław, which had been the German city of Breslau but was now Polish. Breslau, Wrocław, or Vratislavia, a thriving city and the capital of Lower Silesia, has been in various hands through the ages. Lvov had been Polish and Ukrainian, but in 1945 it became Stalin's property.

Poland is one of those places—there can't be so many of them, surely—where a citizen has to move house from time to time to stay in the same country. Conversely, in this part of the world you could live in two or three different countries over the years without moving an inch. In the last 1000 years Poland has sloshed around in central Europe between the Oder and the Dnieper and the Baltic and the Black Sea like a wet oyster.

In a wide shallow part of the Piława we come upon an army tank taking up most of the middle of it. On top of the tank and scrubbing it down like an elephant in the Ganges are three young men with their shirts off. They are Russian soldiers in their tank-scrubbing mode and seem harmless enough, but I remember the look on Basia's face when she warned me not to utter a word in English. So I am a thorough-going Pole now; oh yes, Polish to the core. Maria, sitting in front, doesn't know which way to go around the tank, but the men on the tank say yes, it is deep enough here, and Maria then calls over her shoulder, "*Na lewo!*" I know this means "to the left" and so, as though I am responding to words in my own language that I've known since infancy, I instantly steer us to the left. *Na lewo* and its opposite *na prawo*, oh yes, they are the most familiar phrases in the world to me. That is because I am Polish and the Polish language is my native tongue. I hardly speak anything else. We skirt around the big tank and the friendly boys who don't know that an alien harbouring the English language has just passed under their noses.

After another day of paddling along the Piława—20 kilometres and two portages—we come to a large shallow lake. Our new campsite will be at the edge of this lake among some tank traps. This area is part of the "Russian Polygon", the campground or mock battlefield where the Russians do their Warsaw Pact manoeuvres. As an act of generosity and public relations, in August they allow Poles into this part of Poland for camping and recreation. Our tents are dispersed among some deep ditches that we try not to fall into at night (but which, conversely, make convenient "lonely places" after dark). I am not sure whether they are trenches or tank traps, but they are left over from a big battle in February 1945 when the Russian forces were pushing westward and the Germans were falling back. Some earthworks look more recent than that and are presumably to do with more recent Russian operations.

It is raining when Zygmunt arrives with our tents and equipment, and Maria asks if I would like to find a barn or somewhere to sleep instead of putting up the tent. I look at the light rain and the overhanging trees and think of this theoretical barn, and urge that we put the tent up quickly. We have put it up several times now, and we are getting quite adept at it. With the rain to encourage us, we put up our tent in record time, working in close teamwork, laying out the groundsheet, pegging it down, setting up the two poles and the ropes to secure them, then the brass grommets on the poles, the big tent pegs in place, pounding them in with a rock, securing the flap protecting our little front porch and emergency wet-weather cooking area. In half an hour we've done it all and are only a little damp. We crawl into our dry tent and congratulate each other on our efficiency. We boil up some water for tea with a great sense of achievement and triumph.

Maria and I are getting to be a well-functioning team: we can paddle in unison along an obstacle-strewn river and put a tent up in the rain. We walk in the woods and visit towns and villages. We disguise the fact that I am not Polish when we have to. We have interesting conversations in spite of a certain language barrier. If there is a problem we find a way around it. I have learned a few random but useful words in Polish; I can say some simple phrases and ask our friends for the pump for our leaky air mattresses.

Now, well into our *spływ kajakowy*, it is time for the initiation. This seems to be based somewhat on the initiation of ship

86

passengers when they cross the Equator. Those of us who have not been on the club trip before will be solemnly initiated by Neptune, played by Zygmunt, and his court. The children in the group throw themselves into the preparations, gathering pine branches to decorate Neptune's bower. Some of the women make little decorations to add to the gravity and impressiveness of the occasion. I do not much care for the idea of initiations in general and find the whole thing a pointless exercise. Maria seems to think it is a beautiful ritual only slightly downscale from a Papal Investiture. She calls it a *baptême*—French for "baptism" —but I have learned to take her occasional confusion of the two languages in my stride. "Anyway," I say to Maria, "Neptune was the god of the sea. He has nothing to do with rivers."

"In Poland," she informs me haughtily, "he is god of rivers, too."

But even Maria seems to have some second thoughts about the *baptême*. The air has been full of dark hints about this strange ritual. Knowing looks are exchanged and there are rapid conversations with glances at me. Maria sometimes seems a bit concerned (or conscience-stricken?) and has confessed that sometimes the initiation is quite unpleasant and has been getting gradually worse. It seems to me that 44 is an odd time of life to be introduced to hazing. One doesn't think of it as a continuing threat. Anyway, I am fatalistic about it, and most of the group seem kindly and trustworthy and mature. I suppose the thing will not get out of hand. But then, what do I know of the darker recesses of the Polish character?

The next night I wake up and cough, and Maria is instantly alert and asks me if I have a cold. I say I *am* cold but do not *have* a cold. This is a very subtle semantic distinction for 3 a.m. and I keep saying that I am really not ill. She says she won't let me go through with the *baptême* because I am ill. In the morning she is still concerned and says that if I want to avoid the ceremony she can fix it. "I can say something, true or not true." (Maria! And this on a Sunday morning!)

I impress upon her that I do *not* want any special privileges, as it would not be fair. She goes off to consult with Basia and Teresa and comes back and says it is up to me. I repeat that I don't want to avoid what the others have to do—but add that I won't understand anything that is being said. They can chew over that!

In the meantime, we have to go to Mass. A little group of us walk in to Nadarzyce, where there is a small new church built during the "Solidarity Time", when one of the policies of *Solidarność* was that each village should have its own church. The priest reads a long letter from a synod of bishops asking everyone to abstain from alcohol during August to observe the many important days—nationally significant days, including those connected with Solidarity. The Mass is frankly boring as I can't follow it and am sleepy. Maria helpfully whispers "Credo" or "Agnus Dei" from time to time, to keep me, as she imagines, *au fait* with the proceedings.

Afterwards the Mass-going contingent wanders aimlessly down the main street of Nadarzyce looking for a place to eat. The bar opens at 2:00 and we go in, but there is no food. Maria, however, manages to get some cold breaded pork cutlets and bread rolls from somewhere. When we walk back to the camp, Ula invites us for a meal of spaghetti and mushroom soup with her family and Basia and Krzysztof. Ula has an enviable ability to produce meals, even dinner parties, in the middle of these tank traps in the back of beyond.

The ceremony of initiation differs from year to year, but the general form is that on a certain evening the initiates, all wearing bathing suits, are corralled together and then taken out one by one. The other members, all veterans of their own past initiations, stand about, some holding candles and wearing wreaths of ivy or whatever they could find in the woods. The younger children frolic about being little sea nymphs. If anyone has brought anything resembling a long flowing gown, that is pressed into service. Neptune and his court are wearing all this in spades. The names of the initiates are announced and then they are ritually smeared with some material to mark their new status and given a special new name. Zygmunt and his crew are even now thinking up these nautical names for the new candidates. The only kind of suitable smearing material available to Zygmunt seems to be crankcase oil, but Maria assures me that they won't smear us with much of it, and they will try not to get it on our bathing suits. The more I hear of this initiation, the nuttier it sounds. I can't believe Maria is being so serious about it. She really thinks it's a charming idea: very moving, she says, very beautiful. It is to be this evening, and I'll be glad when it's over.

Magda comes to me in the afternoon and looks worried and agitated. It's because of this silly initiation. "You see," she says—I see she is going to explain something because I am a foreigner and therefore have no idea about the way things are here—"it's the men. Polish men sometimes get drunk and get completely out of control. They're all right when they're sober, but they can be really rough and violent if they get drunk. I'm afraid of what may happen."

And she is really afraid. Whoever she came with hasn't reassured her and must not be a very dependable protector. I, on the other hand, feel that tonight will be ridiculous but not dangerous. That's because I have Maria Wnuk on my side. If anyone offered me physical abuse, I'm sure she would personally take him apart. She has a network, I sense, and is known by most of the other kayakers. She is capable of fixing things so that I can avoid the whole silly business. She and her husband have gone on these trips for years, and she is one of the senior women in the party. Furthermore, I am a foreigner in my 40s and the guest of the club, made up at least partly by courtly hand-kissers. Very few people speak my language and I don't speak theirs; they are not going to say anything rude to me because Maria would give them a royal tongue-lashing if they did, and I wouldn't understand it anyway. And a matron of my age is not going to attract the lascivious attention from young men, drunk or sober, that Magda might.

"Listen, Magda, Maria Wnuk won't let anything bad happen. I think they'll treat me pretty leniently because I'm a stranger. Stay with me and I'll intervene myself if there's a problem."

Some girls slightly older than Magda run past giggling and flirting with some young men. They are the ones who are going to have a problem tonight.

"Another thing, Magda," I tell her, "whatever happens, don't resist. Don't say anything. Just be passive." She seems a bit reassured by all my aunt-like advice, and after being under Maria's mother-hen wing for so long, I want to extend my own wing to Magda. She is a sweet girl and her fear makes me feel protective. (And how far might Maria's original wing be made to go if Magda decided to look out for a still younger girl? I'm sure it would stretch at least that far.)

The initiation is just as absurd as I had imagined it would be. There must be twenty of us new-comers in the little pen of initiates. We are herded together by the children doing their water-imp thing and waving pine boughs. I put my hand reassuringly on Magda's shoulder. "Remember, be passive," I whisper, although it is hardly necessary to whisper in this place where the English language is like a secret code. One by one we are taken out and ritually given a smear of oil on our legs and some kind of incantation is said over us. This must include our new "born-again" names. Some of the flirtatious girls are gleefully hauled off and smeared more thoroughly but Magda and I get off fairly lightly. I have lost sight of Maria in the crowd, lit only by some candles and moonlight.

Now we are supposed to stand respectfully while the rest of the ceremony goes on. There is some kind of speech-making and singing. I suspect that it would be tedious even if I could understand what was being said. Magda and I are still together, and she whispers anxiously that she doesn't want all this dirty oil on her skin. She has delicate skin and this is not going to do it any good. We are standing at the edge of the festivities and near the elaborate backdrop for Neptune's court. I can't see Maria at all, and anyway this is the most idiotic thing I have had to do for a long time. I have been a good sport about it, but there are limits. We can draw back out of the light, such as it is, and duck behind this backdrop and sneak away. I suggest this plan to Magda and we carefully ease ourselves away from the group and into the dark trees. We quietly hurry along to our tent and I get my soap box with a cake of Pears in it. We skirt a tank trap and go down to the lake shore and scrub the oil off our legs. Magda has some on her arms, too. Our eyes are used to the darkness and we can easily see by the moonlight. We are far enough away from the merry-makers that we can talk normally now.

"This is a stupid ceremony!" Magda exclaims. "Look at all this oil!"

"It is ridiculous," I agree. "I guess it's an ego-trip for Zygmunt and his pals."

Magda laughs. She likes *ego-trip.* "This can't be good for the skin. It's filthy! What a stupid idea!"

Magda and I are companions in furtively opposing the silly plans for us. I warm to her. She is less than half my age, but she is an intelligent girl and our escapade is beginning to make up for some of the silliness of the night.

Suddenly Maria appears above us on the bank. "You must come back at once!" she scolds us. "The ceremony is not finished! There is more! Come!"

"But Maria," I say, "We have dirty oil on us. We just wanted to wash it off."

But she is unmoved. "Come back now! Ceremony not finished! You can do this later!"

We are escorted back to the group in disgrace, or probably we are supposed to be in disgrace. I do not feel very disgraced. I feel justified in escaping from this dreary nonsense and I'm an unrepentant rebel. Magda is too, and there is now a definite bond between us. We are partners in crime and we are both happy to sabotage this silliness in any way we can.

The next day Maria forgives me and by extension, Magda. On the whole, the initiation ceremony has been a wonderful success: it has been beautiful and moving and so forth. Maria is a little mystified that I do not find it the sublime experience she does. I tell her I think it's silly, but she shrugs and apparently decides that it is just a strange non-Polish thing about me and can't be helped. I am irredeemably Anglo-Saxon, and the fact must just be accepted. I don't have the necessary Soul.

"Your new name is *Czarująca Pirania*," she tells me. Then she takes out her pocket dictionary to find out what *czarująca* means in English. "It is something very nice," she assures me. "Everyone get fish name, but Zygmunt not know many name of foreign fish. Everyone else has Polish fish name. Only foreign fish they know is *pirania*, but that not very nice fish. Zygmunt add other word to show that this *pirania* is good." She continues to look in her dictionary. "Is very good word," she says, "I show you." She finds it. "Here! *Charming* Pirania! That your new name! You are Charming Pirania!" She laughs at her discovery and laughs at how apt the name is. Other people around us agree that it is an excellent name. So I'm a piranha, but at least a charming one.

Later I'm swimming in the lake. I usually do a front crawl, but now I'm doing a leisurely breaststroke toward the shore, where Ula Mach is sitting writing in a notebook. It comes to me that I know the words for "Look out" and "I am" in Polish. I can say "Look out! I'm a piranha!" I call out to Ula in my most alarming voice: "*Uwaga! Jestem pirania!*" and she laughs delightedly. It's something, but it'll be hard to work it into a conversation.

Chapter Five

Meeting the Locals

The word the day after the initiation is that the next stage of the journey is so pitted with portages that half the group will go today and the other half tomorrow. We are in the second group. The first group will leave their kayaks at the end of the line and come back to camp in the minibus to sleep tonight. Maria thinks they will give us useful information about the obstacles and portages. I don't know what advance information could be useful—except perhaps the phone number of a car-rental place with a roof-rack.

While we are waiting in camp, I decide to give the cooking utensils a really good scrubbing with actual soap, and Maria thinks that the initiation, which she still calls a *baptême*, has had a beneficial effect on me. Afterwards we set off for the town of Sypniewo, which lies at some distance. Half way there we catch a bus and find to our surprise that Ula, Basia, and Krzysztof are on it. We are all strangers to this district (some more than others), but we have somehow made it so much our own that we can exclaim at meeting each other unexpectedly.

In Sypniewo we go to the post office and Maria phones home to check on her family. We find a restaurant where we have a meal of pork tenderloin and potatoes, which is becoming my old stand-by in restaurants now. We buy groceries, and I write a few post cards and have a cup of coffee and watch Maria's things while she does the rest of her errands.

We have been saying that we need a light inside our tent, a safer light that just a candle, and then I see just the thing in one of the shops in the town. It is a sort of hurricane lamp, a red glass jar with a candle inside and a bit of decorative gold around the top. It is exactly the thing to light our tent, but Maria doesn't seem to see its possibilities. I tug at her arm like a child wanting the Cheerios instead of the Weetabix. "Look, Maria, a light for our tent. We could use..."

"No," she says dismissively.

"But, Maria, you remember we said that we needed..."

"Not that," she says. "That is to put on grave in cemetery."

It takes me a moment to realize that these stacks of "hurricane lamps" are votive lights for graves and other memorials. No wonder there are so many of them, now that I think of it. There are crates of them in this shop. Maria must have found it an outrageously lugubrious idea to light our tent with one of these, or perhaps sacrilegious, or both. I have put my foot in it again, but Maria is used to that and is very good-natured about my gaffes. (Later I notice these candles everywhere. The general shortage of everything else doesn't seem to affect them. They are usually red, but I see green ones, too, like port and starboard lights.)

The *spływ kajakowy* is planned to be an alternation between effort on the river and loafing around in camp. Some people like Tomek would probably be happy to spend every day battling obstacles in the river, but there are others who like to cook, eat, sit around, chat, put on cabarets, swim, look for mushrooms in the forest, sunbathe, and sing around the campfire until all hours, and whether Zygmunt has actually sat down and planned it all, everyone's tastes seem to have been provided for in some measure. "I sit in office," Tomek tells me. "Office at work. I look out of window. All year I think about kayak trip! I sit at desk, think about kayak, lake, forest!"

On Tuesday morning the kayaks are taken to a spot below the sluice of the dam and we launch them there. We paddle off, but before we have gone very far Krzysztof has to help us at three different sticky places. In a shallow trickle of the river only a few inches deep we scrape the rudder on the pebbly bottom and badly damage it. I should have pulled it up out of harm's way. It also looks as though we have also damaged the heavy fibreglass hull of the craft, because as the morning wears on, we take in more and more water. It is hard work, with rapids and submerged logs and all sorts of unexpected snags. Briefly the river clears up into placid water meadows and reed beds. There are wild ducks and geese and we coast along for a moment, but just when we think we are having an easy life we come upon a felled tree taking up most of the river, and then branches and bushes are in, under, or overhanging the water in many different ways. Sometimes the river narrows and the current becomes fast and we have to steer very carefully not to get swept into an obstacle or the riverbank. When there is a sharp turn in the river we have to avoid both running aground on the shallow inside bank and being swept out of control in the fast outside current.

The kayak is behaving very sluggishly without a rudder and riding low in the water with the extra heaviness of the water we've shipped, and we are listing noticeably to the left. It is harder and harder to paddle it. I have never understood why we need a rudder anyway, since the kayak can be steered with the paddles, but this rising water is a problem. Now and then we bail out some of it, but it goes from being an inch or two deep to twice that, and we are still far from our next campsite. We paddle all afternoon, but as we are so slow, we lag behind all the other kayakers. Everyone in the group has paddled past us at one time or another. We trudge around bends in the river and plod past obstructions.

Finally, at around 6:30 our kayak is swept sideways into a bushy tree overhanging half the river and it is obvious that in another moment it will tip us out. Before that can happen I jump out and grab Maria by the collar of her lifejacket. Almost simultaneously the kayak tips over and then rights itself, lighter now by the weight of two people. The river is not at all deep here. It comes up to the middle of my thigh, just to the old tennis shorts I'm wearing. I stand on the stony river bed and grip Maria's collar firmly until she is standing beside me. She's a few inches shorter than I am and will feel the current that much stronger. I make sure she can get to the riverbank, which is only a few feet away. Our kayak is now part of the obstacle in the river. I take the mooring cord, hardly more than a string, and tie it to the trunk of the offending tree. It is much too heavy to pull out of the water here. We salvage our bags from the floor of the kayak and then scramble onto the riverbank. Just then the string breaks and we watch our kayak float off down the river, belly up like a dead fish, with more speed than we have been able to get out of it all day.

We are out of the water but our kayak has disappeared and we are on a riverbank covered with nettles. We are wet and muddy and one of my canvas shoes is on its way to the Baltic with the kayak.   More ominously, at the top of the slope up from the river, looming above us, is a chain-link fence stretched between high concrete posts with barbed wire at the top. We can hear guard dogs barking. It can't be anything else but some kind of military installation. It probably goes on for miles. God knows what's on the other side. Armed guards, clean tanks?

I think we should stay where we are and wait for help, but without hesitating, Maria starts climbing up the steep slope toward the fence. I follow her with numerous misgivings. She has a head start and is a few yards ahead—and above—me. When I am about half way up the slope, I hear her actually talking to someone on the other side of the fence! She seems to be explaining our predicament, but to whom? More Russian soldiers? How long can we keep up the charade of my being Polish? Even if I tell them I'm a piranha it's not going to get us very far.

Maria seems to be having some kind of conversation with somebody. It sounds like another woman. When I finally get to the top of the slope, I find Maria chatting to a middle-aged woman wearing an apron and an old dress. It's an odd costume for military personnel, but it doesn't seem to be an army installation after all, in spite of the high chain-link fence with the concrete posts curving outward at the top like huge hockey sticks. Maria turns to me for a moment while the woman hurries off. Maria searches for a word briefly and then says, "Is farm. Turkey farm."

The woman soon returns with a chair and a boy, and Maria hands all our things over the fence and barbed wire to the boy standing on the chair. The farm woman has told Maria how to get around the fence. If we walk along the side of the fence for about 50 metres we will come to the end of it and she will let us through a gate. Every plant growing along the fence for the next 50 yards is either a nettle or a bramble cane, and the vegetation is profuse. Oddly enough, when you are walking through nettles half barefoot in old wet tennis shorts, you eventually cease to notice the stinging of the nettles and the scratches of the brambles and little thorny trees. Your legs take it as read that they are surrounded by stinging, prickly things, and then think about something else.

Maria is striding on ahead, as much as one can stride in these conditions. She is wearing some loose dungarees and is somewhat better covered than I am. She has both shoes on. At the end of chain-link fence there is a grassy yard. The fence makes a right angle and a gate in it leads to a house. We are invited in by the hospitable but bemused woman in an apron. A few more family members appear, attracted by the commotion and curious to see what sort of people can have suddenly turned up at their remote farmhouse. It would be hard to look much more disreputable than Maria and I do, with our wet and muddy legs and three shoes for our four feet. To complete our strangeness, while one of us is a normal Pole, the other is evidently from some other planet. The half barefoot one in the ratty old shorts with the crossed tennis rackets on the leg speaks only English, of all things!

The woman who met Maria at the fence has an adult daughter in the house, and they both invite us in and insist that we use their bathroom to clean up in. Maria quickly gets presentable again, and then I go into a surprisingly up-to-date bathroom (Maria later tells me that they are obviously very prosperous turkey farmers) and begin getting the mud off my feet and legs and then rinsing the mud out of their fine new bathtub. They insist that I put my shorts on their radiator to dry, and they give me a housecoat and some slippers to put on in the meantime. They are very kind once they get over the initial shock of having such outlandish visitors.

This is all very well, but how are we ever going to get to the campsite, wherever it is? When will we be missed? I should know by now that Maria is skilled in talking to people in whatever situation she finds herself in, and she is engaging the turkey farmers in quite an animated conversation now. They wonder if we are hungry and quickly produce plates of sausage, cheese, tomatoes, and cucumbers and mugs of tea. Now that I think of it, I am rather hungry. I had forgotten all about it while we were in the river and then scrambling around on the river bank and following the fence through all the brambles. But now, yes, I wouldn't mind some sausage, cheese, tomatoes, cucumbers and a mug of tea, thanks. We are just sitting down at the table when there is a knock at the door, and to our amazement it is Zygmunt!

We're very glad to see him but it is also a little awkward, as we are just having a bite to eat and I am half dressed with my wet shorts draped on the radiator. There is yet another confab that concerns me but which I cannot understand. Maria will go with Zygmunt in his white van and come back for me later; she will bring some dry clothing (or "closing" as Maria says); I can continue eating and getting acquainted with our hosts. She will be back soon. But how did Zygmunt find us?

(One of the kayakers saw a backrest float past him on the river bearing our number 13. He knew at once that something had happened to us and raised the alarm with Zygmunt. A search party set out and saw us as they passed the farm.)

There are other, temporary, members of the household. The couple who run the farm have staying with them his sister and a nephew and niece from Warsaw. The niece, a schoolgirl of 14 or 15, is brought in and quite plainly would prefer to be somewhere else, anywhere else. She has done a year of English at school, but this is August now and she shouldn't have to think about this boring school subject during the holidays. She had hardly expected, visiting her aunt and uncle here in the wilds of nowhere on their godforsaken turkey farm, to encounter some English-speaking person and have to actually produce English grammar for her on the spot! Yet here was this very person (it must be all a bad dream!) sitting at their kitchen table munching cucumber slices and not speaking any Polish! The girl would like to blend into the wallpaper and is probably hoping that I haven't seen her and won't speak to her.

However, I do speak to her. At length she realizes that however halting her English is, it is the best the home team can offer and serves the important purpose of facilitating communication around the kitchen table. My own repertoire of "yes", "no" "water", "kayak", "coffee", "tea", "may we borrow the pump?"—and not forgetting the information about my piranhahood—is wearing thin and is of negligible value at the present moment. After a while we are having quite a fluent conversation and the girl is getting over her shyness and beginning to enjoy flexing her English and impressing her relatives in this unexpected way. Wine and bread have been brought out, and butter and tomato salad. We are making little jokes and laughing about things.

Just then Maria walks in on this scene of merriment and feasting with some dry clothes she has found in my duffel bag. "Hurry!" she says, as though I have been purposely dawdling. "Zygmunt wait!"

I rather reluctantly go to the bathroom to put on the dry clothes and some shoes and emerge looking less like a boat-person refugee. As I am collecting my damp shorts from the radiator Maria is exchanging names and addresses with the farmers. As the man had told me in German that there was a lot of work in the fields now, I wish him success with it and a cordial *auf Wiedersehen*, and we shake hands all around. The farmer kisses my hand and the rest of the family wave us off as though our visit had been planned and we hadn't just washed up on their riverbank.

Maria and I climb into Zygmunt's van to find five or six men and Zygmunt's son, and also a kayak. This is our kayak, the unfortunate number 13, which has just been found. This must have taken some fancy detective work, because the original finder, a local farmer, had sold it to someone else, who in turn had sold it on to a third party. All this seems to have happened in the space of about an hour. I am curious to know more details, but Zygmunt does not divulge them, or at least not to me.

The new campsite is in a pine woods. Since we were so late and no one knew where we were, Tomek Mach has kindly put up our tent for us next to his and Ula's. They welcome us warmly when we finally arrive and offer us some soup. We tell them about our adventure on the river and the hospitable turkey farmers. We are already the talk of the camp, and when Maria describes our adventure and the turkey farmers, I can follow roughly what she's saying. She is making it into a good story and her audience is laughing appreciatively. She has seen that the farm family were good-hearted people eager to help anyone in trouble, and she gives them full credit.

It seems that we aren't the only ones who have had a mishap. There were three other capsizings today, and even now there are 5 men and boy of 15 missing and no one knows what has become of them. I think the river is a dangerous place, especially at night, and the kayakers might be in real danger. Nobody seems very worried about them. I ask if the police should be notified; I envisage a search with helicopters and searchlights. This causes a great deal of hilarity. The police! What an idea! The police, of all people! They laugh as though I had just told a very witty and somewhat risqué joke. It is funny, but there is something about it that causes knowing glances to flit around the company. I might have mispronounced a word or committed an unwitting double-entendre. They laugh partly at my expense and partly in the gentle way one might laugh at a child's innocent gaffe. It is the most absurd thing they have heard for a long time, and I understand that it is not part of the function of the police here to be helpful to ordinary citizens. No, they say between chuckles, that would not be appropriate at all. The fellows will turn up sooner or later by themselves (and so they do). Once again I see that my instinctive response to a situation is completely the wrong one—grotesquely, hilariously wrong.

But then I recall a conversation I had with Maria before we left Warsaw. "This is a monument to the police," she told me. "We hate it. We would like to blow it up!"

"It is ugly," I agreed. "Who put up this monument to the police?"

"The police of course!"

Tomek and I are sitting on our stools under the tall pine trees one evening. The weather has turned chilly and nobody is tempted to swim in the lake; we're all wearing heavy jackets. (Maria has said to me recently, "Wolves don't wash, and look how healthy!") My pyjama top makes an excellent jacket over a few other layers. Tomek gestures briefly at our surroundings and announces solemnly, "Here is like Hilton Hotel. Very luxurious. Excellent food. Yes. Running water. Air conditioned. And..." he makes a broad sweeping gesture at the ground, "...wall-to-wall carpet."

"Yes," I say, picking up the joke. "Even a nightclub," and I jerk my thumb toward the tents where the late-night revelers sing.

By now there are still more stories about Henryk's idiocies. I haven't forgiven him for his boorishness when he was supposed to be instructing me in the fine art of kayaking. He has now insulted or frightened half the club, and the tales are accumulating. Now he has advertised himself as a masseur and has bruised someone's abdomen so badly that she went to a hospital to have it looked at. He is a menace. We are in a mood to be scathing about the obnoxious Henryk. I say he must have learned massage and kayak-steering at the same school. Tomek remarks on his crossed eyes. I say no, not crossed, but wall eyes that go out this way, and I point diverging angles out from my own eyes. "Still crossed," says Tomek. "Crossed *this* way," and he reaches around behind his head and shows where the sight lines would cross if they were continued in the other direction. We laugh wickedly at Henryk's expense, and it's no more than he deserves.

I have a pair of sandals I can wear, but I'd like to replace the canvas loafers, one of which I lost when the kayak went on its own little expedition. It may have fallen out of the kayak when we did, or it may be in the hands of one of the brief buyers of the boat—who knows? Anyway, I need some new casual shoes, and when we reach Wałcz I go with Maria and a few others to do some shopping, including a visit to a shoe shop. We enter a shop where there are no shoes on open display but only behind a counter. You have to go up to the counter and point to a shoe you want to try on. It is handed over, and as you stand at the counter you are supposed to slip the shoe on your foot. I take a British size 6, which is a European size 39. The closest thing seems to be a dark blue suede rubber-soled loafer. I ask to try it on, but it is a size too small. I hand it back, expecting to be give the next size up, but instead I am handed a shoehorn. Just as official regulations don't always match the situation at hand and some sort of "shoehorn" has to be improvised, so the answer to a missing shoe size is a literal shoehorn.

Wałcz is a good-sized town, rather drab except for a few old buildings. There are lots of shops, however, and Maria, Basia, and I wander about from one small grocery to another collecting butter, meat, tomatoes, and apples. Basia buys a carving knife and looks for a toilet-chain pull. The merchandise is rather sparse in all the shops, so looking for everyday items becomes a treasure hunt. Since the plural of so many nouns is formed with a -*y*, there is a strange diminutive sense of things, even without the real, ubiquitous, Polish diminutive. Light bulbs are *lampy*, buses are *autobusy*, and houses are *domy*. We see a Sony (not the plural of *son*) television, and Basia explains that it costs twice the annual salary of an engineer. We eat at the *Wiking* Restaurant; I have finally persuaded Maria to let me buy her a meal, and I encourage her to choose something expensive. It turns out to be pork and potatoes again, but tasty in spite of its familiarity.

Returning to the pine forest we call home, we speak to a young couple from our group on the same bus who proudly reveal that they have bought a roll of toilet paper. We ask where and congratulate them. (I think yet again that *anybody* could plan production and distribution better than this.) Basia couldn't find a toilet-chain pull, but otherwise our shopping trip was successful. Later there is a comical conversation between our tents when Ula offers to lend us three metres of toilet paper, and Maria says she will pay her back with four metres in Warsaw. So usury doesn't have to be in the form of negotiable currency— although toilet paper has a certain intrinsic value here and with a little more inflation could well become a serious contender.

The next day we go back to Wałcz to check train times and routes back to Warsaw. I finally get the suede loafers, although they are a bit snug. Basia's carving knife yesterday was a real find, although it looks pretty ordinary to me. When Ula admired it yesterday, Basia promptly gave it to her. Now Ula is buying a knife for Basia and Basia's daughter-in-law, who also needs one. Maria has forgotten where we found the carving knives yesterday, and so I guide them to the right shop. The knives are made in North Korea and are bleakly utilitarian to my eye.

There is such an atmosphere among these people of helpfulness and generosity. It seems to be second nature to give people things and share one's possessions and provisions. The scarcity makes it more important to share, just as it also encourages other people to hoard.

The Machs go back to the forest, and Maria and I continue for one last crucial chore: we must find dill for Basia's crayfish we're having tonight. (Krzysztof caught them, little lobsterettes five or six inches long.) They are *homary*, which makes them seem cuter than they are. Maria has solemnly promised Basia that we will contribute the dill. We find a clump of green dill in one shop, but we need the yellow flowering part, too, which we find at another small shop. I am finally understanding the sense of triumph of completing a purchase. As Maria said when we bought my track suit/pyjamas in Warsaw, "In London it is very ordinary, but here it is occasion for joy."

When the time comes for the token *homary*, we take our tea mugs and seats to Basia and Krzysztof's tent. The Machs are also there, and everyone is talking animatedly. I don't mind not understanding it. Maria gives me the gist from time to time. The tail of the crayfish is the only edible part and there is not much of it, but it's the thought that counts.

"When I was a little girl," Maria told me once, "bread was very precious. If I dropped a piece of bread on the floor accidentally, I had to pick it up and kiss it." Now we are sharing food almost for the sake of sharing it—crayfish tails, mushrooms from the forest, hard-sought dill, soup—whatever can be sliced or boiled or fried, just as the turkey farmers did when a bedraggled pair of kayakers washed up outside their fence.

Chapter Six

A Nice Tree Like You

The friendly people on the kayak *spływ* have several times suggested that I should stay on longer in Warsaw after the trip is over. I have told them that my visa is only for a certain amount of time, but they say that it can be extended. They make it sound easy, and I *would* like to spend more time in Warsaw, so we decide to change my return flight to London and extend my visa.

But now it is Sunday and nothing can be done until tomorrow. Maria and I go to Mass at the splendid baroque church of the Order of the Visitation nuns in Krakowskie Przedmieście Street. (A few years later I will have more to do with this place, but I have no way of knowing that yet, and now I can't even pronounce it.) It is magnificent looking, and perhaps Maria wants to make up for those makeshift country churches she has just taken me to. Then again, she may like the grandeur and glitz of it for its own sake. Włodek has been taking it easy in our strenuous absence and today we have left him at home. He has been seriously ill with a heart condition and now he is wearing a patch on his chest that releases heart medicine gradually. After Mass we go to an elegant old coffee shop in the nearby Hotel Europejski (another advantage of the Church of the Order of the Visitation).

Then we stroll through Saski Garden, named after Augustus Sas, the elected Saxon king of Poland, Maria tells me. "Garden" is a misnomer, as the park is one of paths and shady old trees with benches here and there. I think Alastair and I were here eight years ago. We must have sat on one of these benches with sandwiches after we had laboriously rounded up the ingredients for them. There is a big two-tiered fountain, and it reminds Maria of a song. She hums a bit to herself to get the words right, and then she translates them for me: "In the park by a fountain a boy sits near a girl. Then he moves nearer and nearer. Then..."

"He kisses her?" I suggest. It is easy to see how the story is going.

"Yes. He steals a kiss. Then she steals his wristwatch!"

The predictable romantic story has taken a droll turn and we both laugh, even if it is an old joke for her.

Maria Wnuk by the fountain in Ogród Saski, the wooded park in central Warsaw.

We go on to an exhibition of modern art. The images seem familiar. They are rather world-weary: jokey, cynical, superficial, and negative. I find some of it interesting and imaginative, but I always think there is a kind of dead-end quality about this kind of art. I wonder if it is because they are very young artists, or middle-aged-but-never-grown-up artists, and the world-weariness is just an unconvincing pose. Or perhaps this is genuinely the way they see the world and they are clinically depressed. Or maybe they have some real reason to be so glum. Whatever the case, this stuff always makes me want to go and look at Vermeer and Pieter de Hooch, or even the nearly audible uproar of a Jan Steen scene.

In the evening we have a visit from an old friend of the Wnuks', another architect, Witold Dębski. He is also a member of the kayak club and has often gone on the trips but didn't this year. He is in his 60s and a widower. He is slight and wiry, scarcely taller than my 5'6", and has a kind of cheerfulness and energy about him. He has brought a bag of cherries from his garden for us. He has come to see how Włodek is and how the *spływ kajakowy* went and to meet the foreign friend who enabled Maria to go on the trip while Włodek was out of action. He is very courteous and kisses my hand when we are introduced. He speaks reasonable English, which surprises Maria, as she had never had any occasion to know whether he spoke it or not. With each sentence he stops to work out what to say next and composes his remarks carefully. Occasionally some German words slip in disguised as English. Witold, or Witek, was born in Wilno. The city was in Poland at the time, but it is often in Lithuania, and then it is the capital. Witek explains that he began to learn English as a boy during the War in the hope and expectation that Poland would soon be liberated by the British and Americans. Besides being an architect he is an artist, and he tells me how he got started.

When *Snow White and the Seven Dwarves* came out in 1939 he went to see it several times. He was simply entranced by it. He liked it so much that he drew scenes from the film. During the War a Russian soldier was quartered in their house, and he encouraged Witek to draw. The soldier told the boy that he might even draw Stalin one day, as though that were the height of ambition. Witek and the Wnuks marvel at the sheer wackiness of the idea, but they can remember a time when people really said things like that.

Włodek Wnuk,
Witold Dębski, and Sarah.

Monday dawns and we set to work getting my visa extended. First we go downtown to the British Airways office to change my return flight date. There is a long queue there and I have time to read the travel posters and the certificates on the wall saying that this BA office is an outstanding example of the genre. Although it is staffed by Polish personnel, they must have had some British training, because they seem happy to be of service and the windows don't suddenly close just as you are nearing the head of the queue. I get my ticket changed to the following week.

The next step is to go to a certain police station in the Praga district of Warsaw on the other side of the Vistula to extend my visa. This is said by all to be very easy. In the back of my mind is the thought that as my Polish friends have never had to get a visa to their own country, they can't know whether it is easy or not, and they must know that the chances are that nothing is easy. Perhaps they think that everything is easy for foreigners. Anyway, we can do it tomorrow.

In the meantime, we see some more of Warsaw. The Polish language is all around me, not just spoken words as in the pine forest and on the river, but on signs everywhere. It looks like a Scrabble-player's nightmare, but if it is your language it is life and sanity and the world. It has the musicality of comprehension. I know it has elegance and subtlety, even if I can't identify them.

In the evening Witek Dębski appears again because he forgot his keys last night. It wasn't a disaster, because he had duplicates with him. Maria has found them and put them aside for him, and now hands them over with a little joke. To continue our conversation of the night before, Witek has brought a portfolio of his watercolours to show me. He has drawn sketches of buildings and architectural ornamentation. There are many watercolours of the last kayak trip, and he presents me with one. He has even brought some of his old boyhood drawings he was telling me about last night. There is an amazingly skilful watercolour of some dwarves mining diamonds, and he tells me he made it when he was 15. No wonder the Russian soldier was impressed. He was a prodigy of an artist. He would have used his skill professionally when he was practicing as an architect, and now in retirement he is still very serious about it. It is more than a hobby.

Now it is Tuesday and my visa expires. We must go to that police station and get it extended. We take a couple of buses to get there. At the shabby-looking police station in Praga we are directed to an upstairs room where there is, of course, a queue. The other applicants for visa extensions seem to be Polish, except for one Englishman puffing away on a pipe like Harold Wilson. They are far more informative about the procedure than the officials themselves. This is always a symptom of sloppy organisation and a bad sign. A lively discussion about bureaucracy develops and the Poles say that Poland is terrible in this regard. As they are all clearly Poles of some description, I am a little confused. "But where do you live?" I ask a man.

"In the country with the *least* amount of bureaucracy!" he says proudly.

"And where is that?" I enquire, because his answer doesn't sound to me like a very precise definition.

"The United States of America!" he exclaims.

I wonder where he thinks I'm from. He doesn't seem even to be very curious, because the important thing for him in this conversation is where *he's* from. He has also quite obviously never had anything to do with the American embassy in London.

We fill in a form and talk to an official. We are told that a visa extension is dependent on producing extra money, hard currency, $15 for each day of the visa; a week costs $105. This is then converted into a złoty voucher to be cashed at a bank.

But where are we to obtain these external dollars in Warsaw? I have the idea of using my Visa card to get cash. That will be simple. But someone says that the Orbis exchange does not take credit cards. Never mind, we'll try somewhere else.

A young woman who is standing around in the office says that the Hotel Victoria will give cash for a credit card, the only place in Warsaw that does so. This seems to solve the whole problem, and I thank her profusely. I wonder vaguely if she works here, but her English is too good and she seems much too helpful. When I ask, she replies grandly, "I am an American citizen."

This time we take a taxi to the Hotel Victoria, but now it seems that they do *not* give cash for Visa cards. (Ah, what an ironic name for a credit card!) The hotel will take a credit card only in payment for merchandise. In fact, credit cards can't be used even at banks to acquire dollars, but only the local currency, the złoty. We are advised go to the Bank Handlowy. This is the commercial bank in central Warsaw where foreign transactions can be made. (But where were all those proud American citizens at the run-down police station in Praga getting their visa money? I'm more than a little baffled, because they must get it externally, too. Maria has saved some dollars and later Basia and Krzysztof offer me $105 that they have stashed away. Even Teresa has approached me with a sympathetic "To be or not to be." But none of these schemes will work, because the money has to be proved to have come from outside the country. Even if I had brought lots of dollars with me, they couldn't be used, either.)

We take another taxi to the Bank Handlowy, where we get their address and telex number. The bank clerk says that we should go to my embassy, but I can't think what good it would do. I need *money*, not diplomacy, and anyway embassies rightly take a dim view of indigent citizens turning up on their doorsteps.

Although I am using my American passport here, we go to the British embassy, where a Canadian receptionist says we need the *consulate* and shows us on a map where it is. We take a tram there, but it is closed from 12 to 2 for lunch. It is now after one and I see that we can't finish this today. I sit at a handy bus stop until it re-opens, while Maria goes on an errand to Włodek's office. At about 2:00 I go into the consulate and find Poles in all directions. They are both getting visas and giving visas. I stress that I have come on different business and see a Polish employee of the consulate who sympathises about the system and suggests that I borrow money from my friends. I remind him that the foreign provenance of it is the crucial thing, and I haven't any hard currency of my own where I can get at it immediately.

"*That* is the problem!" he exclaims, as though I didn't know. What I really need, I tell him, is the phone number of the Aldwych branch of Lloyds. I write the address on a slip of paper and he goes away to see somebody and comes back with two phone numbers. This is beginning to look like progress, of a sort.

I go out and find Maria in the waiting room. She is not one to hang back just because doors are closed. Living in Poland is a course in assertiveness training—when you aren't learning to keep your head down. Now we take some more buses back to Maria's, where I can phone Lloyds and get them to wire me some money. British banks close at 3:30, of course, so I don't have too much time. I phone them and ask for the equivalent of $105 to be sent to the Bank Handlowy in Warsaw so that I can extend my visa.

But of course they can hardly do anything so dodgy as take instructions about an account over the phone. They must have this request in writing. (I think how many days all this is going to take. I think of the scene at the airport when I try to leave and they discover I don't have a valid visa.) My throat is getting a bit dry with anxiety. The solution now is to phone Alastair, who fortunately works practically across the street from the Aldwych branch of Lloyds. I phone him at work. But he is in another office at the moment. The secretary will go and get him, and I am to phone back in five minutes.

By now it is after 3:00 and the bank is going to close at 3:30. I have hardly hung up the telephone when it rings and it is Maria's sister phoning for a chat. I can hardly ask Maria to get off her own phone, so I practice breathing deeply. The minutes tick by, but Maria's phone call doesn't last long, and I pounce

111

on the phone while trying not to show my panic. I phone Alastair and explain what has happened and ask him to please hurry over to the bank and get $105 wired to me so that I can stay in Poland for an extra week. He has a whole 10 minutes to accomplish this.

Then I tell Maria that we have done all we can do for today. Now "the cares that infest the day / Shall fold their tents, like the Arabs, / And as silently steal away". Now we have a light meal and then go to Tomek and Ula's. They have invited us for the evening, and it is nice to forget about this visa problem for a while. The whole evening is a pleasure. They live down near the centre of town in a street near the river. Tomek's mother lives with them (or rather they live with her—it seems to be her flat). It is a large old flat but with mod cons. Ula managed to be stylish in a kayak and in the woods, and so I am not surprised that at home in Warsaw she is wearing a white skirt and a smart red overblouse and looking very chic. We have a pizza and some Spanish wine bottled in Poland. Later on we have tea and some home-baked cake in the living room.

Tomek is a younger colleague of Włodek's in this bureau for designing hospitals, and the families have known each other for years. I talk to Ula and learn something about her family. She was born in Wrocław but her much older brother and sister were born in Germany, where her parents were in a labour camp during the War. Because of that they now get West German pensions. Her mother was a mathematician and headmistress, but she retired, divorced Ula's father, and went to Vienna to live. The German war pension is apparently enough for her to live on comfortably. Ula tells me that her mother, now in her late 60s, says that she loves Vienna and feels free there. She goes on trips with groups of Austrian pensioners and seems to be having the time of her life. What puzzles me is that at some periods you can't get out of the country except on a very short rein, and at other periods you can move abroad. Of course, I don't know what red tape there might have been at the time, and it would certainly have helped to have a West German pension.

The next day, as I am more or less an illegal alien now, Maria thinks it prudent that we go to some local administrative office to register me as a guest in the Wnuk household. The office has moved, but we eventually find it, a nondescript little place in another block of flats within walking distance of Maria's building. I am startled that everything seems to go smoothly at this little office. I sign something, get a few stamps on a piece of paper, and that is that.

"Let's look in this fish shop. Probably there are no fish," Maria says when we have left the office. She has told me before that fish shops mostly have canned fish and very rarely anything else. Today, to our surprise there is a large package of cold, breaded fishcakes and another container of dried herring. I think Maria is a little disappointed that there is anything at all in the shop, but I assure her that I get the idea. In fact, any fishmonger anywhere in Britain would look like the Harrod's Food Hall compared to this. There are some high, uninviting shelves with a few cans on them behind the counter, which is bare except for these two boxes. Maria tells me that you can get fish only near the coast because there is no transport.

But those Baltic ports aren't *that* far from Warsaw. Suppose they're around 200 miles away. That's about half way across Pennsylvania from the East Coast. At this rate there would never be any fresh fish in Pittsburgh or points west. The refrigerated train car has been in existence since the 1860s to my certain knowledge. *What* is their problem? The run-around with the visa and getting things stamped and queues for everything and the extraordinary shortage of toilet paper! Surely nobody could be this inefficient without lots of planning?

And of course lots of planning is just what they do have, and that is exactly the problem. Someone in an office has flipped a coin scientifically to decide where to allocate things with no thought of consumer demand. Consumer demand is an

113

outmoded concept. Indeed, it is not so much outmoded as outlawed. It is decadent, capitalist, bourgeois, and so forth. I ponder once again why poor countries wishing to create wealth decide to adopt a plan that is the exact opposite of countries that are already wealthy.

And speaking of wealth, Maria thinks I still have too much of it and ought to convert paper specie into merchandise. We go on a shopping spree. Maria takes me by tram across Warsaw to a silver shop, where I dutifully buy a silver ring with an amber set, and to a Cepelia shop, where I find some nice tablecloths. I manage to get a leather pen case for Maria and a few more trinkets for myself. I am still looking for a pricey silver rosary ring for Maria. Next we go to a tape and record shop where I find some nice classical tapes. They are very cheap. I buy a handful of Liszt, Beethoven, and some unfamiliar Polish chamber music that looks interesting.

We return home for a dinner of fish, beef and noodles. It is obviously a tribute to Maria's ingenuity that we are eating fish. When we finish, Maria and Włodek and I take a bus and tram down toward the Hotel Europejski to a cinema to see *Out of Africa*. The cinema itself is hardly marked from the outside. I would have missed it if I had been by myself. We are walking along the street, and then Włodek says, "Here it is," or something like that, and we go up some steps and through a nondescript door.

I like the film enormously for several reasons: the acting by Meryl Streep and Robert Redford, the photography, the period flavour, and the emotional reality. Maria finds the story too romantic and the plot too thin, and she can't identify with Baroness Blixen. I am glad that we could all watch it together, me listening to the dialogue and Maria and Włodek reading the subtitles. I have even learned a new word from looking at the subtitles myself. Baroness Blixen says something about "tomorrow" and there in the subtitles is *jutro. Jutro*, tomorrow. *Jutro, jutro.* We have plans for tomorrow.

The next day is Thursday. I am still an illegal, visa-less alien. Some money is coming slowly from London, perhaps by bicycle and kayak, to enable me to buy a week. I thought modern banking was supposed to be so fast, practically instantaneous. Anyway, I am confident that it will arrive all in one piece, without losing a bicycle bell along the way. We get up early and go down to Centralna Station to catch a train for Puławy, where Maria's childhood home is, the house built by her architect father that got requisitioned by the government and is now some official building, the house where the secret wall safe was, perhaps still is, with the sugar, salt, candles, and matches. The train ride is two and a half hours or so southeast of Warsaw through more fields and forests.

At Puławy we stroll to the home of Hala and Włodek Mleczko where we have a meal and the Wnuks catch up with their friends. We are going to spend the night here, and Hala is extremely welcoming, although she is not in the best of health, as she is diabetic. Maria explains to me that Hala is having great difficulty finding medicine for her diabetes. She has to buy it on the black market when it is available at all, and it is very expensive. Maria wanted me to meet Hala because she, too, is a poet and gives poetry readings to small candle-lit groups. She writes for a small magazine and her poetry often appears in print.

Maria and Włodek and I then stroll around the town and look at Maria's old house. I see that it has been a very pleasant, very spacious, family home. It is a two-storey house with a tile roof in the central European style, and now it is used for council offices or something of the kind. This, then, was the house where Maria's close call occurred. It was during the War; she was out of doors on the wrong side of the curfew delivering a message for the Home Army. As she ran back home a Stuka came after her and opened fire as she reached the house. The door was open and she dashed inside just in the nick of time, and the Stuka made a line of bullet holes all across the house. "If that door had not been open..." she says with a shudder.

115

Maria wants to visit the graves of her parents. Her mother and father died in 1966 and 1972, respectively. Maria puts roses on the joint grave and pulls up some weeds. The gravestone and the image of the Virgin were once in the garden of their home in Puławy, Maria explains.

Next we go to a fine park and the seat of the noble Czartoryski family. We admire the stately home and the memorabilia inside, including, oddly, a chair from Shakespeare's birthplace in Stratford. The house is also associated with Tadeusz Kościuszko, the patriotic hero of both Poland and the United States.

The day has become very hot, and the big old gnarled trees in the park give welcome shade. But Maria is thinking of a long-ago day in the same place, back in the days when it was prudent to put salt in the wall safe and a Stuka might dive at you. Maria chuckles to herself and tells me that once during the War she was walking just here with her friend Misia. Perhaps they were on their way home from a clandestine class. It was a wintry day and snow was falling on the already snow-covered ground. Suddenly the two girls felt so happy to be part of this scene—the deserted park on a grey winter afternoon, the ancient bare trees, the falling snowflakes—that they spontaneously began to dance together. They danced and laughed in the snow all the way down the long avenue of trees. It is the avenue where we are walking now 45 years later on a hot day under the same trees, now thick with August leafiness.

"That was during the War," Maria says, "but we were so happy! Can you imagine?" She surprises herself with the memory. I try to think of those two schoolgirls bubbling over in spite of the German occupation, the dangers they were running every day, and the terrible things that were happening all around them. Happiness can sprout up in such unexpected, inappropriate places, like sunflowers between flagstones.

Now we walk on in the sultry heat to Misia's house. The style of it looks Spanish to me. It is not finished yet, but there are white arches and walls; it is fashionably and sparsely furnished. I meet Misia, a pleasant dark-haired woman, and her husband. Maria reminds me that I phoned their daughter Ania once in London. I had completely forgotten about this, but a couple of years ago Maria asked me to phone Ania and check that she was all right, as she hadn't written home for a while. (The long reach of one's parents! she must have thought. They rope perfect strangers into checking up on you!) Krystyna is also there, the other old school friend from the illegal wartime *gymnasium*. Misia serves us *kolacja*, which has a good selection of salads as well as sausage. This is the doing of her daughter Ania, the one who has been living in London. She is a vegetarian and is into transcendental meditation and has influenced her parents in some new-fangled ideas, like lentils.

Maria Wnuk and her former classmates, Misia and Krystyna.

Ania herself appears and we chat for a moment. She tells me that she first went to London as an *au pair* for an elderly couple in Hampstead.

"They needed an *au pair*?" I ask, surprised.

"Yes they needed someone to do the cooking and generally look after them. They were very old and needed help with everything. The old man ate soup every day. I used to make it on Monday and it lasted all week!"

I am grateful to her for going to London and hearing about lentils and bringing salads back home.

It is after dark when we leave and take a bus back to Hala Mleczko's house.

I wake up on Friday in Puławy, still an illegal, visa-less alien. At breakfast Hala gets out some of her poems and reads us a few and shows us copies of the paper she writes for, an organ of the fertilizer factory where she works. Maria has told me that Hala has no further education, but she is a good-hearted person and serious about her poetry.

After breakfast Maria and Włodek and I catch a bus for another town they want to show me, Kazimierz Dolny. Krystyna comes too and we spend the day together. Kazimierz is a picturesque old town on the Wisła with Renaissance buildings and old churches. It is a pleasing jumble of orange tile roofs, ornate facades, and geraniums. The first place we go is to a splendid restored house on the main square. The square is a large rectangle, a big market space, assuming that is what it was used for. This house was the home of a famous architect and is now a hotel/conference centre for architects and their guests. As Maria and Włodek are both architects and have rights to this place, she makes reservations for the four of us for that afternoon at 1:30. This is to be a special treat for me—for all of us.

This town supports a kind of artists' colony; a lot of artists come to visit just to paint the scenes in and around the town or to run classes for art students. The buildings are of a central European style, and Włodek explains to me the way the roofs are constructed behind the parapets at the top of the front elevations. He draws a zig-zag line; the gutters are located here at the bottom of the V line of the rafters. Włodek is a big man with grey hair and a craggy face. Staszek has inherited some of this cragginess, but not yet the same build. He is slightly older than Maria, and as a young man he fought with the Home Army (the *Armia Krajowa* or AK) in guerrilla actions against the Germans and in the Warsaw Uprising. Maria's term for shooting guns is *pif-paf,* accompanied by a trigger-finger movement. She never did *pif-paf* in the AK, but Włodek did.

One of the sights of Kazimierz Dolny is the house of a famous writer, Maria Kuncewiczowa. She is now a very old lady but still receives visitors. The house is open at certain hours and anyone can go and visit. Maria and Włodek think I should go and announce myself as an Anglo-American poet, but I am not so sure. I think a distinguished literary figure like this has better things to do in her declining years than meet pretentious strangers in her parlour. Anyway, I have never heard of her, and at some point I am going to have to admit this.

We walk on out of town up a long dirt road to a hotel for journalists and then farther up the road, climbing a bit now as we get away from the river. We come to an attractive old wooden house, the writer's home. Maria Kuncewiczowa is or was a renowned novelist, essayist, and travel writer. She lived in London during and after the War, and in the United States after 1956, but then returned to Poland. We four look at the house and then enter the garden. I feel a little nervous about just walking into a stranger's garden, but then the housekeeper appears and invites us in. The author is asleep upstairs and can't be disturbed, but we are welcome to come in and see the ground-floor rooms. Maria announces that I am a writer from London and a member of PEN. We are shown into a charming, rambling house, obviously the home of someone with great aesthetic taste. It looks to me like a bohemian, artistic, hunting lodge. The housekeeper talks about Mrs. Kuncewiczowa and points out some of the furnishings in the house. Maria speaks to her with the same easy aplomb that I have seen her use on everyone from difficult officials to surprised turkey farmers.

Vistors to the house are encouraged to sign their names in a book, and Maria urges me to add my name to it. There is a brief discussion, and it seems that there is no question about it; of the four of us, it is I who am the logical choice to commemorate our visit. I am not quite convinced by Maria's hype, but as I am pushed toward the book I agree to add my name and best wishes to the extensive collection already in the book. Some of the other signatures are those of Susan Sontag, John Ashbery, and William Saroyan, and I meekly write my own on a clean page.

Now that we have worked up an appetite for lunch, we head back to town and the architects'club. The menu is soup, pork, potatoes, green beans and red cabbage. The soup course arrives and we are to serve ourselves from a huge tureen placed on the table. As a special honour, Maria invites me to serve the soup. I ladle it out into a couple of bowls, leaving a margin at the top. But this is entirely wrong! She peremptorily takes the ladle from my hand and tops up all the bowls so that the soup comes right up to the brim. I remember that she has told me that at times during the martial-law period they were actually hungry. Of course they want all the soup that comes along. In a moment the tureen is taken away to another table.

After lunch we all go to look at the old church up beyond the top end of the market place and stroll along the main street and look in shop windows. In a small street at the edge of the churchyard Włodek suddenly stops in his tracks and goes back to a shop we have just passed. It looks like some sort of hardware store and Włodek is highly excited by something he has seen in the window. We three women follow at a distance to see what can be so exciting. Włodek has disappeared into the shop and in a moment reappears with a bulky parcel under his arm. He has found a gas camping stove with two rings instead of the more usual one. A friend of his has been searching everywhere for such a stove and now Włodek has found it for him. He is as elated about it as if he had been looking for it for his own use. Maria knows the friend and the story of the camping stove and is not surprised at this detour in Kazimierz Dolny and is pleased at Włodek's find—pleased for Włodek and for the friend who can now tick one thing off his list.

It seems to me that Poland is a kind of very large treasure hunt. Perhaps everyone has a mental list of the needs of a circle of friends, and perhaps a certain proportion of all the purchases in the country are made on behalf of other people who can't find the desired merchandise in their own patch. This reminds me of Maria's story about Staszek's disastrous cracking of the toilet bowl while he was plastering the WC and the efforts to find a right-handed bowl in Warsaw. The waste pipe had to be attached either at the left or right or middle, and theirs happened to be the awkward style that was unavailable in Warsaw. After many months a friend living in another city located the right kind of fixture and brought it to them. In turn, the national treasure hunt explains a lot about the kinds of things people carry around on trains.

Maria says that the one souvenir I absolutely must take away from Kazimierz Dolny is a wonderful specialty of the town: sculptures made out of bread. This is not bread to eat, although it is bought at a bakery, but bread to keep and admire. The bakery sells folk-art chickens made of a special dough that apparently keeps forever.

"But Maria," I say, "I have to go home soon by plane. I don't know how I would pack this chicken in my bag, and my carry-on bag is already full. Thank you very much, they are charming, but I don't think..."

"You must have these chicken!" Maria interrupts. "Is famous souvenir of here! Every person collect these chicken! You not like to take home? Show Alastair! Hang on wall! Is splendid souvenir!"

"Yes, they are...really nice, really distinctive, but Maria..." I see she is looking disappointed at my lack of taste, but I really don't want one of these things, and packing my bag is going to be hard enough without brittle folk-art chickens in it. "But Maria, how could I carry it? You have to take as little as possible on board a plane."

"You could hold in lap, in little basket," she says defensively. Maria is thinking about a bus trip, and I must stop her before she finds me a little basket to hold in my lap during take-off and landing. ("Fasten your seat belts, please, and ensure that your seat is in the upright position and that all hand luggage is stowed either in the overhead lockers or under the seat in front of you, including any baskets containing bread chickens.") I wonder if she has ever been to an airport except to meet people. Has she ever met anyone there but me? Was her only visit to Okęcie three weeks ago when she met me with the small, impractical, posy? But no, Mrs. Mazaraki comes to visit and smuggles amber brooches.

"But really, Maria, thank you very much for the kind thought, and they are very nice, but really, it would just not be practical to take one of these home, travelling by air, you know."

A few days later my husband asks, incredulously, "You've brought home a *chicken* made of *bread?*" but he doesn't know Maria very well.

After a long walk out along the river on a low dyke, we return to town and catch a bus back to Puławy, where Krystyna has invited us home for *kolacja*. She became a pharmacist after they left their secret wartime school and it was again possible to study subjects like pharmacology. Krystyna was married to a vet but is widowed now. Her husband collected antiques and curios and bought items from his customers. Perhaps he took some of his veterinarian bills in kind, and now her house has an unusual number of odd objects in it. I'm not sure whether she likes these things for themselves, or would like to be rid of them, or keeps them in memory of her dead husband. Although Krystyna's house is modern, there is a certain 17th century air about it. There are heavy, dark furniture, Gothic things set into the wall, brass Russian samovars, and rugs made from the hides of boars and other animals. We are sitting on an antique velvet sofa when Krystyna tells me about her work. She hates it just now.

"It is terrible to be a pharmacist now," she tells me sadly. "I have to tell all customers that there is nothing for them. We have few medicines. They have prescriptions from doctors, but we have not the drugs to give them. All day I have to say them, 'No'."

I can see that this job of disappointing people all day long really weighs heavily on Krystyna. All her training must have been about giving people what they needed to get well—a very satisfying kind of work—but now it has turned into the exact opposite. Once on the kayak trip Ula told me that she had brought some paracetomol with her in her first-aid kit. Nothing unusual in that, I thought, until she told me, "The *only* paracetomol in Poland is in hospitals! Not in *aptcka*. Not at the chemist's." Maria's husband, Włodek, is having treatment for a heart problem, and there are difficulties about finding the medicines. It may help that his son-in-law, Wojtek, is a cardiologist. And Maria's granddaughter, Małgosia, needs various special medications and vitamins, and now the cystic fibrosis is affecting her liver. They hope they can prevent her having to go into hospital again, but it's touch and go.

The problem seems to be that with martial law and its aftermath, the Polish economy is in such a state than the pharmaceutical industry has practically collapsed. Imported drugs or even imported ingredients for Polish-made medicines are now unobtainable, and so the shelves of the chemists' are nearly bare. And it's not just drugs. Things like rubber gloves and bandages are so scarce that surgeons operate with their bare hands, and an accident victim being patched up in a hospital needs to bring his own bandages with him. Rubber and cotton would both have to be imported. I've been hearing little anecdotes and complaints like this since I got here.

I am looking idly at an African mask on Krystyna's wall when she invites us to see some of the other items in her husband's collection. There are pictures and knick-knacks and pieces of furniture. I imagine Krystyna's husband treating some farm animal or pet (she didn't tell us what kind of animals he specialised in) and being given one of these items by a grateful owner. Or perhaps it was a treasured item that the owner didn't want to part with, but the husband made it a condition of the treatment and extorted this loot. But Krystyna seems a kindly person, so I don't want to suspect her husband of anything underhanded.

Just then Maria gives a sudden little cry and lifts her foot sharply as though she has stepped on a mouse. We both look down and see that she has trodden on the small hoof of the goatskin rug we are standing on. I can't help laughing at the shocked expression on her face, but I don't want her to think I'm laughing at her. It's partly because of her startled look and partly because the cause of it is this small, hard, unlikely hoof of a goat not treated but acquired by Krystyna's late husband, one unlikely object among the many in this house. It strikes me as so funny that I can't help chuckling about it for days and weeks afterwards. I try to include Maria in this, but I'm afraid she doesn't find it as hilarious as I do. I just hope she understands the distinction between laughing at her and laughing at the situation.

We return to Warsaw and the visa problem again. We receive a message that we must report to the Bank Handlowy down in the centre of the city. We go to a big marble counter and Maria explains why we have come. Yes, they say, the money from London has arrived; it is here in the bank; in fact it is in an office upstairs. Would we like to see it? For some reason, we are supposed to go and look at it. But have I got this right?

"Maria," I say when the woman at the counter turns away, "why are we going upstairs?"

"To see money," she says. I can't tell whether she thinks this is normal or she's as mystified as I am.

"You mean, just look at it?" I ask. She answers with an expressive shrug that could mean many things.

The woman behind the counter comes back with the secret number we must use on the keypad beside the door that leads upstairs. The door is on the other side of the big marble bank lobby with its cashier windows and attendant queues. By the time we get to the other side of the lobby Maria has forgotten the secret number. We have to go back to the desk to ask the secret number again and then walk back across the lobby to the door. When Maria looks at the keypad uncertainly, the woman at the marble counter calls out across the marble lobby the four secret digits that will allow us entry through the private door. Maria doesn't catch one of the secret numbers, but someone in the nearest queue reminds her.

But before Maria can punch in the numbers, someone comes out, and we take advantage of the open door. A carpeted stairway lies before us, and we go up, unsure which room along the narrow carpeted corridor we are to go to. Maria asks in the first room, and we are directed to a room further along. When we find the international office, they seem to be expecting us, and a bank official ceremoniously opens a desk drawer and produces the paper with the money transfer in my name. We look at it and then go back downstairs.

Now at the big marble desk again, behind which a number of people are busily sitting at desks, a girl is searching for something for us. She is carrying my passport around with her and looking fruitlessly here and there. Maria and I look at each other, because we can't think what the girl is searching for. Then it dawns on me that she is looking for the piece of paper that we have just been looking at, for some reason, upstairs. She dithers around some more and then makes a telephone call and finally someone comes through the top-secret door on the other side of the lobby and hands her the required piece of paper from upstairs. Is this international banking or a folk dance?

Now some more forms are filled in and we are given a brass counter to take to a cashier, where the foreign money is counted out to me. The whole process has taken about an hour.

And now we can hurry over to the run-down police station in Praga to renew my visa, to enable me to have stayed legally in the country retrospectively before it is time to leave.

Maria has a really startling knowledge of the bus routes in Warsaw. She has an intricate map in her head and can get from any given point to any other point by bus or tram. She knows how many buses to take and where to change. We take my passport and our accumulation of official papers back to the dingy police station in a side street across the Vistula. However, the correct stamp cannot be applied then and there; we will have to come back the next day for that.

Maria Wnuk at a bus stop on Nowy Świat.

In the meantime, I go with Maria to visit her older sister, Janina. Janina lives alone in an apartment in another part of Warsaw. I have heard about her, and she was the other person in the family group with the dog, Fysia. Janina has led an interesting life working for the Polish government in Brussels and has never married. Now her little sister, Maria, herself a grandmother in her 60s, looks in on her to see if there is anything she needs.

Maria and Janina and their parents played a lot of bridge together during the War. There was a curfew in place, and in the evening there was not much else to do. They were in a somewhat ticklish situation for much of the time, because their town was on the line between the Russian and German armies. I see them in the house in Puławy sitting around a card table (perhaps it is winter and this is the only heated room; perhaps it is summer and the windows are open). They take turns dealing; they collect tricks and complain good-humouredly about the configuration of cards around the table; something is trumps, someone has finessed, someone is the dummy and goes to make tea. Her father, the distinguished architect, keeps score on the back of an envelope. He plays bridge with his wife and two daughters because they have to do something and because bridge is a part of ordinary life now during these days when so little about their lives is ordinary. A rubber of bridge in the evenings is a civilised thing, and you have to keep in touch with civilised life one way or another.

I can't help pondering the slipshod bureaucracy I have seen and the lack of some goods in shops. On the whole, food seems to be obtainable, and the tomatoes and cucumbers are excellent. I have heard about informal, somewhat black-market, sales of meat, of all things. If it weren't for this black market (and markets of varying shades of grey) in certain necessities, the system would probably collapse, because in its strictly ideological, "scientific" Marxist form it is simply unworkable. It needs all the shoehorns that people can find to accommodate themselves to the system, which reminds me more and more of a car with some superficially fine features but square wheels.

I can't figure out why efficiency seems to be beyond everyone's grasp. Wouldn't everyone's job be easier if they did it more efficiently? Wouldn't the paper-pushers at the police station in Praga have less to do if they stamped the visa while the applicant was there instead of making him come back the next day? Wouldn't the bank employees and their customers be happier and more productive if they cut out some of the pointless rigamarole? Why is it so difficult to get goods into shops in the right amount? And why in the world is there such a chronic shortage of toilet paper? When we got on the train to go to Kazimierz Dolny there was half a roll of toilet paper left in our compartment by the last occupants, and Włodek seized it like someone finding money in the street.

Later as I'm walking along a street lined with saplings, I suddenly notice that they are all silver maples! I must have seen them before, but it's only now that I'm consciously aware of them. Silver maples! As a child I climbed silver maple saplings, and the quintessential backyard tree in Indiana was, in my experience, a silver maple. In the landscape of my remembered childhood there were always a few silver maples around—among the other maples, sycamores, beeches, walnuts, and persimmons. They supplied branches for swings and generous boughs for shade. They become big, solid trees and their leaves turn vivid colours in October. Their crisp leaves fall and curl in the grass until you can't see the grass any more. You rake them into the gutter and burn them there, the thick viscous smoke lying on the leaves until flames spring up and disperse it. That smoke and the crisp chill in the air is the smell of October in Indiana. In the summer the leaves are a rich, dark green on the top side, and on the underside the silvery-grey that gives the tree its name. Silver maples in Warsaw! I walk up to one of the trees and stroke the familiar rough bark. I say under my breath, "What's a nice tree like you doing in a place like this?"

Chapter Seven

Charity Begins Abroad

One of the first things I did when I got home was to look up the number of the charity Medical Aid for Poland Fund in the telephone directory. I remembered hearing about this organisation when it was founded a few years before. They were collecting unused medicines or drugs that had passed their use-by date and sending them to Polish hospitals. I remembered Ula saying to me once that in her hospital they sometimes had to use drugs that were three years past the use-by date. She told me that in her halting English and held up three fingers to emphasize her point.

I dialed the number and the phone was answered by a woman with a voice that suggested well-spoken efficiency and practicality. It was a voice that might have been trained for the theatre or the radio, such was the tone and pitch. I asked if there was anything I could do to help her organisation.

"As a matter of fact, we do need some help in the office," she said. "Can you type?"

"Yes,' I said, 'I can type about 50 or 55 words a minute."

"Could you spare us half a day a week? Perhaps you could come on Friday mornings?"

"Yes,' I answered, "Friday mornings would be fine."

Medical Aid for Poland Fund was founded in 1982 by Dr. Bożena Laskiewicz, Artur Rynkiewicz, and Jarosław Żaba and at the behest of Lech Wałęsa, the leader of the *Solidarność* movement. The medical shortages were serious even then and Dr. Laskiewicz, an ear, nose, and throat surgeon, recruited some associates and before long was sending supplies to Poland. In the early days it was a very hand-to-mouth organisation and the donated supplies were kept in somebody's spare room, but by the time I joined the group, they had acquired warehouse space in Park Royal and an office in Earls Court. The office was run with great good humour and efficiency by Marysia Jaczyńska, whose silky voice I had heard on the phone. Each day there was a different cohort of two or three other women in the office, and somehow Marysia coordinated all these volunteers so that we worked well together, even though she rarely saw the same people two days in a row. My half Friday soon became the whole day. Sometimes if we couldn't make "our" day one week, we would fill in on another day. In this way I got to know some of the non-Friday people. I wonder if even the Poles found their own names a bit unwieldy, because we referred to each other by our initials, certainly in written memos and sometimes in speech. I still think of Marysia Jaczyńska as MJ and Marysia Owsianka as MO. Still, I made an effort to commit their multisyllabic names to memory.

Much of the work of the office took place in Polish, since all the other volunteers except one were Polish. The lone exception was Nancy Rómmel, the elderly widow of a Polish army officer. There was also an Australian who worked for a time on one of the other days, but I never met her. As most of the office workers were retired from other work, they were of an age to be born in Poland before the War; many of them still spoke English with some difficulty and preferred to speak Polish when possible. A few, like Marysia herself, had grown up in England or were the second-generation children of Polish parents and were perfectly bilingual.

Sometimes I had the feeling that I almost understood Polish. I used the words for "coffee" and "tea"—*kawa* and *herbata*—and I caught random words in the conversations around me when my office colleagues were in their Polish mode. Once I heard MJ on the phone discussing a *delikatny problem*. Unfortunately, I knew only that the *problem* was *delikatny* but none of the intriguing details.

These Poles were very considerate of my linguistic handicap. They tried to stick to English in my presence unless they really had to say it in Polish, and then they apologised beforehand. If the talk had fallen into Polish and got stuck there, sooner or later somebody would come to and say, in one language or the other, "Oh! Listen! We've been speaking Polish and Sarah's here!" Whereupon the talk would be wrenched back into English until some other Polish imperative came along. If I left the office to go around to the loo, I would hear Polish again before the door had closed behind me. I got used to hearing the Polish language in the background as I stamped letters or logged the incoming post. There would be a steady susurration of sibilant Polish sloshing about the room. I stipulated only that they translate the jokes.

The office staff tended to be all women, and Marysia managed to blend her rag-tag mixture into a surprisingly coordinated team. The men in the organisation tended to be concentrated in the warehouse and in the task of collecting supplies from various hospitals, donors, and wholesalers in the Greater London area. Our work in the office was usually to receive requests for, and offers of, help. We also bought medical equipment from wholesale suppliers. Marysia, whose voice was equally mellifluous in English and Polish, was to be heard ordering a consignment of hypodermic needles from an English supplier or discussing in Polish some problem about the distribution in Przemesl. The state Polish haulage firm, Pekaes, took lorry-loads of goods back to Poland on their return trip once a fortnight. Some sort of mutually advantageous agreement was arrived at that enabled Medical Aid to send many tonnes of supplies to selected centres in Poland and enabled Pekaes to avoid having an empty lorry on the road. A large map of Poland on the wall showed where we had already sent lorries and where the next one was going.

On warm days I rode my bike to the office and chained it to the railing or sometimes carried it down the area steps and left it in the downstairs hallway. The office was poorly ventilated, and to get a breeze going I would open the bathroom window on the east side of the building and wedge open the office door with my bicycle pump. One summer day there was a bus and Tube strike and I was the only one who could get to the office even though I lived about ten miles away. I kept the office open that day, although I was too new to MAPF to be of any real use. Polish-speakers who phoned must have felt put-upon to have to express themselves in English, especially if they had become used to MJ's effortless bilingualism. A man phoned and told me in a thick Polish accent that he was sending us a truckload of equipment from Paris. I couldn't understand why a truck would be coming to London from Paris if the destination was Poland, but the man with the thick accent seemed to think that it was quite normal. I dutifully wrote down his message as well as I could and left it for MJ to figure out. The next day when competent staff were back in the office, she immediately realised that it was from a keen MAPF supporter in the Polish community in Perth. His Polish accent with an overlay of Scots had made "Perth" sound to me like "Paris". I tried to leave the telephone to others after that.

MJ usually presided on the phone. She would break off a conversation with us about the filing system or the photocopier to take a call and speak at length in Polish, her voice rising and falling and performing all the consonant clusters so musically that I forgot how unpronounceable the words seemed to the eye. A moment later she would be arranging a purchase of catheters from a medical equipment supplier in south London, now in her sleek radio-announcer English voice.

MJ was a sculptress, in fact. She had trained at St. Martins School of Art and Hornsey College of Art. She and Kazik had two children and had lived in Italy and Kenya, where his civil engineering work had taken him. When she had to spell words on the phone—"B for Bertie, R for Roger"—I noticed that she usually used place names and that N was Nairobi. This may be an international convention for all I know, but I always imagined that she said it because she had lived there.

In any office there are conversations and coffee breaks, but these sociable moments at the Medical Aid for Poland office were fascinating. We made *kawa* or *herbata* for each other and added *mleko* (milk) or *cukier* (sugar) to taste. Sipping a mug of tea under the wall map of Poland, I heard anecdotes about people's lives long before they had found their way to this office in Earls Court. They were older than I was and had had bizarre adventures during and after the War. Teresa had spent part of her childhood in Siberia where her family were deported by the Soviet invaders of her part of Poland in 1939, and then later she had gone to school in India when the Soviet Union switched sides and they were allowed to leave Siberia. She used to say that her life-long habit of traveling had begun early, courtesy of the USSR. Marysia Owsianka had lived in the grounds of a hospital in Warsaw during the War. Her mother had written an interesting memoir, which Marysia was now translating. Urszula, a jovial grey-haired woman who had a surname that provokes awe among Poles because of the famous scholars and artists who have borne it, had trained as a nurse and then worked in a Soviet lab on a project to study typhus. As a junior staff-member, she was assigned the task of caring for the collection of lice needed for the experiments. They were kept in small containers like match boxes with one gauze side. To feed them she fastened numerous boxes to her thighs and sat for an hour while they ate their fill. "It itched, you know," she told me, "so I sat and read Agatha Christie novels to take my mind off it."

Later I heard that after the change of government in Poland a representative of an organization of former landowners had approached her about getting her ancestral Lithuanian estates back. With her illustrious name on their letterhead—or wherever they planned to use it—they would have sound credentials. She serenely picked up a flowerpot and indicated the contents. "This," she said, "is all the land I own now."

Hela was a taciturn woman who would arrive early in the morning long before the rest of us and do the bookkeeping. She didn't say much to me, preferring to speak Polish to the others in a throaty rasp as she chain-smoked. Several of the people I knew were on the Executive Committee, which met every Wednesday evening and included some of our office staff and some of the warehouse staff. The meetings must have all been conducted in Polish, but Marysia Jaczyńska produced the minutes of the meeting in impeccable English by the next day when I typed them up. I assumed the English was a legal requirement for a registered charity. Dr Laskiewicz would preside at the meetings, and sometimes she made a lightning visit to the office when she wasn't doing *delikatny* operations at her hospital in the Surrey suburbs. She would give us scraps of paper on which she had written highly abbreviated messages from or to well-wishers. If they were in English I would compose a letter, guessing what she wanted to say about, for example, "Fr Kowal. hosp—wchr thanks."

For a time Nancy Rómmel and I wrote a little newsletter to be distributed to the supporters of Medical Aid for Poland Fund about once a month. It was small and we ran it off on the photocopier, and later it was superseded by a smartly produced illustrated quarterly or triannual magazine edited by Marysia Owsianka. She wrote well—indeed had written a charming book about bees—and was a skilful magazine editor. Nancy and I would describe some of the projects Medical Aid was involved with: the hospital to which we had sent an incubator; the dental equipment we had dispatched to a city in southern Poland with the last lorry; the used clothing we were collecting; the small cheque we had received from an elderly man who had known Polish airmen in the RAF and revered their memory. We crammed it onto a couple of folded sheets of A4 paper, which we then stapled together. We used two columns per page and there was no scope for interesting layout. Marysia's production later was a vast improvement on ours.

One Christmas I joined some Polish émigré ladies who were selling hats at Shepherd's Bush shopping centre. One of them had acquired some seconds or overstocks and we could sell them with all proceeds going to MAPF. They were in all sorts of materials and styles. I could see, just by the way Magda handled the hats, that she was very expert and had handled many hats in her time. Picking up a scrap of fur and fingering a fragment of veil, she told me, "You can make a hat out of *anything*!"

At the first Christmas party at POSK, the Polish community centre in Hammersmith, I wanted to be given a job as the guests arrived, and I was hastily put on the desk at the door where the name labels were. I was supposed to write the guests' names on a sticky label for them, but I instantly abandoned the attempt when my first customer was MJ's sister-in-law, Oleńka Chrzanowska. After that I generously allowed the newcomers to write their own names.

At the Christmas parties there was always a tombola with donated prizes and tickets at a pound for five. Dr. Laskiewicz would give a speech thanking everyone and giving a summary of our activities and successes in the last year. One of our patrons, Baroness Caroline Cox, might stand up and describe a visit she had made to Poland. We would sit at tables and drink a glass of wine and eat a glazed doughnut or perhaps a slice of poppy-seed cake. Whole cakes were also available to be bought, thanks to Grodziński's bakery. Everyone would sing traditional Polish Christmas songs, all of them different from English ones and therefore unrecognisable to me as Christmas carols. Ewa Brzeska would direct the singing with cheerleader-like verve. Her husband Kazik often appeared in the office. He was Kazik Brzeski to the Poles but Ken Breski to non-Poles, who were deemed incapable of the Polish version of his name. In the office we called him KB anyway.

After I had been with Medical Aid for a few months, Marysia Jaczyńska told us that a new volunteer was going to arrive and join the Friday group. The new person was Polish and had been living in Sweden but was now in London. She sounded like a capable and welcome addition to our Friday team. I could do only the jobs that didn't require Polish, and only a select few understood the filing system. The next Friday the new volunteer appeared and was introduced. She told me in good English that her name was Małgorzata, but as that would be rather difficult for a mouth used to English, I could call her the English equivalent, Margaret. In Sweden she had been known as Margareta. She didn't look like a Margaret to me, so I made her spell her first and last names for me so that I could remember them syllable by syllable. I feel people should be called by their right names and not some foreign version of it, unless they particularly *like* to have different aliases. It should never be just because nobody tries to pronounce it.

Małgorzata Koraszewska and I soon became friends. We shared an interest in language and translation. Sometimes when we should have been filing papers or typing letters we were comparing Swedish adjectives with some interesting parallel in Old English. She had been working for a Polish publisher based in London, but the company was closing down and she had looked for something constructive to do with her new spare time and happened upon Medical Aid for Poland Fund. We went out for sandwiches at lunchtime and brought back things for the others, like the rock-hard pears that Marysia Jaczyńska liked.

Małgorzata's husband, Andrzej, was a radio journalist with the BBC Polish Service at Bush House and had been specially headhunted to London from their home in Lund in southern Sweden. As Polish speakers in Sweden, they had both done some translation work between Polish and Swedish and, to my amazement, had also done social work in that culture so different from their own. Their leaving Sweden was unremarkable in a Europe of fluid borders and international employment opportunities, but their arrival in Sweden 18 years before was a story I found riveting.

They had left Poland under a very unpleasant cloud. In 1968 there was a particularly repellent government decree that Polish Jews were now unwelcome in their own country—insofar as there were any Jews left after the Nazis' depredations and the wholesale emigration of most of the survivors. Anything that was wrong with the society or economy, which was most things, was somehow all their fault. Małgorzata, who was Jewish, lost her research post at the Polish Academy of Sciences, where she was working toward a doctorate in sociology. Her widowed mother was similarly given a curt notice at her work that her services would no longer be required. Andrzej was making a name for himself as a dissident journalist and was in bad odour with the regime, too. They stuck it out for a while, hoping that things would get better, but nothing improved. When they had a chance to go to Sweden, they left Warsaw to start new lives in more congenial surroundings. They were deprived of their Polish citizenship and, until they qualified for Swedish citizenship five years later, they were stateless.

Małgorzata and I were almost exactly the same age, give or take a couple of months. While I had been born in a placid 1943 in Indianapolis in the most ordinary circumstances in St. Vincent's Hospital under the supervision of my mother's obstetrician, Małgorzata had been born in a village in Uzbekistan, to which her parents had been deported from the then Polish city of Lvov by the Soviet occupiers of eastern Poland early in the War. ("For six years we were hungry," her mother told me later, summing up the whole experience.)

Over the *kawa* and *herbata* in the office, fascinating details of the others' lives came out in little remarks and anecdotes. I knew from early on that I was going to get much more benefit from my association with Medical Aid for Poland than the charity would have from me. I met people I never would have met otherwise. I went to Christmas parties and ate *makowiec* (poppy-seed cake) and heard unfamiliar Christmas carols. I went to send-offs of our lorries at the warehouse, surrounded by crowds of Poles who were working selflessly for anonymous fellow-countrymen. Many of them visited Poland regularly to see friends and family and could report back what the situation was like.

However, I knew from Maria Wnuk that the situation was changing so rapidly now in 1989 that mere visitors couldn't keep up with it. Sometimes I felt it was a positive advantage to *know* that I was ignorant of the day-to-day political shifts in Poland. I felt caught up in their fervour but yet apart from it. I wasn't Polish myself. When the priest came to bless the lorry and asperse it with holy water, I did not cross myself and utter prayers. I had no family and no history in, and no cultural connection with, Poland. My family history was North American for 300 years and Scottish, Dutch, and French before that. There wasn't one Pole in the works. And yet I felt an attachment to these people and their cause. I had begun to think of my friends collectively as "my Poles". I'd been to their native country, camped under their pine trees and fallen in their river. And I'd once met Maria Wnuk on a train to Wrocław.

Chapter Eight

Gimme Twentyish Hectares

The Berlin Wall has come down. I remember watching in disbelief, aged 17, when it was appearing in instalments on the evening news at home in Indiana that August of 1961. It seemed to me such a bald acknowledgement that to keep people in the country Walther Ulbricht had to build this ridiculous physical wall, penning them in like livestock. What a public admission of defeat! The mortar was barely dry when they were shooting people who tried to escape over it. There were people who wanted to get out of East Germany so badly that they were willing to brave minefields, guard dogs, and armed sentries. If I hadn't known it before, that told me the essential truth about eastern Europe.

A couple of years later on a summer tour of Europe I was with a group of students in Prague, and one evening in a beer garden I danced with an East German, Hartmut Süss, a likeable engineering student of my own age. Afterwards he and two of his friends walked three of us girls back to our hotel, where we took pictures of the group and exchanged addresses. Hartmut and I corresponded for several years, during which we both moved several times and he got married. In the beginning he wrote in English, but when I took a course in German for reading knowledge as a requirement for grad school, he wrote in German and I answered in English. We described our studies and various hobbies and student activities. He had warned me that our letters would be spot-checked by the authorities. Our letters could have been broadcast over loudspeakers in the Alexanderplatz and there would have been nothing compromising about them. Boring, certainly, but nothing that couldn't have been public knowledge, as far as I could see. He was always doing lab reports to do with industrial ceramics and I was always reading medieval English literature. Some zealous Stasi man may well have been keeping files on us and recording our syllabuses for all I know.

If you don't live in a state like that, you don't always know what might be compromising or illegal. I tried to send Hartmut an, as I thought, innocuous copy of *The Reader's Digest* to help him with English, but it turned out to be too hot for the Stasi and it came straight *zurück*. I then sent him the more interesting articles a few pages at a time enclosed in letters. Another time a letter was returned because I had written "East Germany" on the envelope instead of "German Democratic Republic". I sent Hartmut articles from *Der Spiegel*, which I could buy—I was living in Philadelphia by then—but he couldn't. Once I sent him a small cloth American flag, and he wrote exultantly that it had got through. I could see that he was delighted with this triumph, but now, after all we have learned about the Stasi, I doubt if it went unnoticed. In the late 60s our correspondence stopped, but it didn't occur to me to wonder if he had been penalized for writing to someone in the West. When you're a student and you have eight different addresses in five years you lose touch with people.

But now the Berlin Wall was coming down after 28 years and Germans were tearing it apart with their bare hands. In other countries of eastern Europe unworkable and iniquitous governments were finally imploding, and the popping sounds accompanying the process were sometimes gunshots and sometimes champagne corks. I was in Scotland at Christmas and was finally reading the Penguin edition of Marx's *The Communist Manifesto*, which I had read about in a government course once but had never actually read straight through. I even waded through all the prefaces. At the rate things were falling apart in eastern Europe—that was the Christmas that the Romanians overthrew the Ceaușescu regime—the *Manifesto* would soon be as irrelevant in Europe in reality as it was intellectually, but I felt a need to read it while it was still being taken seriously somewhere. Now, reading it cover to cover, I was amazed to see how redolent of the 1840s it was. It was 1848 in amber. Here was a reaction to early Victorian Britain and a comically off-base prediction of what was "inevitable". It was an analysis of an industrial society before many major reforms and adjustments had been put in place, but Marx had extrapolated from the downside of early urban industrialism, called it "science", and made some really ludicrous prophecies. It was no more scientific than phrenology and homeopathy. Why hadn't this been obvious to everyone else who had ever read it? Was it obvious to me only because Marx's bright ideas were crumbling to pieces in the newspapers and every night on television?

But then I thought of Hartmut and the suspicious police state he lived under and the Wall that trapped people inside a "workers' paradise", and I saw that whatever theory underpinned that practice had to be hopelessly flawed. A one-party state has corruption and failure built into it, and Marxism in power can only be a one-party state. It was no wonder it was all falling apart now, and not before time.

From time to time one of the members of the Medical Aid for Poland Fund (or MAPF, as we always abbreviated it) would go as an "escort" on one of the lorries. This person would meet the representatives of Caritas, the Catholic state-approved charitable organization in Poland entrusted with local distribution. Sometimes a special consignment was earmarked for a certain place within the city or region, and the escort might be delegated to deliver it personally. All the escorts wrote reports of their trip which were then presented at a meeting of the Executive Committee. I would normally have been too junior and too non-Polish to be allowed to act as an escort, but in early 1990 the Executive Committee let me go because I was going to write an article or two about it for a newspaper. (In the end, the paper didn't print it because there was suddenly too much news from eastern Europe; every day there were stories about the upheavals that had been going on all winter after the fall of the Berlin Wall the previous November, and most of those stories were more momentous than news of a charity sending a truck-load of medical supplies and used clothing to Upper Silesia.)

A documentary about the pollution in Poland, "Poisoned Inheritance", had recently been shown on television with an appeal by Jeremy Irons. Money had come rolling in. One of my jobs in the office had been to help log all the contributions. One of the hospitals shown in the documentary was a children's hospital in Zabrze near Katowice, and after the delivery in Katowice I was to go on to Zabrze with the parcels for that hospital on behalf of a similar medical charity called, with extraordinary hubris, Angels International. I was also taking a copy of the video of "Poisoned Inheritance" to show in Katowice with strict instructions to remember and bring it back.

Sarah Lawson, Adam Siedlecki, and Dr. Bożena Laskiewicz with the Pekaes lorry bound for Katowice, January 1990.

At the warehouse in Park Royal the staff have been busy colour-coding hundreds of parcels. The tarpaulin on the right-hand side of the truck is rolled up and the boxes and crates are being stacked carefully and systematically. Alastair comes to lend a hand. He has a nodding acquaintance with several of the MAPFers. I am given a clipboard to keep track of the various consignments within the larger shipment, because later I may need to know what the packages contain and where they are. As the packages are stowed in the container-sized truck, I see that only an *idiot-savant* could remember where everything is, but I do my best with the clipboard. Dr. Laskiewicz is overseeing operations (ear, nose, and throat ones during the week and this one on alternate Saturdays), and the other officers of MAPF, like Artur Rynkiewicz and Wanda Sarnecka, are doing their well-practiced jobs labeling the packages. A photographer has come along from a local newspaper in South London and wants the driver and me to pose loading the truck, as though it were all our idea and we were doing it by ourselves. The Pekaes driver, Adam Siedlecki, obligingly gets into the trailer and pretends to receive a bulky bag I hand him from the ground. The picture and quite a long article later appeared about this South Londoner (me) who wanted to help Poland, and so under the auspices of Medical Aid for Poland was going with this truck full of medical supplies accompanied by Mr. Siedlecki. "The pair" were going to deliver it to Katowice in Upper Silesia.

Finally everything is loaded and the tarpaulin is lashed down and we're ready to be off! I climb up steps like a stepladder into a surprisingly comfortable Renault cab. It is like sitting in a roomy easy chair. It is a good thing that it is comfortable, because it is going to be home for the next three days.

We sat high above the ordinary traffic and bounced gently on our wide, well-sprung seats. Behind the driver's and passenger's seats were two bunk beds. Adam Siedlecki was a big man with a broad, friendly face. He had driven Pekaes trucks all over Europe and the Middle East. We drove down to Dover and had our manifest checked by Customs and then drove onto the ferry to Zeebrugge. We were carrying 17,218 kilos of goods in 998 boxes and bags. While we were delivering it to the diocesan charity office in Katowice in Upper Silesia, there were batches of things that were to be sent on or collected from Katowice. Eighteen parcels, for example, were destined for a home for handicapped children in Kochłowice near Ruda Śląska. Some of that was washing powder and sweets, but there were supplies of a more medical nature for the children's hospital in Zabrze, like syringes and cannulae and IV sets. There were a few wheelchairs and 347 bags of used clothing. Our 32-tonne lorry was packed tight with all this, and when the manifest turned out not to tally by one parcel, I was surprised that it was out by only one. The shipping agent checked it numerous times and finally, shrugging, altered one number, and lo, it tallied after all.

We had a meal in the truck-drivers' section of the ferry. (The arrangement was that the MAPF escorts always paid for the drivers' meals in western Europe. Pan Adam paid for my meal in East Germany because I had no East German marks and he had a supply of them. We acted as host and hostess for each other on our respective sides of Europe.) One great advantage of being a woman truck driver when the rest are men is that you get a cabin to yourself on cross-Channel ferries. At 1:30 a.m. the wake-up alarm sounded. I was dressed, orange-juiced and back in the cab leaving the ferry at about 2:10. That night there were gales in England and Belgium and the Channel between, and our ferry was the last to cross before the next few were cancelled.

There were always little jokes in the MAPF office about women escorts "spending the night with strange men" when they travelled to Poland with the lorry drivers. There were about as many women escorts as men; in this respect the gender division of labour in MAPF did not apply. The roomy Renault cab might well have served as a place of assignation, but it could also be as chaste as you liked. I climbed into my sleeping bag on the top bunk fully clothed, but pan Adam changed into his pyjamas. It was unimportant whether I got a good night's sleep or not, but I was glad that he was going to be comfortable and get as much rest as possible for the drive the next day. The gale rose and our cab began to sway and lurch with the gusts of wind. It rocked like a rowboat in the Minch, it rocked like Emma Bovary and Rodolphe's carriage, and it woke me up. I saw out of one half-open eye that pan Adam had pulled back the curtains that had

144

been closed over the cab windows and was driving to a more sheltered spot in the lorry park between two other trucks.

The next morning we freshened up at the office by the lorry park and ate breakfast in a drivers' canteen, where pan Adam talked to some other Pekaes drivers. Some English drivers were going to wait out the gales, but we were going to press on to the German border. As I was looking at some audio tapes, one jumped out at me. I don't know any truck-driving songs, but this one had a roadmap as an illustration on the front, and it happened to be a map of central Indiana, where I was born and grew up. I figured that whatever it was, it and a Trini Lopez tape could be my contribution to entertainment in the cab.

Pan Adam and I had a very sketchy but sufficiently effective means of communication. I knew a few words of Polish and he knew a few words of English, and we both could cobble up a sentence in German. We spoke in this hash of languages as we drove along, and I sometimes had recourse to a small Polish/English, English/Polish dictionary I had brought with me. I showed him my new tapes and he put the trucking songs in the tape deck. I thought he would like them, because he had some other similar tapes. They were tuneful songs about life on the road, and I liked one of them, "Gimme Forty Acres". It had a catchy tune, and the point of the song was that the speaker, a somewhat inept truck driver, needed forty acres to turn around in. He got into various scrapes on the road and had to turn the truck around and then the chorus kicked in with, "Gimme forty acres to turn this rig around. / It's the easiest way that I've found." I explained to pan Adam that this driver needed about 20 hectares to turn his truck around. (Later I did some calculations and found that it was more like 16 hectares, but I claim poetic license.)

We had an easy drive across Belgium on Sunday. It was a sunny day and the wind had abated. It was like a Sunday outing, driving along high above the roadway listening to the bouncy music. We stopped short of the German border because lorries aren't allowed on the *Autobahnen* on Sundays. The plan was to have a nice meal at the motorway stop in Belgium, have an early night, and then get underway very early the next morning to cross the border, pass through customs, and get across the Ruhr before the rush hour. Pan Adam had done this many times before and knew the timing. We stopped at about 4:30 in the motorway service area. Now we could relax for the rest of the day. We chatted and had a nice restaurant meal of *coq au vin*, for this was the French part of Belgium. We talked about Ernest Hemingway, because pan Adam was reading *For Whom the Bell Tolls* in Polish. He showed me pictures of his wife Zofia, and his two teen-age children, Katarzyna and Aleksander.

We were at the West German border by 5 a.m., but most of the other truck drivers in Europe had had the same idea, and there were already dozens of them at the customs office all wanting their papers checked. Pan Adam was irked at the delay, but I took this opportunity to phone the MAPF office and leave a message that we had reached the German border; this too was one of the duties of a lorry escort. We drove in the dark through the Ruhr, the *Autobahn* gradually filling up with traffic and all the other lorries that weren't allowed on it yesterday. By the time the sun came up we were nearly across the Ruhr and the traffic looked like a rush-hour to me.

Now, snacking in the cab, we sped across West Germany as far as Garbsen, where we made a rest stop. For a key deposit of 20 marks I was given a shower cubicle and adjacent dressing room and a huge fluffy towel. After two days on the road, in the same clothes since Saturday morning, I had rarely so luxuriated in a hot shower and a change of clothes. If this motorway stop had a fan club, I would have joined it.

Near the border with East Germany pan Adam stopped again at an Aldi cut-price supermarket where he stocked up on goods that couldn't be found farther east. One of the great perks of being a Polish truck driver was that you had chances to buy rare merchandise like German coffee and chocolate and that perennial favourite, toilet paper.

146

When we arrived at the East German border that afternoon in late January 1990 the barbed wire and the watch towers were still there, but no one was on guard. There was a border post at which we had to pay a fee for a transit visa through the country, but that was all. The road suddenly deteriorated and was no longer a four-lane *Autobahn*, but had just one lane in each direction. Now we really did bounce along, skirting south of Berlin on the road to Cottbus. We stopped for lunch at a simple establishment along the road where there was a buffet of cold salads and good beefsteak and chips.

East Germany rolled past us as we continued down the old pre-war highway. It was as straight as any Roman road. Now and then the rolling farmland was interrupted by some ugly signs of heavy industry. On the whole, East Germany looked a lot like New Jersey to me. Silver birch and fir trees sometimes lined the road. The sun was setting behind us in flares of red and orange. Soon the trees were silvery in the full headlights of the Renault cab. We listened incongruously to Johnny Cash singing about the ups and downs of life in Tennessee. By early evening we reached the Polish border at Olszyna.

Now for the first time pan Adam had to open the tarpaulin on the side of the lorry and take out random parcels as directed by the customs officer. He seemed unduly suspicious and insisted that Adam throw down a certain box. It turned out to contain hypodermic needles for Zabrze, and he seemed to conclude reluctantly that we weren't smugglers after all. I sat in the cab for an hour or more listening first to a programme of polkas and then to a German news report from Leipzig about a street demonstration. It was the evening news and was remarkably frank. There were other demonstrations all over East Germany against the caretaker government and in favour of a united Germany. The German Democratic Republic was on its last legs. I thought of my old pen pal Hartmut and wondered what he was doing now. It would be his children who were taking part in these demonstrations!

Our passports were at last returned after careful and lengthy study. I changed £20 into złoty and found myself looking at a pile of cash well into six figures. I was now equipped to buy the Boardwalk and all four railroads.

Here at the border was a truck-drivers' hostel, where we spent our third night on the road. It was something like a basic youth hostel, and once again as a lady truck driver I had the privilege of private quarters. Following my instructions from MAPF, I asked pan Adam to phone or telex this church charity office in Katowice with our estimated time of arrival.

We were to start at first light the next morning, and so I was up before dawn had quite cracked. In fact, I was up and ready to go before pan Adam was. We sat in the receptionist's office having coffee and some Dutch biscuits he had bought at the Aldi yesterday. The cafeteria in the hostel didn't open until 8:00 and it was only 6:20 now.

"But now it is 7:20 in eastern Europe," pan Adam assured me.

"What?" I said. "I thought it was the same as western Europe." I was sure that when I had gone to Poland before I had changed my watch by only one hour.

"No," he said decisively, "it is an hour later."

I slipped off my wristwatch and quickly moved the hands an hour later to 7:20 a.m.

"But," he continued, "in Poland it is 6:20, like in western Europe. At Soviet border it is one hour later."

Of course. Poland wasn't "eastern Europe". If you're Polish, Poland is "the Heart of Europe" or "central Europe", but not "eastern Europe". There is lots more of Europe east of Poland. Indeed, on the map Warsaw is almost equidistant between Brussels and Moscow. To think of the Soviet bloc as "eastern Europe" was to skew simple geography. I slipped my watch off again and reset the hands.

Now at 7:30, western European and Polish time, there was a magnificent sunrise in the East. The eastern sky was a vivid display of orange, pink, and pale blue. The pink crept west until it touched East Germany a few hundred yards away. There was a light rime on the grass, and the orangey-pink clouds in the east cast the shadow of their colour on it, so that an orangey-pink glow seemed to be on everything. I looked up and down the road, empty except for a few Pekaes drivers getting underway. This straight road was entirely in Germany when it was built, merely an uninterrupted continuation of what we were on all day yesterday. We began to drive directly into the cold winter sunrise down at the end of this endless road.

I am constantly riffling through my little yellow Langenscheidt dictionary. I look up words and pronounce them at pan Adam. We talk about the crops and animals that we see. At other times we listen to pan Adam's tape collection, which includes Theodorakis and the Polish Christmas carols I have heard at MAPF Christmas parties. We listen to the trucking songs, and once again I am amused by "Gimme Forty Acres". I am sure pan Adam, who has a sense of humour, would like this song if he could understand the words. As we lurch over the old German road I transcribe the chorus and then copy it neatly when we stop for lunch. As I thought, he finds it very amusing when we go over the text together. Back in the truck he plays it five or six times, taking out the cassette and running it back each time. Finally I make a very juddery copy of all four *stanzas* to copy neatly later.

This road is supposedly a "motorway", but the surface is uneven and potholed. Pan Adam laughs and calls it "Polish rodeo". I tell him, more or less in Polish, that if we went on day after day, by the time we got to Vladivostock I would speak perfect Polish. He laughs and says yes, and he would speak perfect English.

We skirt Wrocław and chunter along to Opole and then enter the Katowice conurbation. The sun is shining brightly, but there is a haze hanging over everything. Katowice is famous for its mining and heavy industry and its health problems caused by

149

pollution. Pan Adam seems well informed about this and tells me that women may have 10 pregnancies but only three live births. The rates of birth defects and childhood leukaemia are shocking. Houses are pumping out black coal smoke and I see plumes of yellow smoke coming from industrial chimneys. The grubby, down-at-heels look of the place in this pale winter light reminds me a bit of the Glasgow I knew in the 1960s. We wind through city streets, and also, surprisingly, through farmland and past gardens. There are the usual tatty cityscapes: endless right-angled blocks of flats in grey concrete and mud where there should be sidewalks. Bauhaus-derived design and concrete may work somewhere but not here. They are the twin visual curses of the East Bloc. ("Bloc" indeed—concrete block.)

We reach the curia in *ulica* Jordana, and pan Adam goes to announce our arrival and enquire about where he is to park the lorry for unloading. Meanwhile, as there is nothing else to do, I make a clean copy of the verses of "Gimme Forty Acres". A rather rag-tag band of lorry-unloaders appears, some of them children of only 10 or 12. They tackle the lorry from the back, not the side, as it was loaded in London. They plainly know what they are doing, so I leave them to it, having first extracted a crate of a dozen boxes of powdered soya milk that Dr. Laskiewicz had said I could take to my friends in Warsaw.

Fr. Malcher is in charge and understands the rather complicated colour code. Of the 998 cases in the truck, some parcels are being picked up by other people for other destinations: huge boxes marked with red, yellow, and green tape go to Poznań; 14 parcels marked with blue tape are from the Eastbourne Polish Relief Appeal and go to Kraków; another 16 parcels are marked with yellow and red and are a consignment that I am to take personally to a children's hospital in Zabrze.

While the expert unloaders were busy with their task, I sit in the cab with pan Adam going over the new verses of "Gimme Forty Acres" to be sure he understood them. I doubted if this text had been used for an English lesson before.

When he finally got unloaded
He was glad to leave the town,
Yeah, he was very happy goin' back to Alabam'.
When up ahead he saw a sign
That said, "You are northward bound,"
He said, "Gimme forty acres
And I'll turn this rig around."

This trip from London to Katowice with a Polish lorry driver had been pleasant and interesting and I enjoyed his company and our inventive communication. When Adam Siedlecki left to go home to his family, I gave him some Cadbury bars, some Mr. Kipling pies, and both cassettes. He gave me his Christmas carol tape as a souvenir.

Fr. Malcher is a friendly, somewhat stocky, energetic priest who is in charge of Caritas in Katowice, a man really committed to the work of helping people. He is eager to show me the pharmacy that Caritas runs and introduce me to the pharmacist. This pharmacy is in the basement of the curia and is only open on Thursdays, but very early on Thursday mornings a queue forms that extends up the stairs, out the door, and down the street and around the corner. People come hoping that the pharmacy may have the medicine that they have been prescribed. They come from all over the diocese. Sometimes they are lucky and sometimes not. The pharmacist is Mrs. Depta, or rather Dr. Depta, as she has a PhD in pharmacology. Poland seems to be full of capable, well-trained people who lack the tools to do their jobs. Dr. Depta takes me into her *apteka*, where there are shelves like library stacks full of medicines. She tells me that the biggest need is for surgical gloves, needles, and catheters for both adults and children. She needs antibiotics, but a pressing problem is a treatment for intestinal worms in children. The *apteka* also dispenses Gerber baby food for sick children.

Later I am served a *kolacja* of scrambled egg, cold cuts, bread, and slices of red pepper in oil. Fr. Malcher finally has a chance to sit down and talk. We get acquainted and he tells me about his nephew, who died of leukaemia at 22 in September. The priest is full of admiration for his nephew, because he was very brave and prepared his family and his girlfriend for his death.

On that sombre note I am shown to my room at the hostel beside the warehouse where the boxes and bags from the lorry have been stored. It's a bare little room with two beds. The shower remains resolutely ice cold (unlike the one in Garbsen, which is now a wistful memory) and there is no plug in the sink. But then, I'm not in Poland to have a luxurious life. I'm up the next morning shortly after 7:00, and breakfast is an exact replica of last night's *kolacja* and very good. Now two seminary students arrive to show me the sights of Katowice. Have they been dragooned into this, or is it a treat for them?

Marek and Witek are boys in the fourth year of a six-year course. They are trainee priests and are already wearing dog collars. I put them at their ease and we chat and joke as we walk along. Suddenly to my surprise they both go down on one knee and cross themselves. They stand up again and point to a student friend of theirs crossing our path a block or more ahead. He's carrying a bulky sort of monstrance and is on his way to a sick person in hospital. "He is carrying the body of Christ," they explain.

We stroll on toward the centre of Katowice, and I am struck again by how much the old streets, blue with winter light and coal smoke, look and smell like Glasgow in 1967. I even have a brief flicker of *déjà vu*. We go into a department store and look at all four floors of it, then in a street by the railway station we find an open-air market selling great chunks of raw meat for 13,000 or 14,000 złoty per kilo. The idea of eating something you've bought at a smoky, dusty crossroads like this gives me a whole new appreciation of canned ham.

It's a cold, damp day, and I want to take the boys to a coffee shop. We find a nice *kawiarnia*, and Marek succeeds in buying all three coffees, which was not my intention. Witek carefully wraps his scarf around his neck and tucks it into his coat. This is not because he has a sore throat or is protecting his singing voice, but because seminary students are not supposed to be in a place where alcohol is available and he is very conscious of the responsibility of a dog collar.

We sit over our coffee and I ask them about their studies. They are both taking an exam on Saturday in Old Testament studies. Hebrew isn't a required subject, but Witek is taking it anyway. They are serious, bright, rosy-cheeked young men who are going to follow in the footsteps of people like Fr. Malcher, doing their best with what they have for the needy of the diocese. On the way back to the curia they show me a Carmelite convent and the adjacent church of SS. Peter and Paul, and then the splendid round cathedral. I give them each a Cadbury chocolate bar to help them with their studies and wish them success with the Old Testament.

I then throw some overnight things into a nylon travel bag and go with Fr. Malcher to a home for handicapped children. There are no children there yet because the place is still being built, all by volunteer labour, so the progress of the building is somewhat fitful. It was a farmhouse and now a new wing is being added. There is to be a ramp for wheelchairs. Fr. Malcher is bubbling over with the ambitious plans for the place and shows me what it will look like when it's finished. In the meantime we are served a fine lunch in a more-or-less finished kitchen. This home for handicapped children is going to be a self-sufficient working farm when it gets going and even turn a profit. The residents are going to learn how to care for the animals. I am taken to a barn with 10 bullocks that will be used for meat and on the way back to the house I notice a rather baffled-looking sheep.

Sarah and Fr. Malcher with the minibus loaded with supplies for an orphanage.

Fr. Malcher is a man with ambitions and plans, and the next day he's going to show me another ambitious project up in the mountains south of Katowice. We set out in Fr. Malcher's parish's Mercedes Benz, Fr. Malcher and I and pani Stefania and her daughter Mirella and a black labrador puppy. He has some other errands to do first, and then we head south on a main road toward a house in the mountains where youth leaders are trained. As we drive along I am invited to name the puppy. I take it as a considerable honour to be asked to do this, and I give it some thought. I tell them that I will name it after my husband, whose name is Alexander. (This is the second time I have falsified his Scottish name for the benefit of Poles, just as Małgorzata tried to simplify her name for me. It's not that they couldn't pronounce *Alastair*, but I am sparing them the explanation and digressions about Gaelic. I am not consistent, I know.) This is an international name with noble connotations and I think they'll like it, and I wonder how exactly it might be spelled in Polish. They take to it immediately and call the puppy Alex. This is to be a kind of "souvenir" of my visit. But just then the car starts to sputter. Do things go wrong with Mercedes Benzes?

Something has gone wrong with this one, because we lose power and coast to a stop at the side of the road. Fr. Malcher sees a church not far away and goes there to phone for a repairman. Fr. Malcher is an employee of a concern with many branches. Pani Stefania and her daughter and Alexander and I wait for an hour or more as a foggy evening begins to come on and we sit in a car without lights at the side of a busy road. I am not very happy in this situation, but pani Stefania and I make conversation in German. Her German is not much better than mine, but we muddle along. (My German should be improving, and perhaps it is, with all the practice I get speaking it with Poles. There is certainly enormous scope for improvement.)

When Fr. Malcher finally reappears he has a young repairman with him who goes straight to a fuel conduit which is accessible from inside the car, under a housing between the driver's and passenger's seats. From his toolbox he takes out a bicycle pump. He disconnects the fuel tube and gives it a few shots with the pump and reattaches it. Fr. Malcher tries the ignition and the car starts at once. He thanks the mechanic and we continue on our way in a diesel Mercedes Benz that has just been repaired with a bicycle pump. I am completely mystified.

"There are impurities in the petrol," Fr. Malcher says.

"Is there rust in the tank?"

"Yes, but it's mainly from water in the petrol. You see, filling station managers add water to the petrol. This produces a chemical reaction that makes a salt of a sandy consistency. It goes into solution and then collects in the fuel tube. A diesel has more filters, and so the problem is not so bad. Petrol-engine cars have worse problems. The dirt gets into more places." Fr. Malcher changes lanes and slows down for a stoplight. "This is a Polish story," he adds.

Now it's completely dark and there's a thick fog. We drive through villages and eventually come to a house and I think we've arrived, but we're only changing cars. We leave our Mercedes Benz at a house where Fr. Malcher greets the householder and transfers our bags and parcels to the new car, and then we go on in a Toyota four-wheel drive jeep with snow chains on the rear wheels. Now the road deteriorates to what seems to be a dry riverbed tending steeply upward. We lurch over big rocks and around boulders and the headlights of the jeep bounce from one obstacle to another. Now and then there's a sharp turn and the headlights pan across gnarled trees at the side of the road, if indeed it is a road. Finally we turn off onto another track and arrive at a house.

The lights are all on and we are greeted by the housekeeper, Fr. Malcher's mother, who has some food ready for us. Fr. Malcher's brother's four children are staying in the house, too. This is another house that has been built or remodeled by numerous volunteers, some more skilled than others. Before we eat I am shown to my room upstairs. It is a chilly but somehow cosy little room under the eaves. There is a toilet near by, but the bathroom is somewhere else. I hurry down to the dining room where *kolacja* is being served. At the top of the stairs there is a sizable hole in the floor. You can see the rug on the floor below through this hole. You could drop Alexander through it. There is no indication of how it might have been made, and I wonder what they could have dropped to make such a hole, like characters in a cartoon film who are hit by a heavy safe that makes a safe-shaped hole in the floor.

We have a plate of cold cuts and cheese and some vegetables and then chat after the meal. We're sitting in a long rectangular room with knotty-pine paneling. Fr. Malcher tells me about a summer camp he runs for deprived children in the Katowice area. They are from such poor families that some of the children arrive with only the clothes they are wearing. When the clothes have to be washed the children go to bed until the clothes are dry again because they have nothing else to put on. "My dream," he tells me, as though it is an ambition that cannot be realized in the near future, "is to have two tracksuits for each child so that they can have something to wear while the other one is being washed. One for night and one for day."

Bed-wetting is a serious problem among the children, and he tells me how he helps them. "They're embarrassed and ashamed of their bed-wetting, so I say to them, 'Let's not tell anyone else. I'll help you make your bed with a dry sheet. We'll do it quickly and then no one will know!' After that they're not so tense and afraid of wetting their beds, and the problem often disappears."

Fr. Malcher has all the facts and figures at his fingertips. Of the children at his summer retreats, 70% have health problems, mainly the result of environmental pollution. He also attributes the health problems to other contributing factors like bad nutrition and no exercise at school. There are no clubs, he says; the children have no alternatives to watching television. There are asthma and bronchitis, scoliosis, and also speech impediments and difficulties. He tells me that what seems to be an orthopaedic problem often turns out in fact to be neurological. All the local doctors say that children should be out of Katowice for *at least* two weeks every year. The summer camps run by Caritas need 500 volunteers, and they have to keep recruiting new volunteers because young people marry and have families and can't give up their annual vacations so readily. All year Fr. Malcher collects clothing for the summer camps.

On top of everything else, there was the problem with lice. About 30% of the children had lice when they came to the camp. Fr. Malcher and his staff, however, had a tactful way of dealing with it. All the children wear caps, but some are treated for lice, so it is not obvious who has lice and who doesn't.

"We tell the leaders that there are three rules: (1) Love the children, (2) Love the children, and (3) Love the children!"

In the Katowice diocese the most important social projects are these holidays for deprived children, care for handicapped children, and care for impoverished old people. They live on small, inadequate pensions in bad housing and often with their grown children in small flats. Caritas is building an old people's day centre for people to come to once a month; it is to be called The House of Monthly Renewal. Fr. Malcher's dream—he is a man full of big dreams—is to have one such house in each *decanat,* an area of ten parishes, of the diocese. This house could contain the office for the Caritas leader and could perhaps be used for weekly training meetings for parish Caritas workers. There is some money from the West German government to build "social structures". Bishop Domin is in the Federal Republic now discussing it.

Yet another plan is for parish kindergartens. Fr. Malcher longs to provide children from problem families with a happy place to play and eat nourishing food. He hopes to break the cycle of anti-social, alcoholic families. But that isn't all. The kindergartens have to have teachers, and he has another plan to build a school for girls to train in a two-year course as kindergarten teachers. State training institutions did exist, but Fr. Malcher feels there is room for improvement. Lots of room.

"The state-run institutions train them to do a job, like caring for farm animals. It is not a vocation. Caritas says that children are human, a child is a child of God."

After *kolacja* and the Mass Fr. Malcher says for the household, I go to take a shower and get ready for bed. The shower has also been installed by volunteer labour, and it must have been difficult to know where exactly to put it. Someone finally made the decision to install it in the front hallway. It is in a little closet with two glass inner doors. After I solve the problems of how to close all the doors and keep my clothing dry and get the water to the right temperature, I have a very good shower. Nothing is seriously inconvenient if you can have a hot shower now and then.

The next morning I look out into the clear mountain air and see a stunning panorama from the house. I have some nice toilet soap, and I give it to Fr. Malcher's mother, aged 85, our hostess and the provider of *kolacja.* Pani Stefania takes a picture of Fr. Malcher and me at the car with Alex, who is going to stay here. Then we drive back down the road that is more than ever like a dry riverbed in the daylight. I'm not at all sure that it is really a road; my dry-riverbed comparison may be the literal truth. We reach the house where the Mercedes is parked and drive on back to the curia, making it this time without the help of repairmen with bicycle pumps.

In the following days I visited two or three orphanages including the one in Kochłowice. They were rather spare, unadorned places that tended to smell of disinfectant. The children seemed to be kept as healthy and happy as possible in the circumstances. The institutions contained an abnormal number of handicapped children, because their families had dumped them there, mortified at having produced a defective child. The children had toys and companionship, but lived inevitably bleak lives. The high levels of pollution in the air and in the soil meant that there were more miscarriages and births of handicapped children in this area than in other parts of Poland, I was told. In Katowice and surrounding towns in the 1950s and '60s, workers had been encouraged to come from other areas with the promise of spacious accommodation and good pay. Something huge and filthy, like a coking plant or an iron-smelting plant, would be installed in the middle of a residential area so that the workers would not have far to go to work. As a result, if the workers had little gardens nothing could be grown in them because of the very high levels of substances like cyanide (used in copper smelting) in the soil. As the region was honeycombed with coalmines, there was also a problem with subsidence and large cracks in the fabric of buildings.

In the home for handicapped children in Kochłowice, the greatest needs were for warm socks and laundry markers. Some children didn't have house slippers but wore socks indoors, and there weren't enough to go around. They needed cream for bedsores, toilet soap, and ordinary disinfectant. They had one kind of disinfectant, but it smelled worse than whatever it was supposed to kill. Although it was only about 6:00, the children were being put to bed for the night. One boy had a leather tube strapped around his hands like a skinny muff. When I asked about it I was told that it was to prevent his scratching his eczema in his sleep. The children's lives seemed dismal, waking or sleeping, but the staff seemed to be doing their best with what they had.

The day has come for the trip to Zabrze. This children's hospital was featured in "Poisoned Inheritance", and sympathetic donors contributed numerous parcels of medical equipment and playthings for the young patients. I go in a minivan with a driver. Zabrze is in this same industrial conurbation, but it is a few miles away. While the driver and some men from the hospital are unloading the van, I am taken to the office of the director. I am greeted by Dr. Bożena Hager-Małecka, a capable woman who runs this hospital and has also represented this district in the national legislature, the Sejm. She offers me tea and seems somewhat ill at ease. A man appears who speaks a little English. They are waiting for an interpreter to arrive. Dr. Hager-Małecka says, half to herself, that she never studied English, but French. This is cheering news, and I tell her in French that we can use that language, if she likes. She brightens up considerably, and when the English interpreter arrives he finds to his chagrin that he is *de trop*.

But Dr. Hager-Małecka has another reason to feel ill at ease. She cannot understand why we chose her hospital. I explain that there was a documentary on British television featuring her children's hospital and then many people wanted to support it and send medical supplies. However, it emerges that she considers her hospital a bit of a showplace and not at all the sort of institution that should excite any kind of charitable inclinations abroad. The idea of some foreign charity sending gifts to *her* hospital is downright insulting. It looks as though we have made an embarrassing gaffe here and I try to paper over it with personal cordiality. The conversation turns to Medical Aid for Poland Fund itself, and I describe its work in general. They want to know how it transports the goods from England to

Poland, and I explain that the Pekaes trucking firm carries it for us on their return trips.

"Ah!" the man exclaims. "Ah, you see," and he chuckles a bit, as though he is going to explain some simple law of physics to a child, "they are cheating you. They are getting money from you. How much do you have to pay them?"

I do not care for the tenor of these remarks and reply, "I don't know about that side of the work. It is arranged by other people." And that is the end of this discussion because I really don't know anything about the details of the agreement with Pekaes, but I doubt if anybody is being cheated; in fact I had never thought of it before. What intrigues me is that the man's first thought on hearing about it is that someone is operating a scam. There must be something dishonest in it somewhere; that it might be a mere agreement for mutual benefit does not seem to occur to him.

Dr. Hager-Małecka gives me a lecture about cancer in general and the health situation in Upper Silesia in particular. First of all, she assures me, it is just not possible to say precisely what elements cause cancer; it is not even possible to say that the rate is higher in Silesia than the rest of the country. There are five or six coking plants in the immediate area. There are heavy metals—manganese, cadmium, and lead—in worrying concentrations. The lead levels in children's blood are very high: 53% as compared with 12% in London and 8% in Scandinavia. She herself detected this chronic lead poisoning as long ago as 1974! The problem is that the body absorbs lead instead of beneficial metals like magnesium, zinc, and iron. So zinc levels are lower in children with high concentrations of lead in their bloodstream. The lead comes from car exhaust (for there is no lead-free petrol yet), water, the soil, and food. Interestingly, in general—in Britain, the US, and Poland—children in higher socio-economic groups have lower lead concentrations; there is a correlation between frequent bathing and lower levels of lead in the bloodstream.

"The factories must be closed, but the main thing is to get the children out of the toxic areas," she says. Concentrations of benzopyrene and formaldehyde both lead to high rates of infant mortality, as do polluting dust in the air and lead.

This children's hospital in Zabrze is in fact one of the very best in all of Poland. Dr. Hager-Małecka took a small hospital and recruited good doctors from other hospitals, and soon she had the biggest children's hospital in Silesia, with 265 beds. About 12,000 inpatients are seen in a year. When Dr. Hager-Małecka was the representative for this district in the Sejm, her fame was good for the hospital, but she doesn't sit in the Sejm any more. Now, she tells me, she is somewhat out of favour politically and is concentrating more on medicine.

"I was never a Communist," she remarks, in case I was wondering.

In the end, I am treated to a guided tour of the hospital. Dr. Hager-Małecka proudly shows me the accommodation for cancer patients undergoing chemotherapy. There are side-rooms for their parents to stay the night so that they can be with their children all through the ordeal. There are brightly coloured decorations on the walls of rooms and corridors and a cheerful atmosphere throughout. I leave Dr. Hager-Małecka with a friendly farewell and a promise to tell people in London what a fine hospital she has, and so I do.

But a few months later in London there is an unpleasant moment when I go to a party for charitable organizations and meet the self-important organizer of Angels International. She has with her a doctor from the same Zabrze children's hospital where I delivered the mini-van load of supplies. The Angel demands to know what happened to the supplies I was supposed to deliver. This doctor—and here she perfunctorily introduces Exhibit A—had never heard of these supplies from London! What, then, has happened to them, the Angel wants to know. I say that I had no control over the supplies after they entered the hospital. Exhibit A now confirms that she knew nothing of any medicines or parcels from London. The Angel looks at me angrily. Where are they? What have I done with them?

Of course it was highly unlikely that Dr. Hager-Małecka and her staff would want to noise it around that they had received charitable gifts from abroad. Everything would have gone straight into the storeroom with no comment about its origin. Of course this doctor wouldn't necessarily know where anything had come from. And why should she, unless she was the hospital quartermaster? It was too complicated to explain then and there to the self-appointed Avenging Angel, so I merely repeated that I could not be responsible for what might have happened to the material after it had left my hands. And it was true: someone might have filched it and sold it on the black market for all I or the Charity Commission knew.

Chapter Nine

The Million-Złoty Coat

Fr. Malcher and his staff at the hostel in Katowice kindly helped me get a ticket and put me on the train to Warsaw. In the train station in Katowice I saw a pile of bashed-up boxes with red crosses on them and a sign saying "Polish help for free Romania". It's not that Poles have so much to give, but rather there is a generous impulse to give the shirt off their backs, even in Katowice. One's own need is not a sufficient reason for not wanting to give to others.

I couldn't very well take the case of soya milk powder with me on the train, so I took the 12 individual canisters of powder and stuck them here and there in the folds of my sleeping bag, like raisins in a Swiss roll. I still had only two pieces of luggage: my duffel bag and an unusually heavy sleeping bag, which is making its second trip to Poland. Staszek and Mirka meet me at the Centralna in Warsaw and we went to his parents' flat in Żoliborz. Mirka was expecting their second child and so far, to their great relief, everything was normal with her pregnancy, but she went for regular scans. This child was going to be a little boy.

Staszek and his family live with Mirka's mother in Celestynów and now Maria and Włodek live alone in the flat. Again I am given Staszek's old room. I hear tea and a snack being prepared in the kitchen as I begin to unpack. I am going to surprise them with the soya milk. "Staszek," I call, and he appears in the doorway. "Here is some soya milk for Małgosia," and I hand him one of the canisters. He seems very pleased and goes to show his mother. In a moment I call him again, and when he comes I ask him how long one box of soya powder lasts them. A month, he tells me. I thought they might get through it faster, and I'm glad that my supply will last them a whole year. This will be a real load off their minds, because they've never been sure when and where they could get the next batch of it, and it seems to be essential to the little girl's diet. She in unable to digest the protein in cow's milk.

"Well," I say to Staszek, here is another month's worth." He beams at me and takes the second canister away. I gradually deal out the other ten canisters to him until the whole dozen are stacked in Maria's kitchen. When they have so many worries, it's a real pleasure to relieve them of one of them. Maria calls me to the table and I leave Staszek's room, steadying the skis behind the door as I go.

Maria and I go out to Celestynów to visit Mirka's mother down at the end of a little potholed street at the edge of a woods. Małgosia is a lively little girl in a red plaid skirt bouncing around her grandmother's living room when her other grandmother arrives with me in tow. We all go off for a walk in the woods and Małgosia romps on ahead of us. I walk with Maria and then with Mirka and Staszek and enjoy the winter woods, big bare deciduous trees. On the return walk to the house, five-year-old Małgosia rides on her father's shoulders high above the rest of us and laughs delightedly.

Małgosia Wnuk, aged 5 in 1990, Maria's granddaughter.

What she likes best of all is to do what she calls "rock-and-roll dancing". She has seen it on television and now she tries it at every opportunity with Staszek when he comes home from work. They face each other and hold hands and hop vigorously from side to side. Staszek plays along and seems to enjoy it as much as his little daughter does.

Mirka takes me with her to the clinic when she goes to have her scan. I have never seen anybody's scan before, but I have been getting so used to the medical world now that it seems quite natural to watch it. I can't tell whether the equipment is the absolutely latest thing or not, but it looks pretty sophisticated to me. Mirka bares her midriff and oil is applied to make the scanning gadget move more smoothly, like a slick sanding block. And there on the screen is the shadowy form of their son-to-be, like a little astronaut floating through space so far away that the television reception is snowy.

Maria, who knows all the bus routes in Warsaw by heart, takes me to the Litewska Street Childrens' Hospital, where I have to deliver a parcel to Professor Roma Rokicka-Milewska in the haematology department. Before I left London, Małgorzata Koraszewska entrusted me with a box of a dozen sternum-puncture needles to take to her. They are like hypodermic needles but much heavier and more solid because they have to penetrate bone. They have been at the bottom of my bag all this time and now I am going to present them to this doctor. Maria phoned her for me and told her we were coming.

Professor Rokicka-Milewska greets us warmly and is thrilled with the sternum-puncture needles and offers us cups of tea. She tells me a bit about her work. She has child haemophiliac and leukaemia patients, and she says that it is impossible to keep from infecting them with hepatitis because all the hypodermic needles have to be used over and over. Although the needles are "disposable", she can't afford to throw them away. The needles get dull with so much use, and the doctors don't always have the smaller size suitable for children and often have to use adult sizes on children's veins. Just as Fr. Malcher dreamed of having two tracksuits per child at his summer camp, so Professor Rokicka-Milewska dreams of having one needle per patient. "I don't mean non-disposable ones," she says, "I just mean I wish I had as many needles as I have patients so that at least each child would have its own needle. It could still be used over and over, but at least there wouldn't be any cross infection."

My duties to MAPF and Małgorzata are now over, and Maria Wnuk is entertaining me. One Sunday afternoon we have a jolly reunion with several people from the kayak club: besides Maria and Włodek there are Tomek and Ula and Basia and Krzystof and Teresa. As a joke Włodek goes and gets a couple of kayak paddles (mixed in with the skis behind a door somewhere?) and we snap some pictures of each other holding them. They look ridiculous in a living room with tea things on the table and we laugh hilariously. Ula uses make-up, even in pine forests, and I have brought her a selection of eye-shadow from Boots, and she is delighted with the little present.

Setting aside the kayak paddles, we are talking about the dizzying changes in Poland in just the last few months. Until recently most people thought that nothing significant would change politically in their lifetime. They had learned, either from the disaster in Czechoslovakia in 1968 or from other similar episodes, that a Communist Party in power has little inclination to relinquish any of that power and that a party shored up by the Soviet Union is pretty much unassailable. But now impossible things were really happening! There was apparently no further danger of being arrested for being a supporter of *Solidarność*; it was now an accepted political party in a new multi-party Poland! Ula summed it up for me. She turned to me at the table and said, beaming, "Can you tell how happy we are?"

During the martial-law period when Solidarity was outlawed, a number of my Polish friends were in danger of being arrested and thrown in jail. Many of them were resigned to it and took it for granted that it was a distinct possibility, even probability. One day the police came to the Machs' block of flats when they weren't at home. The police asked a neighbour where their basement storage room was, and then they broke the lock on the door and searched it thoroughly. To the disappointment of the police, the room contained only old bicycles, prams, camping equipment, skis, and similar items. What the police didn't know, and what the neighbour either didn't know or didn't say, was that the Machs had two storage rooms, and the other was full of all sorts of illicit leaflets and incriminating material. When they came home and found out what had happened, they treated it as a joke, but a scary joke.

Things were certainly looking up, but later on when there was an independent Sejm for the first time in 50 years, I did wonder about Polish priorities. They were reorganising their country and putting new democratic institutions in place, so it seemed obvious to me that the very first thing they should do was to agree on a constitution setting out what these institutions were and who did what and for how long. How was the new government to be structured, how was power distributed, how were laws made and enforced and interpreted? How were elections held and what were the electoral districts and how were those boundaries decided upon? What were the limits of power; what were the ground rules?

But it seemed that none of that figured on the agenda when the Sejm began to meet. The most important item was discussed first, and presumably by common consent this most important item was this: that the national symbol, the heraldic white eagle, should have its gold crown reinstated. The crown was removed by the Communists along with the gold claws and two five-pointed stars at about the eagle's elbows. All these things had to be put back in place before anything else was done. Later in the decade there were some fairly bizarre developments in Polish administrations, but I found that I wasn't really surprised by most of it.

But now most of my remaining days in Warsaw are spent in non-medical ways, except when Ula invites me to see her hospital and meet her colleagues; I am given a white coat and see behind the scenes and look at her blood-monitoring equipment. Maria and Włodek and another friend of theirs, Alicja, and I go for a long walk in a near-by woods. It is a cold bright day, and we have a little "picnic" at a campfire place. Maria has brought along some bread and sausage. We roast the sausage over the fire and have hot sandwiches and coffee from a flask. It's a nice little snack after our trek through the woods, and a break before we trek out the other side and catch a bus home.

I am beginning to get the hang of the buses myself. Buying the ticket is the tricky part, but sometimes Maria has a supply of tickets and gives me one. I know a few words, but they still don't quite stretch to telling someone at a kiosk window that I want to buy a single or return bus ticket. (There are some countries where too much language is required in public places, and this is one of them. There are few opportunities to swan around in a shop examining the labels on things and deciding to buy them in a language not locally spoken. Decimal money and Arabic numerals are fortunately international and I am deeply grateful for them.)

Now I get on the right number bus and I know what stop I want to get off at. I punch my own ticket at the ticket-punching gadget. The bus is crowded and I have to stand. When I realize that my stop is approaching I have to manoeuvre toward the door. I think I might know the word for "Excuse me", but in my concentration on getting to the door I can't remember it. I inadvertently elbow people aside and step on feet, all the time trying to remember the exculpatory word. I think of certain syllables. It goes like *psham*, but there is more to it. There is an *r* in it somewhere. *Purzh*? Possible syllables come to me, but not connected together in a whole word, not a word that I can say with any confidence. I mouthe some trial syllables to myself as I continue rudely trampling people and get to the door. When it opens at the bus stop, I get down onto the kerb and away from the crowd in the bus. And as the bus pulls away, I remember the word!

"*Przepraszam,*" I say feebly to the retreating bus and its pushed and trampled passengers.

Today I am going with Staszek and his father to see a house Włodek has designed for a man who is building it himself. Designing private people's houses for them is quite a lucrative side-line for an architect. On the way, as a special treat for me, we are going to Żelazowa Wola, the birthplace of Chopin, well to the west of Warsaw. Chopin's father worked on a large estate and the family had a comfortable little cottage on the grounds. It is set in a wooded park and a stream flows nearby. The house is full of Chopin memorabilia and pictures and furniture of the period. By the time we get there I can pronounce *Żelazowa Wola*. Literally it means "iron will". This seems a funny place-name to me, but there is a district of Warsaw called Wola, and there is another town in Poland called "Steel Will". (I think "Steel Wool" would make as much, or more, sense.) In Polish it seems to sound perfectly normal, but I keep wondering why a place should be any kind of "will".

Back in the car, we drive on and cross the Vistula on one of the few bridges in the area and get to the house. There seems to be no one around, although a little shed where we stop the car seems to have some life in it. A woman comes out and then a couple of men, perhaps father and son. Or perhaps they are brothers. They seem to have knocked off work for a while in favour of a leisurely vodka break. Staszek remembers to introduce me to them, and one of the men undertakes to kiss my hand when I offer it. The result is what you might expect from a friendly golden retriever. He slobbers all over the back of my hand, and I can't think how to wipe it off unobtrusively. I fall behind the group slightly and feel for a Kleenex in my pocket. There is a downside to this courtly habit.

We walk up a long path to the new house. The outside walls and roof seem to be finished, and now they are working on the inside. They seem to be building it like the man in the old story who builds a yacht in the basement and then can't get it out. They are building the house from the inside, and the wood shavings are knee deep in places. We are shown where the bedrooms and bathrooms will be. It is going to be quite an opulent house if and when it is finished, and if they manage to get all the wood shavings out of it.

Back in Warsaw, Maria has contrived to get tickets for the event of the season. It is a performance of *Götterdämmerung* in the splendid opera house. I don't have the heart to tell Maria that Wagner is not my favourite composer. In fact, if I made a list Wagner might come in around 150th on it, and that would be because I didn't know the names of 151 composers. It is being sung in Polish and performed in modern dress. It is the cultural high point of the winter, and I am genuinely grateful for Maria's thoughtfulness in getting us tickets for it. But all the same, I wish it were something else.

We go, and I do my best to appreciate it. I get a programme, which contains the whole text in both Polish and German on facing pages. The programme was printed before the season began, and that was long enough ago that with inflation this substantial paperback text costs the equivalent of 4 pence sterling. I follow along and try to keep track of the outlandish happenings on the Rhine. Siegfried comes on. Brunhilde sings. Shady characters wearing boots and long overcoats appear and skulk around. (It turns out that the audience likes this touch, because Wagner's unpleasant dwarves somehow suggest the Polish secret police, who are now being quickly phased out.) In the end there is general destruction; things fall apart, the centre cannot hold, and the performance comes to a crashing conclusion. But the opera house itself is a magnificent building with impressive polished brass and chandeliers.

Now I tell Maria that there is one more thing that I would really like to see if it is at all possible. At the theatre in the Palace of Culture and Science the famous film director, Andrzej Wajda, is directing a very imaginative production of *Hamlet*. I would particularly like to see this, because I collect productions of *Hamlet*, and for once I don't even care what language it's in. When we inquire at the theatre, the tickets are sold out, but Maria goes into her dealing-with-officials mode and tells the box office that we absolutely must have two tickets because I am a distinguished visiting foreign scholar who has written a doctoral thesis on *Hamlet*, and it is imperative that I see this production.

I understand just enough of her presentation to cringe. "Foreign" is right and you could make a good argument for "scholar", and "visiting" is undeniable, but the rest is not perfectly accurate. The box office takes Maria's phone number, and to my surprise we get a phone call later telling us that the tickets are available. I suppose they must be ordinary returns, but it looks like another example of Maria knowing how to get results.

Wajda's *Hamlet* really *is* a high point of the season, for me, at least. Hamlet is played by a well-known actress; the scene is largely set in Hamlet's dressing room in a theatre, the audience therefore sitting behind the scenes facing the "audience" that would be watching the play out front. The troupe of travelling players appear in modern dress, although the rest of the characters are in Elizabethan period costumes. Wajda has taken extraordinary liberties with Shakespeare in the staging, but I am fascinated by it and can overlook the Wagner.

Maria and I do a little shopping. The inflation just now is something to behold. When she showed me their new colour television set, she said, "This is because of inflation!" so it benefited her, if not the seller of the television set. I would like a suede jacket, and I find just the right thing in a leather shop. It's a slightly bloused brown suede jacket and it costs exactly one million złoty, but it's a steal at the price.

It was easy to be a millionaire in Poland that winter. The suede jacket worked out at about £11 sterling, but I'll always think of it as my million- złoty coat.

Chapter Ten

Nobody Called Smith

I went back to Medical Aid for Poland and wrote articles for a couple of magazines and a report for the Executive Committee. I continued to go to the office on Fridays and help out with whatever I could that required a knowledge of neither Polish nor the filing system. I got to know my Polish friends better and gradually met still more. I was such an anomaly, being involved with Poland yet being so excessively non-Polish, that there was even a small write-up about me in the Polish daily paper in London, *Dziennik Polski*, complete with my last passport picture. Headlined with "Why I Am Helping Poland", the story was in the form of an interview. It was just as well that my gormless remarks were in Polish so that I couldn't read them, but then it is odd not to be able to read what you have allegedly said.

One day when Bożena Laskiewicz was in the office she mentioned that she had seen the article about me in the *Dziennik Polski*. "I was reading it in the theatre," she remarked, and I pictured her in her seat at the National Theatre skimming the *Dziennik Polski* before the house lights went down. But it quickly dawned on me that when a surgeon speaks of doing a thing "in the theatre" it's not about the National, after all. Then I was left with a second odd image of Dr. Laskiewicz peering over her surgeon's mask at the newspaper.

Lech Wałęsa and Dr. Bożena Laskiewicz speaking at the send-off of the 200th Medical Aid for Poland Fund truck in 1991.

Polish priests from Caritas and even Bishop Domin came to visit; every year there was a Christmas party at which the Poles around me sang the lovely, lilting Christmas carols that were on pan Adam's tape; trucks were sent off from the warehouse in Park Royal; requests continued to come in from Poland. One day we had a request for some extremely expensive piece of equipment. It was something that was beyond the budget of most British hospitals and was completely out of the question for our organisation. Some of the staff wondered how on earth this Polish hospital consultant could have dreamed that we could supply such a thing, but it made perfect sense to me. If everything was subsidised and assigned an arbitrary price, how would they know the relative value of anything? If the value wasn't understood but it seemed that everything was available in the West, then why not ask for the Moon?

With the change of government in Poland in 1989 and later, a new ambassador came to London and was invited to a reception by MAPF. We were offered the use of an elegant flat of one of our supporters who lived in a block of flats between Whitehall and the Embankment. The planning of this reception confirmed me in my belief that Marysia Jaczyńska was an organisational genius. We volunteers were assigned to a number of committees with specific jobs to do. On the afternoon of the reception I went to Hanka's in Fulham to make canapés. Hela Rankowicz, Hanka Groszek, Marysia Owsianka, and I sat around Hanka's kitchen table spreading bread and crackers with butter or cream cheese and adding a further decorative topping. After a couple of hours we all changed clothes and set out for Whitehall with a carload of canapé trays. It was a Saturday and Hanka could park reasonably near the door. In relays we then carried the trays into the building, up in the lift, and down the hall to the flat. We put them in the kitchen or on tables in the living room, where other committees dealt with them.

A committee of MAPF men were busy covering the tops of the antique furniture with neat sheets of clear plastic so that they would not be damaged by carelessly placed glasses. Earlier committees had been arranging the room while we were making canapés in Fulham. The flat was going to make a fine setting for this reception for the new ambassador. There were chandeliers in every room including the kitchen.

Before our guests arrived and I went into action on the checking-people-off-the-list-and-taking-their-coats committee, I had a free 20 minutes. Małgorzata Koraszewska, who had been working on one of the committees in the flat and had not yet taken up her position with the showing-people-into-the-lift-and-giving-directions committee, was sitting on an antique chaise longue smoking a cigarette and I sat down beside her. She looked around at the opulent flat and some of the chandeliers and said, "You know, maybe it's my communist upbringing, but I don't really feel comfortable in a place like this." Then she took a thoughtful drag on her cigarette. "But on the other hand, it wouldn't help all those homeless people if this flat were shabby."

When the time came, Małgorzata went off to join her new committee at the street entrance and I positioned myself inside the front door of the flat with my new colleague with the clipboard. We welcomed numerous distinguished guests from the embassy and the resident Polish community in London, and I stowed all their coats in a bedroom near the front door. As more and more people came, I realized that I could never match up the people and their coats again, but to my relief that wasn't necessary. When they got ready to leave they found their coats by themselves.

When everyone was checked in and de-coated, we joined the group in the living room and heard speeches by the new ambassador and Dr. Laskiewicz. At certain times in the past the embassy had been a bit hostile toward MAPF because the state (still clinging by the fingernails to Lenin, perhaps) didn't want it known that they needed any outside help. We wanted to get off on the right foot with this new man and his diplomatic team. Dr. Laskiewicz spoke from the heart about her concern for the doctors and patients of Poland, and the new ambassador, Tadeusz de Virion (scion of a distinguished French-Polish family of lawyers) answered in kind. He and his wife, an Indian academic, were indeed a breath of fresh air at the embassy in Portland Place. They were a gracious couple who welcomed our efforts, and relations between MAPF and the Polish embassy remained warm.

Alastair surrounded by people not named Smith: Marysia Jaczyńska, and in the background at right, Marysia Owsianka, summer of 1990.

Małgorzata Koraszewska at the Jaczyńskis' garden party in Muswell Hill.

Sarah at the Jaczyńskis' garden party.

I saw a good deal of my Polish friends outside the MAPF office, too. Once Alastair was looking through his appointments diary and said, "Let's see—we're going to the Koraszewskis' on the 7th and then the Groszeks' on the 14th, and the Jaczyńskis' on the 21st...Don't you know anybody called Smith?"

When I went to China to teach at Suzhou University in the academic year 1991-92, I kept in close contact with Małgorzata by letter. Some of my letters ended up being translated and broadcast in an occasional filler slot called "Postcard from China" in transmissions of the BBC Polish Service. I don't know what the Polish listeners made of my impressions of China, but it seemed to be an acceptable series. I was always afraid that I would cause an international incident by offering some mild criticism of the People's Republic of China, but Małgorzata asked, "How many Chinese people listen to the BBC World Service in Polish?" Probably not very many, but what about the Chinese legation in Warsaw? But they still dismissed the possibility and insisted that Poles would find my observations interesting.

"The listeners will be interested in what this Anglo-American woman notices about China. Don't worry." So I continued to write my unexpurgated impressions to Małgorzata. Andrzej would "commission" them after the fact, and Małgorzata would translate them. One was about the experience of being foreign in China and the tolerance it gave you for foreigners who got lost or muddled in London. I sent silk blouses and scarves from Suzhou to Małgorzata and other friends in MAPF and also to Maria Wnuk. The silk scarf I sent to Maria in Warsaw was the only one that failed to arrive.

By an odd coincidence, Maria Wnuk and I became widows in the same year. At Christmas 1992 she wrote me sadly that Włodek had died. He had had heart trouble for many years, and now at the age of 70 Włodek was dead. Włodek the AK resistance fighter and post-war hospital architect was a taciturn man I had not really got to know. He was a man of few words and hardly any of them were English. He looked rather dour, but I could see that he had a sense of humour. I relied on Maria for my knowledge of him. Alastair had been having some bouts of depression, but no one could have predicted that they would end in suicide. His mother and I were stunned, as were his co-workers at college. His funeral was on a Friday, and Dr. Laskiewicz had the office closed so that the staff could attend it. Several of my Poles came across London to pay their respects, and I was deeply touched by their gesture. Before Alastair's mother went back to Scotland the college had a very affecting memorial service in the chapel.

In the following spring, Małgorzata invited me to go with her to Lund, where her mother still lived. She had first suggested the visit six months before, but I was still too occupied with Alastair's death and the practical aftermath. I took to Mrs. Jakubowicz at once. She had been unwilling to uproot herself yet again at her time of life to follow her daughter and son-in-law to a strange city with a new language, so she had stayed in Sweden. Małgorzata was in frequent contact with her mother by phone, and twice a year she went to Lund to visit her. I met several of

Małgorzata old friends in Sweden, both Swedes and transplanted Poles, some of whom had also been refugees twenty years before.

Now I saw the Swedish side of my Polish friend I had met in London. In her fifteen years in Sweden she had made many firm friends and made sure to see them again during her biannual visits to her mother. I enjoyed meeting the old friends and imagining those fifteen years, during which Małgorzata had done such an extraordinary variety of jobs and had experienced the horror of losing her teen-aged daughter to leukaemia. At first she had worked as a cleaner in a hospital, but had taken a diploma in social work at Lund University and then later had lectured Swedish social workers about Swedish family law; at other times she had done social work among one-parent families and unmarried mothers in Malmö. I was full of admiration of her, and still am, for going to a strange country, learning the language from scratch, beginning as an unskilled hospital cleaner, and working her way up to impressive heights of social work expertise.

Małgorzata told me once that as a refugee hospital cleaner in 1970 or so she was sitting reading a book waiting for an operation to finish so that she could clean the operating theatre. A young nurse, perhaps accustomed to less intellectual hospital cleaners, spoke to her encouragingly and told her that she should think about getting an education; she was probably capable of some higher training. When the nurse had finished her speech, which Małgorzata found irritatingly condescending, she told her that in fact she had an MA from the University of Warsaw and had been well on her way to a doctorate when she had had to leave the country. When she told me about it 30 years later, she was still a little ashamed of having been rude to the nurse.

"But what else could you have said?" I asked. "It was only the truth."

"She was just trying to be helpful," Małgorzata said. "She probably just thought...but you know, it sounded extremely condescending to me, so I was rude to her."

"Yes," I said, "but it was only the truth."

Mrs. Jakubowicz told me something about her life. She was born in 1914 and her family, the Wahrsagers, lived outside Lvov, then a Ukrainian city. They lived in a woodland clearing, as she told it, where there were only two other houses, but it was part of a *stetl* composed of Ukranians, Poles, and Jews. During World War I they had to flee to what later became Czechoslovakia or they would have been caught in the fighting. The family returned to Lvov after the war, impoverished to the point of destitution. They lived in what amounted to a street-market stall and made small cardboard boxes for shoe polish. Later they did the marginally more lucrative work of making the shoe polish that went into the boxes. From this extreme poverty the family's life gradually improved and Anna Wahrsager went to a local school in Lvov, now a Polish city (for Poland had come into existence again), and did well at her academic subjects. Polish was the language of instruction. She learned German and Ukrainian at school and spoke Yiddish at home. In 1941 Anna and her husband were deported from Lvov, by then a Soviet-occupied city, to the far south of the Soviet Union to the borderlands of Uzbekistan and Kyrgyzstan. Being deported to Uzbekistan was at least better than the fate that met more than 60 of her relatives who fell into German hands and ended their lives in the gas chambers of the Nazi death camps. Between the Soviet invasion in 1939 and the summer of 1941 she had learned enough Russian to get a job. She worked in an office in Uzbekistan, and her monthly salary amounted to a pittance—hardly enough, she said, to buy a loaf of bread at the end of the month.

So that was where my remarkable friend Małgorzata was born: in the village of Osz in the Soviet Union during the hardships of wartime deportation. When they were eventually freed in 1946 Mr. Jakubowicz was dead and his widow, her sister, and her little daughter made their way to Warsaw to pick up the pieces of their lives. Now Mrs. Jakubowicz got an office job in one of the government ministries and Małgorzata went to school and then the University of Warsaw. It was when she was half way through her doctoral research at the Academy of Science that the bottom fell out of things yet again. Małgorzata might have left Poland then, except that Andrzej, being "Aryan", was not allowed to leave and they refused to be separated. When it was finally possible for Andrzej to leave too, the couple and their little daughter and Małgorzata's mother all bolted for Sweden.

When Mrs. Jakubowicz had finished the training given to refugees in Sweden to enable them to become productive citizens, she was given a job transcribing and indexing old handwritten Swedish records. She was in that office for the rest of her working life, and when she retired her co-workers gave her an affectionate retirement party and signed a certificate as a memento. In her kitchen in Lund she showed me the certificate she had been given in appreciation for her work and the card signed by all her co-workers. The contrast between her work experience in Sweden and her curt dismissal in Poland was not lost on her, nor on me, either.

Chapter Eleven

Charades

Maria Wnuk had always wanted to be a journalist, even as a girl, but her parents had decided that she should study for the more worthwhile and more honourable profession of architect. Architects, they reasoned, were not required to spread propaganda and lies. (This is after her clandestine secondary schooling and the façade of the tailoring school. The War had ended and Poles were trying to remember what normal life was like.) Now as a widow reorganizing her life, she decided to take up journalism seriously. She enrolled in a course for aspiring journalists in Toruń, a university city in north central Poland. She went there twice a week for two years and then began writing regular pieces in a Sunday Catholic newspaper. Sometimes she wrote a column of homely observations of a grandmother. For recreation she went with groups of fellow artists on painting holidays to the mountains or the seaside. She kept me informed about her children and grandchildren. Staszek and Mirka's son, Paweł, was growing up. Małgosia's condition seemed stable. She was taking part in a test of a new drug that was doing her a lot of good; the drug would have been prohibitively expensive were she not part of the test. Maria's daughter Agnieszka and son-in-law had three growing boys and still lived in their new house outside Warsaw.

I was also keeping in touch with Magda Lachaut, the girl on the kayak trip in 1988 who had been frightened of the initiation ceremony. She finished high school, passed her Matura exam and entered the University of Wrocław. For a while she was studying art history, and then she changed to French and English. One summer she and a student friend, Justyna, came to England to pick fruit in Kent and I took them to Hastings for the day. Another time she came to London and I took her to Bush House to meet Andrzej and see the Polish Section. Magda sometimes asked my advice about her studies and her life in general. I dispensed advice to my young friend from the wisdom of my advanced years, and before long I was an Honorary Aunt.

One day Małgorzata phoned me to tell me about a volume of poetry someone had sent her from Poland. This was surprising in itself, because I knew that Małgorzata didn't care much for poetry. She didn't even read the stuff Andrzej wrote; she didn't read the stuff I wrote; she didn't read the stuff anybody wrote. Now she was telling me about this Polish poet, Jan Twardowski, whom she actually liked. He was an elderly priest in Warsaw and wrote poems from a fresh angle.

"I think some of his poetry really ought to be translated into English. I can do a rough draft, but I need a poet to turn it into poetry in English. Would you like to try, if I do the rough version?"

It sounded intriguing. I had never tried collaborating on translation before. I liked being singled out as a Poet who would be essential to the project. I agreed, and one weekend I went to stay with her and Andrzej in Kenton and we worked on her drafts of 10 or 12 of Twardowski's poems. We got into the poems on the Friday evening and made a good start. All day Saturday we worked on them, with breaks for meals and coffee. We started a pattern then that we were to continue off and on for longer than we could have suspected. We sat side by side at her big dining room table with a creative untidiness of papers and books around us. I like to work on a clipboard with ink in two or three colours. Małgorzata supplied a variety of Polish/English and English/Polish dictionaries. Sometimes our translating sessions resembled a game of charades.

"This word," I would say, "what register is it? Is it the normal term?" And she would describe situations in which in would be used. "What kind of movement exactly is this supposed to be?" I would ask, and then we would demonstrate the verbs in question. What was the difference between *walk, stroll, sidle, slink, strut, shamble,* and *saunter?*

Twardowski's poetry is full of various unlikely animals. He sometimes invents words or uses some strange locution that Małgorzata assured me sounded odd in Polish. Should we make it sound odd in English, too? Would readers merely think we were clumsy translators? There were cultural peculiarities. There were allusions to bureaucracy that struck a chord with Poles but not with English-speakers. There was special significance attached to a gold tooth that completely passed me by. There were proverbial sayings and plays on words. Małgorzata explained things so thoroughly that I got a free crash course in Polish language and culture. The inflections of Slavic grammar were a revelation, and I marvelled all over again at the MAPF office staff and their casual fluency in all these case endings.

The whole weekend was a delight. We worked diligently on a dozen or so poems by Jan Twardowski and printed out clean copies so that I could go home and do some fine-tuning. In the end we had turned those Polish poems into acceptable English and they were published in the International PEN magazine (called *Pen International*), the very prestigious *Modern Poetry in Translation,* and the Catholic weekly, *The Tablet.*

Several months later Małgorzata rang me with the news that she had acquired a new book by Jan Twardowski and had found some new poems she liked. Would I like to have another go at them? One in particular she liked, and she read me a rough translation of it over the phone. It was his poem about a tiny figure of Death with a minuscule scythe who comes for the canary. The wit and the imagination of it made me laugh and I quickly agreed to another translation weekend.

Altogether, we translated almost 50 poems by Jan Twardowski and got his permission to publish them wherever we could. More appeared in *Modern Poetry in Translation* and a considerable sample of them were published in *The Month,* the venerable Jesuit journal. The editor of *The Month* asked me to write an article about Jan Twardowski so as to put his work into a context for the English reader. Now I was in a fix, because I needed some critical and biographical material and it was all in Polish. I asked Małgorzata to find me some material on Twardowski's life and publishing history and give me the gist. As we now had so many of his poems transformed into English, I could write a general commentary on those. It was good to assemble what I knew about our poet and get it down on paper, because it helped me understand who he was and what he had done.

Andrzej and Małgorzata Koraszewski with Marysia Jaczyńska at a launch for my collection of poems, Below the Surface, at the Barbican Library, 1996.

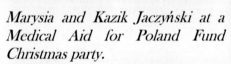

Marysia and Kazik Jaczyński at a Medical Aid for Poland Fund Christmas party.

Maria (Marysia) Jaczyńska in her living room, one of her sculptures at the lower left.

188

During those years in the mid-90s I had stopped working at the MAPF office, but I was still in touch with many of my old colleagues there. I was always invited to the annual Christmas party and heard the now familiar Polish Christmas carols, although I still couldn't sing them. I saw Teresa Glaser occasionally; she was reviewing films for *Dziennik Polski* and would invite me along to some of the showings. I went over to New Malden to see Marysia Owsianka and her beehives. (She was a devoted beekeeper and had written a charming and informative book from the point of view of a bee, *The Legend of the Hive*.) Marysia Jaczyńska had taken studio space and was producing a series of sculptures, including a head of Hanka Groszek's daughter Oleńka. Then and later I went to some of her exhibitions and one-woman shows.

Ania Bentkowska had come to MAPF at about the time I was leaving. She had come to Alastair's funeral in 1992 with the rest of the office staff, and I was touched by her gesture. She was married to Jan Kafel, an English-born Anglo-Pole, and they had a schoolgirl daughter. Ania was an academic art historian and had an active professional life first at Birkbeck College in London University and then at the Courtauld Institute. I saw her sometimes when I met up with my other Poles, and sometimes I would run into her at the British Library. She was on the editorial board of a quarterly journal called *The Art Book*, and she later asked me to review the catalogue of an exhibition about Cleopatra at the British Museum for it. Since then I have reviewed several books in its pages.

And of course Maria Wnuk and I continued our correspondence and our odd closeness in spite of our distance literally and figuratively. Realistically, we had very little in common, but I liked her because she was brave, good-hearted, generous, and honest. She was intelligent and had a nice sense of humour. She was also a domineering mother hen, but I forgave her easily.

I got a letter from Ula Mach one day asking me if I knew what "DFC" meant. Her mother had gone to Northolt on the west side of London and looked at the monument there to commemorate Polish airmen in the RAF who were killed during the War. She found the name of a young Pole she had once been in love with, and these initials were after his name. She delegated her daughter to find out what they meant, and Ula contacted me. Well, I didn't know. I was neither British enough nor old enough nor military-minded enough to know, but I telephoned the Imperial War Museum and asked to speak to the librarian and asked him what "DFC" meant. That was how I learned about the Distinguished Flying Cross and its significance as an award to officers of the RAF. Ula Mach was grateful, and her mother, Frau Wall, the Viennese matron late of Wrocław, had her curiosity satisfied.

Chapters Twelve

A Step Ahead of the Floodwaters

Maria had been inviting me to go on another kayak trip with her and her club, and in 1997, I couldn't think of any reason not to join her again. She wanted to go just for the camping and outdoor living, and I could find another kayaking partner, perhaps Witek Dębski, whom I had met in 1988. We made plans by mail; she gave my name to Zygmunt, who was still the captain of the club and the guiding spirit behind it; I got out my old Chinese-made tracksuit/pyjamas.

I arrived in Warsaw in early July and was met at the airport by Maria in a taxi. We went back to her flat, familiar now in spite of the seven years since I was last there. I was installed again in Staszek's old room, but when I looked behind the door the skis were gone. He and Mirka were at the Baltic seaside with their children. I settled in with Maria and we took up our friendship where we left off the last time we had seen each other.

Poland is one of those countries where you often have to explain that, while the food in front of you is absolutely excellent and delicious, you do not actually want any more of it because you have had enough, even more than enough. While I am eating, Maria draws my attention to all the other things on the table that I am not eating, so that if I put honey on my bread she reproachfully mentions the cheese, and if I put cheese on my bread she says, "Ze honey, why you are not eating ze honey?" We are talking about teeth one day and she says, "My mother lost her teeth in ze First War. She was starving. Later she and my father, they came to Poland and they said, 'Bread! Meat!' They could not believe how much food there was!" Now when I have had twice as much for breakfast as I usually eat, she pushes the last of the yeast doughnut balls at me. They are really good and we have been eating them every day, but I don't have any room left for them this morning. I eat them, though, because Maria sternly reminds me about them as though I am a charlady who has forgotten to hoover under the bed.

Maria often throws a French or German word into her English and sometimes unidentified syllables that may be Russian. They are like the sand in your sandwiches at the seaside—bits of grit which definitely aren't sandwich but pass unnoticed if there aren't too many of them. Some days her English is very gritty and some days we manage without much foreign decoration. (She pronounces the *g* in *foreign*.)

Maria takes me to Mass at a highly ornate church in Krakowskie Przedmieście Street. It is one of the more magnificent churches in the city, and in fact was Jan Twardowski's church before he retired. He still lives on the premises, as it were, because there is an adjoining convent of the Visitation nuns and he has a flat there. The baroque period was plainly (or not "plainly") a time of vigorous church-building in Poland. Once again, like the statuary that intrigued me when Alastair and I were in Wrocław, here are Bernini-like figures that look as though they were caught doing the twist in a quilt by a strobe light lasting three and a half centuries. Some of Father Twardowski's poems are about the unfortunate concentration of gewgaws in churches to the detriment of the deeper meaning of Christianity. In one poem the altar is described in terms of a coffin on little rat paws, and I look around to see if anything matches that, but the high altar is too far away to be sure about its base.

Another day we go to visit Maria's daughter, Agnieszka, at her new home. We take a bus out beyond the outskirts of Warsaw and walk along a country road until we come to a very nice, spacious, two-story building. Indoors it is modern, in the Polish/Scandinavian style of bare floorboards and light wooden furniture. Her two younger boys are about 6 and 8, but the older one, Kuba is away. They are as shy as chipmunks and spend most of their time out of sight in another room and then behind the furniture when they venture into the living room, where we are having tea. At length one of them, Matteusz, shows me a book he is reading at school, and the boys get much more communicative. Finally they forget that there is a scary stranger in the room and they are bouncing around like normal children.

Staszek is delegated to take me to the Old Town one Sunday afternoon. It's nice to see Staszek again. His command of English means that it can be somewhat more relaxing to talk to him than to his mother. I like the Old Town because it is picturesque and you can see what Warsaw used to look like. I wonder how much of pre-war Warsaw looked like this. A great many of the buildings would have been much later than this, since the old square was here in the 17th or 18th century and one of the aids in reconstructing it was a picture by Canaletto. Now there are shops of all kinds and high-quality tourist traps. Even in 1980 it was an attractive place. Staszek and I walk around the Old Town Square and the side streets. The Old Town is not very big. You can see every inch of it in under an hour, and that includes some window-shopping.

Stanisław ("Staszek") Wnuk in the summer of 1997.

Although I was here seven years ago and visited the Old Town and did a few touristy things, I am thinking about my visit in 1980. There was something called Hortex at one end of the main square that resembled a normal outdoor café. You could get ice cream there and other tasty things. Now very little of the square is without a colourful umbrella advertising a local or imported beer, to say nothing of Coca-Cola. The bigger shops and ones with international pretensions take all the main credit cards now. I go into a shop and buy a pair of amber earrings for a friend in London, and the saleslady knows all about the sliding credit card gadget; she doesn't look askance at my wanting to buy something with plastic; it is possible to export amber without a special license or visitors from abroad to help you smuggle it out of the country. This is a recognizably commercial Europe and not the grey, suspicious, craven, incomprehensible dump I remember from former years when I was trying to buy stamps, find a usable WC, or locate a sandwich. Staszek tells me that people don't remember how it was before. But the memory has to be tucked away somewhere if *I* can remember it so clearly.

I am relieved both for myself and for the Poles that modern western ways of doing business have finally caught on here. No one sidles up to you in the street now wanting to change worthless złoty for something else, *anything* else: dollars for preference, then deutschmarks, then pounds sterling, and oh, just whatever you've got in your pocket, please. The złoty can hold its head up again in the money markets, and you don't have to search for ways to get rid of it. ("The złoty used to be a strong currency," Maria once told me. "Before the War it was as strong as the Swiss franc!")

Staszek shows me an eating place nearby that I would have loved to find in 1980 when we searched for inexpensive restaurants, or any restaurants. This is a place with several western fast-food chains all under one roof. There are Burger King, Kentucky Fried Chicken, McDonald's, and one or two others. It is plainly a delightful novelty here, and the place is well patronised. A family, probably Vietnamese, are sitting nearby with a big KFC tub on their table. Staszek goes off to get us some food at one of the counters, and I keep thinking of Warsaw 17 years ago when public eating places were so hard to find. (I asked Maria once where people used to go to eat, and she looked at me blankly and said, "At home".)

I look around at the people enjoying themselves and suddenly wonder where the Marxist hamburger is, or was. Or the Marxist Model T Ford, for that matter. Here are these families, perhaps on a low income, but they can have a meal out at a place like this. This is part of democracy: the ability of everyone in the population to enjoy eating out. This innocent enjoyment was not on the menu here in the dour old days. Meals could be bought in student or workers' canteens, or, at the other end of the scale, fine restaurants for hard-currency tourists and the *nomenklatura* of the Party. The real proletarian revolution happened years ago in the United States, but not everybody noticed.

It is customary all over Europe to decry "the spread of McDonald's" as though it were a dangerous fungus, but in fact these places serve a very useful purpose. In the United States they are essential for the long-distance traveller, or even the person out for the day on far-flung errands. At least the chains are a known quantity. Their uniformity, so disdained in Europe, is the whole *point*. You know what you are getting. If you are from Ohio and are travelling in Oklahoma and you see a familiar sign, you know what to expect. You don't have to take your chances with the local hash house or even get far off the Interstate to find it in the first place. Would Europeans rather get lost in the suburbs of Tulsa looking for a really charming little bistro for a lunch stop when they are in a hurry to get to Wichita? No, and they have taken all these fast-food places to their hearts and erected some of their own. At the same time, the Europeans who have access to more expensive restaurants have found a golden opportunity to be snobbish and anti-American and health conscious all at once. The hamburger, which is no more than a steak sandwich in a different shape, can be made to sum up all that is most reprehensible about what they have chosen to import from the US. Of course you shouldn't eat one at every meal. Hamburgers should be compared to their equivalents rather than to an ideal diet. Cold pork pies and Scotch eggs have not caught on internationally but hamburgers have. Now there's a puzzle.

Back in Maria's flat, we are watching the weather reports on television. A strange thing has been happening. Down in the Tatra and Sudeten Mountains in the far south of Poland there have been torrential rains. It has rained day and night, dumping a whole month's worth of water on the mountains in the space of only a few days. Some of it has run off into Czechoslovakia and caused havoc in the river systems there. Some of it has run off into the Neisse basin and flooded large areas of eastern Germany, but most of it seems to be making its way inexorably down (in terms of land level) or up (in terms of the map) into southern and western Poland into the tributaries of both the Odra and the Wisła, but especially the former. As the crest of the floodwaters reaches the flat farmlands below the mountain ranges, the rivers overflow and houses are ruined and livestock swept away. We are wondering how this will affect Wrocław. I am planning to go there for a few days to see Magda, and a large contingent of the kayak club comes from Wrocław.

We make plans anyway for me to go to Wrocław. With luck much of the floodwater will have spent itself on the farmlands and by the time the crest of the Odra gets to Wrocław there will be less of it and it will be held in check by the stout flood levies built by the Germans when it was Breslau. Magda comes to Warsaw and I am handed over to her at Warsaw Centralna station like a child in the care of grown-up relatives. (Like Mariusz, in fact, the little boy on the Warsaw-Wrocław train in 1980, the polite lad with all the cookies and crackers.) They decide that on the whole it would be better to get a one-way ticket instead of a dated return ticket. Two singles cost the same, and I gather Maria foresees that I might not spend the whole week there, after all.

Magda and I have a pleasant trip to Wrocław. The train is a bit faster than it was in 1980 and we chat and catch up with each other's activities. Outside, as Poland goes past, I see some flooded fields. We are getting into the Odra basin and the district around Opole is looking very marshy. Wrocław, in spite of its low-lying position on several arms of the Odra, is still dry underfoot. This is my first time here since 1980, and I have completely forgotten how we got into the city from our youth hostel in the boating club where all the swallows and martins swooped. Only the main square looks familiar, with its Gothic town hall where the strange canteen-like restaurant was in 1980 with the meat that was not really meat but turned out to be meat. The fine old market square around the town hall is really impressive. It is like the square in some prosperous old Flemish town, complete with Flemish-style gables. All the tall narrow buildings have been freshly painted for the Papal visit of a month ago and they are still so bright and shiny that we could be in Antwerp in 1650, if we just keep our eyes on the upper storeys and ignore the modern shops at street level.

We tour the town by tram and foot and Magda is an admirable guide. Her English is excellent. It was pretty good nine years ago when we first met, but in the meantime she has done an MA in it at the University of Wrocław and she has read widely in all sorts of things on and off the syllabus. I am really getting acquainted with Wrocław now. Magda is also an interesting informant in general. She tells me, as we are talking about popular foodstuffs, that until very recently there has been only one breed of cow in Poland, a milk breed. Beef comes from old milk cows, so beef is not very popular. Of course, before the War people were interested in breeding cattle, but during the communist time they weren't, and the skill was lost. Now they are starting to import beef breeding stock. (I think of the placid, shy Herefords we had in Indiana and wonder if that might be the breed they are importing.)

Magda has heard all my sob stories about the lack of restaurants in Poland. She is a civic-minded Vratislavian and sets out to demolish my poor opinion of her city's restaurants. At mealtimes or coffee breaks she shows me the wealth of international restaurants and coffee shops now on offer. On one of the islands in the Odra there is a charming old mill with traditional Polish dishes. Then there are numerous exotic restaurants—Egyptian, Chinese, Mexican, Japanese, Vietnamese, French, Italian, Turkish; about everything you can think of except possibly Eskimo, but I wouldn't rule it out. After every two or three such restaurants Magda drives her point home.

"You see, there are a lot of interesting, high-quality restaurants in Wrocław now. Whatever it was like all those years ago, now there are fine restaurants everywhere."

One afternoon we go to one of her coffee shops, a student hang-out that is bare, smart and colourful in a Germano-Scandic kind of way. The coffee is very good and made with a proper, shiny, Italian coffee machine. We're enjoying our drinks, I've said how impressive the place is, and I am gazing at a vivid orange wall when Magda whispers that this was a favourite place to come when she was seeing a previous boyfriend. She's hardly been back since they broke up. She doesn't want to run into him here in their old haunt.

But Paweł turns up! He even comes over to our table and there is a frosty pause. In the awkwardness of the moment he greets us stiffly and says that at the local radio station where he works there has been an important announcement about the imminent flood. It is expected to hit Wrocław tomorrow or the next day and be more serious than anyone expects. He feels it is his duty to tell as many people as possible, he says. I gather he wants to give the impression that he would never re-open old wounds if it were not a national emergency. He bids us farewell and retreats to his table across the room.

During the rest of the day we can't help noticing that there are sandbags at basement windows and at ground-floor doorways. On the big island, the Ostrów Tumski, around the old cathedral there are piles of sandbags. In fact, we can't get into the cathedral at all because it is all sandbagged for the siege. On the bridges between the islands and the rest of the town crowds of people stand and marvel at the water level. It hasn't quite reached a dangerous level yet, but it is much higher than usual. The talk everywhere is about how much higher it is supposed to get and whether the old German flood-prevention barriers will hold. The general opinion seems to be that they will hold, but it is all pretty touch-and-go. It is like some previously neutral city awaiting an inevitable attack.

We were a bit uneasy at whichever exotic restaurant we favoured that evening, and we went back to Magda's flat in a thoughtful mood.

The next morning Magda's mobile phone rang several times. Some calls were about business, as her travel agency was arranging a tour of Barcelona, but other calls were from friends. One friend who lived near the river reported that some streets were already flooded. We heard that the electricity in the centre of town had been switched off. We discussed the situation and decided that it would be sensible for me to get back to Warsaw on the first possible train. We ate breakfast quickly. While Magda was on the phone I tried to rinse my cereal bowl and found that the water had been shut off. Suddenly, after all the loafing around during the past couple of days, we had a sense of urgency. There was no time to lose.

I pack up my things quickly and Magda dresses. We hurry to the tram stop but have to wait for several valuable minutes. Then we trundle down to the centre. Trams are not running from the direction of the islands, so we hurry for a few blocks, Magda carrying my bag, then hop on another tram which gets us near the big crenellated train station. We hurriedly buy a ticket and race to the platform. We are just on time—but the train isn't. When it finally arrives it is fairly full, but Magda hurries along the train looking in at the compartments and finds a six-seat compartment with only a young mother and her daughter in it. I am increasingly in awe of Magda's skill as a travel arranger. She installs me in this compartment, and I thank her profusely and promise to give her a glowing recommendation any time she wants one.

The train leaves 20 minutes or more late, and in fact this is the last train out of Wrocław for many days. We gradually accumulate three more women in the compartment. On the outskirts of Wrocław we see some high water and a flooded street or underpass, but nothing worthy of the evening news. This train is on a more northerly route than the previous one. We return via Łódz instead of Opole, and the low-lying fields along the track seem remarkably dry. We see sandbagged levies and people standing on top looking at the high river. This flood business is a strange waiting game.

The little boy in my compartment is about two or three, a cute little fellow with a rosebud mouth and fluffy pale brown hair. I think he's travelling with three doting relatives, but the fourth person, on whose lap his stockinged feet rest, was already in the compartment when the others arrived. They're getting on like a house on fire. The boy sits mainly on his grandmother's lap and occasionally his mother takes him out to the toilet. The grandfather sometimes takes him on his lap. The child gurgles and chatters in a cheerful high-pitched burble all the way to Łódz. But who is the passenger who played the acquiescent footstool to the boy? Perhaps she is a kindly, motherly stranger like Maria Wnuk, befriending a little boy on a long trip.

I have been back in Warsaw now for nearly a week, and every day the floodwaters have ground on down the valleys of the Odra and its tributaries, and today, July 18, has been declared a day of national mourning. In Wrocław Magda has had to move out of her flat for the duration and take refuge with her parents. Apart from everything else, this must be an embarrassing blow to a young woman of 26 who is beginning to live her own life away from the parental nest. She tells me by phone that things are awful in Wrocław. Her parents' street is still dry and they have gas and electricity, but they have to go and queue for water. By a great stroke of good luck, they have just found a source of water where there wasn't a queue and they filled up buckets and every other container they could carry. Her flat, the place where I stayed only a week ago, is in the flooded area. There is no electricity and the lift doesn't work. She tells me that the water is up as far as the traffic lights. She can't get over it.

"You remember the traffic lights out in the street? *That's* how high the water is! This has never happened before in *history!* It's not even in medieval chronicles!" They're waiting for the second crest of floodwaters. I tell her to keep a diary.

Maria finds it blackly ironic that so many of our kayak club members will be coming from Wrocław, which has been flooded, and Szczecin, which is waiting its turn at the mouth of the Odra to be flooded, only to go and swim and kayak in other rivers. And as if that sort of water worry weren't enough, the water is turned off this morning in our block of flats, and water has to be carried from another building. Camping would not be less convenient. It was turned off for a good reason, however, because they are repairing a pipe somewhere. Maria asks me if this also happens in London, and I say it does.

We are about to leave for our camping and kayaking trip. Staszek is back from the seaside and is going to drive us to the first campground up on the Radew River, which is part of the coastal Baltic drainage area and therefore far away from the water drama farther south. Witek Dębski will come over and we'll all go together. Staszek now has a larger four-door car. I sit in front and Maria and Witek are in the back seat.

As we speed along there are billboards advertising restaurants, of all things. There is strange graffiti in English, complete with misplaced apostrophes (*skinhead's*). I wonder if there is an international graffiti-English. English still appears on clothing in the same sort of nonsense phrases that I observed in 1980, but now graffiti-English also employs odd, nearly meaningless, combinations of obscenities and other unlikely words. "Neighbourhood Asshole" is written in large capital letters on a block of flats in north Warsaw. It could be the latest rock group, for all I know. We get into the intermittent Polish forests, the birch and pine that Alastair and I cycled through in 1980. Tall birch trees stand like a herd of albino giraffes grazing on bushes in the sky.

Sometimes over the years Maria has suggested that I might learn Polish, and she is right. It would take some of the responsibility off her and everyone else I have to depend on for communication. She tells me I would pick it up fast. I doubt it, but it is nice of her to say so. I have some words and phrases. I have a dictionary. My Polish is like a cairn that people leave another pebble on as they pass. It grows gradually, but it still doesn't amount to much.

In English dictionaries the last few letters of the alphabet fizzle out like the top treble keys of a piano. There's not much to them, and the really meaty stuff has come long before. But in Polish dictionaries the first few letters are the least interesting. The alphabet is just revving up before the serious stuff from about G onwards. It really gets into its stride later with the *Prz*'s and the *Szcz*'s and is still going strong when it hits the Z's. I am still a tepid observer. I have taken the lazy way out. I have collected enough English-speakers that I can neglect learning Polish. I can play at learning a word here or a phrase there without buckling down to the task of understanding the grammar and getting to the stage where I can use the language and talk to people in it and read magazines and books in it. I know I'm missing something, and most of my Poles know that I know that I'm missing something, but they have resigned themselves to my indolence. They are taking it with a good grace and I'm grateful to them.

Chapter Thirteen

Surgeons in the Forest

Polish drivers make me nervous. The roads are narrow and everybody wants to get around whatever is in front of them at all costs. They seem to tailgate until there is a chance to whiz around the offending slowpoke. The fact is, Staszek makes me a little nervous. He is skilful and confident, but I cringe a bit at the narrow margin he leaves between us and oncoming cars. And sure enough, finally he miscalculates and has to drive off the road to avoid a collision. We come to rest on a steep slope on the left side of the road. I get out of the car with difficulty, as I am climbing out of it uphill, and Maria and Witek somehow scramble out of the back seat. Staszek must be very embarrassed, and the rest of us are too mortified on his behalf to say anything to him about his dangerous driving. (Or "bad luck", in case the others don't think he was driving dangerously.)

The car is at too much of an angle to drive, but in a moment several other cars have stopped. Someone has a rope, someone else has a sturdy Land-Rover sort of vehicle that can pull us back up onto the road. In no time there is a little impromptu team of young car-reclaimers, presumably all strangers to each other, all tying this rope to Staszek's front axle and pushing it up onto the road as the Land-Rover eases the rope taut and then pulls. The car begins to move and then regains the road. The team untie the rope, Staszek gingerly tries the starter motor and the car starts. Everybody shakes hands all round and then gets back into their three or four cars and drives off. We also get back in the car, which doesn't seem to have suffered from its off-road trip, and continue on our way. There is an awkward silence in the car. I keep thinking about the little team that assembled in minutes. Would that happen in Britain? Is this a common occurrence in Poland?

As we get closer to the appointed camping place and rendezvous, Maria, Staszek, and Witek confer about the exact location of it. Finally we come to the right turn-off and Staszek goes off on a much smaller road and through a few villages. Then he turns off onto a still smaller road, and after a few miles we find an even smaller, lavishly unpaved, road leading directly to the campsite beside Lake Hajka.

A number of tents are already in place, but many more campers will come later. There are a lot of cars, unlike the *spływ* nine years ago when hardly anyone came by car and Zygmunt's van was the only motorised vehicle at our disposal. Staszek himself is an old hand at these kayak trips and knows some of the people. Some of the older ones greet him and remember when he used to come as a boy with his parents. We unpack the car and eventually Staszek drives away again. No one has said a word to him about the way we were nearly killed on the road.

Maria and I look for a place to pitch our tent, while Witek goes about pitching his own tent in a very professional way. He is pacing around a small patch of ground and concentrating hard. The area he and Maria have chosen is strangely corrugated and doesn't look particularly comfortable to me. In fact, what it looks like is graves. Knowing what I know about Polish forests, I can easily believe that they are graves from any one of numerous historical periods, but the thought seems not to occur to either Maria or Witek. Witek brings pine boughs and lays them carefully on his patch and then he lays his ground sheet over them, so that the floor of his tent will be springy even before he puts his air mattress and sleeping bag on it. Maria and I get our tent up with a minimum of trouble. The old technique comes back to me and she has probably always had it. She loves living in a tent and cooking over a gas stove at the front flap. It has its cosy moments, especially in the evening when you don't have to go back to town to go indoors. The indoors is out there with you, with a doormat miles square.

We are in a clearing at the edge of the forest with the lake down a path past some other tents. It glitters at us through the row of trees along the edge of it. (All the days we were there, Witek would take his water colours early in the morning and go along the lakeside to a quiet spot and do a few impressionistic sketches, which he would then show Maria and me later in the day.) In the other direction is the forest proper. The floor of the forest is as springy as a shag-pile carpet on a trampoline. It is green with grass and moss and brown with layers of pine needles. The trees are spaced several feet apart and are like bare columns, as the branches only start about 30 feet up. It looks like the cathedral in Córdoba.

That first night there is a gathering around a campfire of the whole group—the three sections from Warsaw, Wrocław, and Szczecin. The Mach family—Tomek, Ula, and Ania—are in a neighbouring tent to ours, and seeing them again is nicely familiar. Basia and Krzysztof are there, and Teresa—old friends from nine years ago. The Machs' daughter, Ania, is now a young woman of 18 or 19 and is a self-assured student-to-be who now speaks excellent English and is an accomplished translator for me when I get into difficulties in conversations with her parents or anyone else. Ania is a real godsend. The Mach group includes a nephew of Tomek's and Ziutek, an ex-brother-in-law of Ula's. At first his connection to them is not clear to me. He looks like a gruff former Party official, but knowing the Machs, I suspect that he isn't. We all sit around this campfire on various chairs and logs until it gets late and chilly. People sing with and without a guitar accompaniment. Teresa asks me if I can sing a song, but I emphatically cannot. I can't think beyond the first line of any song, and when it comes to the crunch, I can't sing even that. Out of pity, or to sing the song I should have, Teresa and a couple of others do a startlingly adequate rendition of "It's a Long Way to Tipperary". I wonder how on earth they know the words. Finally we go back to our tents with the welcome mat of the world which might or might not have been pitched on a graveyard.

To get some practice in a kayak I go out with Agnieszka, one of three or four of Ula Mach's medical colleagues on this trip.

(Henryk, the oaf from Wrocław, is not with us this year.) We paddle all the way to Mostowo and back, stopping at Rostowo to buy bread. Her husband Wojtek and 7-year-old daughter Ewa are near us in another kayak. We go through a low sluice at Rostowo and cut off into a canal instead of the Radew River proper. We then come to a strange sight. It seems that the end of the canal is completely blocked by an unlikely bungalow that extends right across it! The view from the front of the kayak is positively surreal. As we draw closer the impression doesn't change, but some others from our group are at the right-hand side of it at a little landing place. When we get there the situation becomes clearer. It is a hydro-electric plant.

The "bungalow" is the top storey of a 4-storey power station. The river drops 40 or 50 feet and turns turbines inside this building. We look in and see rods and cogs turning like a corner of *Metropolis*. It is German-built and dated 1921. This area could have been part of the Danzig Corridor, and anyway, this whole area has a German imprint according to Witek, who was pointing out typically German architectural features in the towns we passed through on the way up here, like the sleepy-eyed dormer windows squinting out from under rows of roofing tiles. This small power station is one of several in this region. They got a bit dilapidated but were privatised and are now contributing to the national grid. With the help of some men in the party we portage down some steps and a steep embankment to the river below where it comes out from its work among the turbines in the power plant. It rushes out as though it is glad to be released from its unexpected employment.

Maria and Teresa and I walk into the nearest town for some supplies and stop for a drink at a café there. They teach me the Polish saying, a humorous euphemism for a toilet: "The place where the king goes on foot". I say it a few times and, as I have a notebook with me, they solemnly give me a Polish dictation test and congratulate me when I get it right. I am awarded a 5 out of

5 and Maria writes "very clever pupil!" on my "test paper" and signs it "Prof. Maria".

On the way back Maria remembered something we have been trying to think of. On our last kayak trip we had a code phrase to mean the-hidden-place-in-the-woods-that-you-find-to-attend-to-your-private-needs, and now it comes back to Maria. "Lonely Place"! It amused us both, and this private joke was a little bond between us. We revive it now, no worse for its neglect for nine years, waiting for us where we left it.

One morning as I was waking up I heard a conversation outside the tent and grasped the general import of it. They were saying something like, "Would you look at that tick on Ziutek! That certainly is some tick! My heavens, that is definitely a tick!" I had somehow picked up the word for "tick", *kleszcz*, if not, fortunately, the thing itself. I quickly dressed and went to look at Ziutek's famous tick. It had fastened onto the thickest part of his calf and he looked oddly vulnerable, standing there in his shorts with everybody exclaiming about his tick, which he could see only by craning his neck around awkwardly.

Nobody seemed to be doing anything about it, and I suddenly remembered something I had read somewhere about ticks. You have to kill them with a hot match and then they slide out. If you fail to kill them first, the head is left in the wound and gets infected. (More recently I have also read that none of this is true. Anyway, I was about to put it to the test.) I hurried back to the tent for Maria's box of matches and returned purposefully to Ziutek. Everyone gathered around to see what I would do. I struck a match, blew it out, and touched the hot match-head to the tick. Then I carefully grasped the bulbous little body and pulled it out of Ziutek's calf. It came out like a knife out of a sheath and then lay like a textbook specimen in the palm of my hand. There was a general sound of approval and an exclamation from Maria, who had followed close behind to see where I was going with her matches, which she usually guarded carefully.

Perhaps Maria was relieved that I had finally found a niche in the kayak club. Instead of merely being Maria's clueless foreign friend (a "charming piranha" if anyone remembered the idiotic initiation ceremony of nine years before), I was now a recognized expert at removing ticks. The word quickly got around. Ania Mach had two ticks on her leg and I removed them in my practised way. People I had never met before from the other sections of the club would approach me about their tick problem. A man came to me with his small son, who had a tick in his arm.

"I have heard that you can treat *kleszcz*," he said in English. I saw that the tick was already dead and half destroyed, but before I could do anything, Maria was at my side striking a match. I solemnly touched it to the remains of the tick and then eased it out with my fingernail. The boy was brave, like a cowboy having an arrow removed. He and his father were grateful, and Maria followed me around with her matches like a theatre nurse with a set of scalpels. Basia and Teresa had now heard the *kleszcz* story and had dubbed me a "*kleszcz*-ologist" and were telling everyone what a skilled "surgeon" I was. I began to carry a pen knife and matches with me everywhere as the tools of my profession. I was expecting many more "patients", since everyone kept running around in the woods in shorts and bathing suits. The embarrassing thing about my new fame was that there were real surgeons in the party who must have thought I was an absurd upstart.

Even at the time I didn't know exactly where I got this stuff about killing ticks with hot matches. My best guess is that as a child I found it in my older brother's *Boy Scout Handbook* and thought it was an interesting bit of lore. The fact was—and I carefully left it unmentioned—that I had never seen a tick before in my life. Anyway, can it be true? Can the head come off so easily? If you were stuck into your grub, so to speak, and a really strong force was pulling at your abdomen and thorax, wouldn't you let go of your food? Wouldn't you let go before your *head* came off? This habit cannot be advantageous to ticks as a species. Doesn't it make you wonder what makes ticks tick?

Lake Hajka wasn't the most salubrious place. Maria and others who had waded or swum in the lake came back to the camp with leeches stuck on them. Others who strolled around in the woods in skimpy attire got numerous ticks, some of which I was called to deal with, but like medical pioneers before me I had shown others how to do it, so I was not called every time. Once Maria came to me with a tick, or part of one, in her leg, and I carefully dug it out like a splinter with my pocket knife. The exposed flesh strolling about in the woods must have looked to the insect life there like breakfast, lunch, and dinner, also elevenses, tea, supper, between-meal snacks, and definitely *kolacja*. For my part, I wore long sleeves and kept the legs of my jeans tucked into my socks.

But the pine forest was delightful. It was wonderfully green and shady with shafts of soft light filtering down at a high angle through the sparse branches. There were little pine cones underfoot on the spongy, mossy ground. If it rained, the water soaked into the humus and before long it seemed dry again. It was a delight to wander among the trees inhaling the pine smell with only the sound my muffled footsteps and the snapping of twigs underfoot. I could see why Tomek Mach spent the rest of the year in his architect's office dreaming of the annual camping and kayak trip.

Zygmunt had welcomed me and re-introduced himself and exchanged a few words with Maria, but except for that I hadn't seen him since we arrived. Zygmunt still made all the decisions about the movements of the club. During the previous year he had chosen the route and arranged the campsites and presumably worked out a time scheme, but nobody but Zygmunt knew what it was. He was inscrutable and everyone else was apparently satisfied to be in the dark. There might have been a tentative itinerary somewhere, or maybe not. We went on enjoying the campsite from day to day, going out for little excursions of a few hours in the kayaks, vaguely waiting for Zygmunt to give us the word to move on. The situation was somewhat exacerbated by the fact that Zygmunt was known to have a serious alcohol problem. He had become a bit erratic latterly. I asked Maria how serious it was, exactly, and she loyally defended him: "Zygmunt drink from time to time," she said carefully, and then added, "from morning till night."

We are still in the camp a couple of days later when we celebrate Krzysztof's name day. His name day, July 25, is always a feature of these camping trips, because Zygmunt always schedules them at the end of July and the beginning of August. So every year Maria picks a bouquet of wildflowers and every year his friends gather in their shorts and bathing suits to sing *"Sto lat"* to him. Maria, Witek, and I look like a little family group because we are all wearing some white swan feathers stuck in our kayaking caps. Witek found them on one of his early-morning watercolour forays. (Every year Zygmunt issues the kayakers with caps, and this year they have a camouflage pattern on them. Our zany swan feathers make them look like Mercury's helmet with overtones of Pinocchio's ears.) Krzysztof's wife, Basia, has arranged some little cakes for everyone and we bring our own coffee cups and drinks. This morning Maria has her bouquet of wildflowers and she has also written a poem, which Witek has illustrated and everybody (we and the Mach group) signs. Maria says, "You will write a poem in English?" It is a question, but it is also an order, so I write a few lines. They start out in a *Hiawatha* rhythm but soon degenerate into unusually amorphous free verse. My little poem meets with general approval, and I declaim it for Krzysztof and the dozen or so others. It sounds better than it is.

Afterwards there seems to be a lot of leisurely messing around and gourmet lunch preparations. The weather is looking a bit dubious. Eventually we break camp and load all our gear into the big truck. *Just* when Witek and I go to our kayak it begins to rain and there are rumbles of thunder. We wait a bit but get underway in a light rain. I am really frightened to be in the middle of a lake with lightning around. I explain this to Witek so that he will know in case I seem withdrawn and panic stricken. Every time the thunder rumbles I think how exposed we are out here in the middle of all this flat water. I wonder what it feels like to be struck by lightning. Sometimes people are struck by lightning and live. Witek seems completely unconcerned and I wonder what comforting secret he knows that I don't. Whatever he knows, I can't guess it, and I try to stay calm and ignore my terror.

The local paper will say "Foreign Woman Struck by Lightning. An Englishwoman, Sara Lansom, met her end yesterday in a freak accident on Lake Hajka when she was struck by lightning while paddling a kayak with pan Witold Dębski, a noted architect and watercolourist. Mrs. Larsow was visiting friends in Poland..."

I find it helps to—not sing exactly—but *think* a song. The song I think is: "I've got a mule, her name is Sal, / Fifteen miles on the Erie Canal." The rhythm of it matches our paddling, and so as we go across this terrifying lake on our way to the more sheltered Radew River, assuming we will ever get there, I concentrate on remembering the words. I probably last sang it with the words in front of me in the sixth grade at Speedway Elementary School in the days when I wasn't yet so afraid of lightning. (Tornadoes, yes, but not particularly lightning. My fear of lightning suddenly arrived one day several years ago when I was cycling in rural Normandy and couldn't find a safe shelter during a series of thunderstorms blowing across the coastal plateau.)

> I've got a mule, her name is Sal,
> Fifteen miles on the Erie Canal.
> We've hauled some barges in our day,
> Filled with lumber, something, hay,
> Hauled them all the wa-a-a-a-y
> From Albany to-o Bu-uh-ffalo-o-o...
> o-o-ow bridge! Everybody down!

Low bridge, for we're goin' through a town.
Well, you've never known your neighbor
And you've never known your pal
If you've never navigated o-o-o-on
The Erie Canal!

I could have sung this when I was asked at the campfire singalong. Well, no, I couldn't have sung it, but I seem to know most of the words, at least. "We've hauled some barges in our day, / Filled with lumber, da-dum, hay... Filled with lumber, *coal* and hay." Coal! "I've got a mule, her name is Sal..." I concentrate hard on the Erie Canal all the time we're paddling in the lake, out in the middle of this very large lake, with thunder rumbling overhead like the Little Men bowling in the Catskills.

Chapter Fourteen

Hail and Farewell on the River

Witek and I paddle along until we reach a mill at the end of the lake and are helped to portage around it. We continue on the Radew River proper, a meandering bucolic stream, quite shallow in places with lots of reeds and weeds. There are not just willows growing aslant it, but everything overhanging and in it. It is an obstacle course most of the time and there are three more portages: two big obstacles and a sluice. At the portage places we meet up with others. I notice that Witek is helpful to other people and when we need help there always seem to be someone to lend a hand.

When we are not avoiding obstacles or carrying our kayak around fallen tree trunks, parts of the Radew are absolutely idyllic, shady with oak and other deciduous trees and then sunny with vivid reflections of trees in the water. Zygmunt has chosen a river that is about as picturesque as it is possible for a river to get. But then, much of Poland is a land of meadows, forests and rivers.

Witek and I communicate in English and German. Witek may start in English, but it often turns into German. I speak a slow and careful English to him, and when that doesn't work, I make a stab at German. This seems to be more or less adequate. Witold Dębski is a small, wiry man with a neat white moustache and beard. The Dębskis are an old armigerous Polish family, and Witek has an indefinably dignified air, even when he is wearing ancient track-suit bottoms with a bandana around his head. He can be grave and courtly, and I can imagine him in a trim business suit and tie or in a uniform with decorations. He is missing a front tooth, but even that does not diminish his essential dignity.

When we approach any difficult obstacle, say a pile of brushwood that looks like a beaver dam, I hear him mutter, "Hum! Hum! Hum!" under his breath as he devises a strategy for dealing with it. Sometimes the strategy involves me getting out of the kayak to make it lighter. Sometimes he studies the current to see if we can use it in some way, or he examines the shape of the obstacle to see where the best point is to tackle it. He has obviously had a lot of experience with obstacles in rivers, and no doubt elsewhere.

After only about 10 kilometers we come to our camp on high ground above a river landing. Zygmunt has just barely had time to get to the new campsite with his truck and put up the club flag before the first kayaks start arriving. Actually, he didn't get there in time, because we find out later that 10 kayaks had gone on, overshooting the landing place before Zygmunt got the flag up. Some of the kayakers realized their mistake and turned back, but by nightfall some of them are still missing, including Barbara and Krzysztof. Maria and I are a bit worried about them and wonder what could have happened. The night is cool, and Maria reminds me that they were wearing only their bathing suits.

Maria is an early riser, and the next morning before I am quite awake she tells me that the adventures of the night before have had a happy ending. Basia and Krzysztof had returned at midnight in high spirits. There had come a time in the evening when they realised that they had somehow missed the flag and would have to turn back. They had come to a bridge where there happened to be a restaurant. As they hadn't had much to eat, they quickly decided to stop for a meal before going back along the river to look for our campsite. When they moored the kayak and got up onto the roadway, they discovered that this wasn't just any old restaurant but a very grand and exclusive one. Although they were still wearing only their bathing suits, they walked in and got a table and had a fabulous meal. To top off the story, they recognized, sitting at another table, none other than the *Marszalek*—the Speaker—of the Senate! He was

214

accompanied by a young lady and a few security agents. Maria relishes the whole story and the happy outcome. "And zey were in zeyr bazing suits!" she exclaims.

We have another day in camp. Now it is Ania Mach's name day and Witek has done a watercolour especially for her. I give her a little book by Penelope Lively that I have been reading. Ania's ease with English is all the more remarkable to me when I think of our communication problems in 1980. English was an arcane subject on the school curriculum then if it was there at all. A few words had leaked out somehow and had got themselves embroidered on shirts or stamped onto sweatshirts in some distant developing country whence they had been imported into Poland. They were talismans rather than words.

Witek asked me why *watch* (noun) and *watch* (verb) are the same word, but I couldn't tell him. That's just the way it is. Any language is going to be a mystery to foreigners, because we native speakers spend our lives in the full-time job of arranging our language to suit us, as you might make alterations over the years to some inherited furniture, but with the general advice and consent of the people around you. Then you visit another language and find that they, too, have been constructing their own system of things that makes sense to them, if to no one else. Why, for example, in Dutch is the word for "eyeglasses" and "toilet seat" the same: *bril*? Why does *slof* mean both a house slipper and a cigarette carton? Well, that's just the way it is.

Our last day on the Radew before we reach the confluence with the Parsęta is a long day of paddling around obstacles. Twice I have to get out of the kayak and make my way on foot through weeds and nettles to meet Witek farther on. The second time I get back in the kayak I am easing myself into it from a fallen log when I slip and scrape the inside of my left leg on rough bark. Unfortunately, I have just been developing some varicose veins in exactly that place and it throbs ominously as the day goes on.

My right knee is also abraded, but at least there aren't any surface veins there.

We sit on kapok life jackets in the kayak, and after an hour or two they become unbelievably hard. Granite, I feel, would be like a plush cushion compared to that kapok. I notice that some other kayakers have provided themselves with inflatable seats. The kapok is all right at first, but there comes a moment when I feel that my hip bones are in direct contact with it, having penetrated the thin flesh that has separated them. (But that flesh is far from thin. Where is it? Why isn't it making a padded cushion? How could any substance known to man be as hard as this kapok?)

Witek and I in our kayak are like dancing partners anticipating each other's movements. We see an obstacle at the same time or the need to correct our course and we both stroke on the same side at the same time. We keep in a rhythm together—usually set by me because he can see me and I can't see him. We do a dance in which no one leads all the time and we are both going in the same direction.

Witek and I are sizing up a large obstacle in the water, a pile of branches and logs, when Tomek and Ula Mach come along in their kayak. There are a few other kayaks in the same position we are in: hanging around in front of the obstacle trying to figure out what to do about it. Ania Mach and her cousin are in another kayak, also presumably hatching a plan.

Tomek is like a bull deciding what to do about a matador. Ula sits like a figurehead in the front seat of the kayak while Tomek charges, as it were, straight at the brushwood. He flails with his paddle, using the impetus to launch the kayak out of the water and into the brush, where he flails some more, furiously paddling through the leaves and branches. The kayak continues to move in small increments until Tomek somehow by dint of force and will-power slashes and elbows his way through the "beaver dam" with a wildly windmilling paddle and gets it back in the water on the other side. Beyond the barrier comes a triumphal shout and we all laugh and applaud. I can't see myself

216

as a figurehead or Witek as a charging bull, so I climb out and trek through the undergrowth to a sandbank along the shore 50 yards downstream.

It is early evening when we reach our stopping place. Our campsite is outside Karlino and our flag is draped over a bridge at the edge of town. To my surprise I see that Maria is on the bridge directing people where to stow the kayaks and how to find the campground. Zygmunt is busy elsewhere, and she is in charge of corralling the kayakers. And she is doing it with a will (an iron will? a *żelazowa wola*?), taking charge like a traffic policeman. The camp isn't very close to the river, and I am stiff and chilled now as the evening is drawing on. Maria is busy at the bridge, but eventually we get our tent put up, and we have the ritual *kolacja*. It is nearly dark and I still haven't cleaned up my sore, muddy legs. Maria is rather dismissive about my scratches and bruises, and I notice that she has no sign of varicose veins herself. I, on the other hand, imagine fatal blood clots forming minute by minute. Maria says that of course everyone always has a few scratches and bruises when camping and kayaking; it is perfectly normal and nothing to get excited about. She seems to think that the extreme commonness of bruising will somehow make my aches and pains disappear, along with my concern about blood clots.

I sleep badly and ache all over. The next day Witek takes a fatherly interest in my bruised leg and gets some arnica to put on it. We walk into Karlino and he points out interesting little architectural features I would have hardly noticed. When we come to a chemist he goes in and gets two different kinds of arnica to reduce the bruising. Back at our camp he dresses my abrasions and I nap for much of the afternoon. When I wake up, I wonder if I should go in the kayak at all the next day. Kayaking, I reason, is like cycletouring in that if you are tired and not at your best it can be dangerous. (But then, cycletouring is *not* like kayaking on a placid river.) I go to my authority on all medical things, Ula Mach. Her specialty is blood clots. Or anyway circulatory problems in pregnancy, but I feel she will be deeply informed about veins. Ula's specialized medical opinion is that I should wear jeans the next day instead of shorts. Anyway, we will be on the Parsęta, which is wider and might have fewer obstacles and so would be an easier river. I decide to wear trousers the next day and brave the new river.

The next day the plan is for me to meet Witek on the other side of the town, where he will bring our kayak to a low sandy spot on the shore. On this leg of the trip, so to speak, I am wearing some protective denim between my skin and the great outdoors. The Parsęta is indeed a much wider, slower river and it looks like plain paddling. It is a sunny morning, and when we dash through a low weir, it is like the splashy ending of an amusement-park ride. I get drenched, but the sun is warm and I am soon dry again; even my jeans are nearly dry by the middle of the day.

However, the weather then becomes truly awful. There is a headwind, then a side wind, then rain, then really heavy rain with hailstones. For the heaviest downpour we shelter by some willows, but they don't afford much protection. We don't have adequate rain gear for such a downpour. Some other kayaks go past, their cagouled occupants apparently prepared for any eventuality. Meanwhile, the hail throws up splashes on the brown river like the hooves of invisible horses on a dusty road.

The wide Parsęta is not very fast. Tomek must find it a tedious stretch of water. All the way along the river after the weather clears again we play a stately leapfrog with other kayakers who are dawdling or stopping for a break or overtaking us as we dawdle or stop. We usually hail each other, and Witek exchanges some remarks with them. I think to myself that "Hailing on the River" sums up the day, one way and another. We see a few fishermen on the banks, and we try not to disturb their fish. The Parsęta is not shady, as the smaller more clogged Radew was, and so not as startlingly beautiful. The Parsęta is murky and muddy, broad and full-looking. We see swans swimming on the river, flying and taking off. The swans walk on the water and flap and flap and eventually get airborne. Witek says their wings make a particular sound, but I can't hear anything special. We have also seen storks flying. They are like swans but more so, with a startling wingspan.

As we approach the new campsite there is another low weir, a shallow doorstep in the river, and we take it squarely, throwing the water up to the left and right like an exuberant Roman fountain.

Now we are encamped in a large meadow, rather far from the "lonely place" facilities. In an adjacent field there are two chestnut horses, but they are quite unlike the horses I used to see on the roads in 1980, stolid draft animals plodding along pulling scruffy haywagons. These horses now are plainly not there to pull anything. They are sleek saddle horses and are for more up-market pursuits than Old Dobbin was, who has anyway now given way to the tractor. The neighbouring farm is mechanized and the wagons seem to be "store bought" as opposed to the poor contraptions we saw on the country roads on our way to Szczytno 17 years ago, which looked home made, as though the farmer had bought the wheels, axles and flatbed and then just put anything along the sides to keep the hay bales from falling off. They were sometimes rough tree branches such as the kind Tomek charged through, except that the farmer had usually removed the leaves and hacked off the smaller side branches.

There is activity overhead in the sky. There was sometimes a loud buzzing of fighter planes yesterday and last night, now presumably NATO planes rather than the Russian jets of nine years ago. Last evening there was also an odd thing I had never seen before. There was a rainbow, but only a scrap of it. There were dark clouds covering most of the sky, but where they stopped half way to the horizon there were vertical stripes of colour protruding below the edge of the cloud like a Highlander's stocking flash, red at the left and fading a bit at the right where indigo and violet ran together. It was clear, but a patch rather than a rainbow and not at all curved.

Maria has decided that we should end the trip a day or two earlier than the others and get back to Warsaw, and I find I am quite willing to abandon the tent and the outdoor living conditions. What I am really looking forward to is a shower in Maria's bathroom. We also have an appointment with Jan Twardowski at the convent of the Sisters of the Visitation, and I want to prepare for our meeting. As Maria is going to be our interpreter, I want to prepare her, too, for the questions I intend to ask him. I need to go to a bank for some cash and pay Maria what I owe her for our groceries, and I need to phone Swissair to reconfirm my flight. Maria has her own reasons for wanting to return early, but I don't think any of them coincide with mine.

Zygmunt drives us to Kołobrzeg, a town on the coast at the mouth of the Parsęta. It is one of the resort towns along the Baltic, but it is as dreary as Worthing on a wet Sunday. Rain has been pouring all day, and we get out of the van and into the train station as fast as we can. The trip back to Warsaw is fairly uneventful. The train goes east to Koszalin, where lots of backpackers get on with their very up-to-date-looking backpacks: nylon with light metal frames and bedmats. The train turns south toward the capital and we traverse the flat, wooded plains of northern Poland. Some of the little stations we pass still look derelict. Perhaps they will still look derelict a long time from now; there is a lot of catching-up to do and not everything is going to progress at the same rate. Now we pass fields of hay, barley, potatoes, and even dark green stands of tasselled corn. What are they doing here? They startle me even more than the silver maples in Warsaw did. Our campgrounds always seem to be very sandy, and I have formed the impression that all of Poland is covered with a light, thin, sandy soil, but there are fields of rich loam, too. These cornfields prove it. Our train compartment is new-ish looking and comfortable. I go out of the compartment and into the corridor. Getting past other passengers there is like changing places in a small boat, edging past each other from stern to aft and back again.

Chapter Fifteen

A Visitation to Father Twardowski

Maria has made some phone calls and arranged for us to go to Father Twardowski's flat beside the Church of the Sisters of the Visitation on Krakowskie Przedmieście. I'm excited about meeting "our poet". I wish Małgorzata were with me, since she is really the main translator. Everything in our work depends on her knowledge of English, because otherwise, if it were my sole responsibility, the poems would have to stay in Polish. She always insists that my name should come first on our by-line, but I have never thought that this arrangement gives an accurate impression of our division of labour. I go along with it only because it seems to be the conventional thing. Maria is looking forward to our visit, too, because she, like practically every other literate Pole, is a great fan of Jan Twardowski. New collections of his poetry come out all the time, and collections of his previously published poems appear in new guises—all his poems on cats, dogs, love, flowers, motherhood, the seasons, and so on. You can't go into a bookshop anywhere without finding at least one title by Jan Twardowski.

I have various reasons for wanting to meet him, but in particular, I need to get his permission to publish our translations. We could have translated anything at all by anybody, but to publish it, if it is still in copyright, we need the permission of the original author. We have his permission for one set of poems, but I'm hoping for something like blanket permission for all our translations, and we also need his go-ahead for a project to publish a postcard. I take some offprints to give him of a few pages from *Modern Poetry in Translation* and also a souvenir coffee mug with "English PEN" on it. I also sketch out some questions I want to ask him, together with several flattering references to his poetry. I want to rehearse some of this interview with Maria, but there isn't time.

I would really like to stage an informal interview with him. I have in mind asking him about his use of animals in his poems and his personification of abstractions. I'll ask him what poets have influenced him. I may not have heard of these poets, but I can worry about that later. I will suggest some main themes of his poetry and ask him to elaborate on any others. To make it easier for Maria when the time comes, I have written out three discussion points and a long preamble about our work with his poems and the details of publication. We don't have a publisher yet for a full collection, but we will need his permission before we can do anything. I want to be sure he understands Małgorzata's part in the translation work so that if she needs to write to him he will know who she is. I can read all this to Maria sentence by sentence and she can translate it for Father Twardowski. Even though we haven't had a chance to practice, this may work out all right if we just take our time.

Fr. Jan Twardowski in his room at the Sisters of the Visitation convent.

Jan Twardowski's flat is a spartan but comfortable suite of rooms reached through a side door and up some stairs. An elderly stooped man in his eighties, he greets us warmly. We sit in his pleasant little parlour and Maria chats easily with him. I say that I have offprints and a little gift for him. I see that my interpreter is going to have a problem when she repeats my words verbatim in English to Father Twardowski.

I take out the notebook with the questions I am going to ask, but the conversation veers off at other angles without me. I explain about the postcard and ask for his permission. By now Maria is addressing me in Polish and the priest in English and getting thoroughly flustered. She would just prefer to chat to him in the normal way, in Polish, without all this bilingual bother. They are getting on very well together. I see that all my carefully composed praise and my thoughtful questions are never going to get an airing. At this rate there is no way I can dictate my items sentence by sentence and have a little discussion. Also I am not sure that Father Twardowski hears very well in either language.

To my great relief, Father Twardowski speaks some halting English, and we manage much of our conversation and the business about copyright permission without needing Maria's help. He gives me a little signed yellow hardback volume of his collected poems and a copy for Małgorzata. (This book is very valuable to us later when we continue our translations, because it contains all his best poems.) We drink tea together, and he seems pleased to meet us and I am certainly delighted to meet the man whose poetry I have been working on and trying to recreate in English. Maria is also very moved to meet one of her favourite poets, even if she does sometimes forget what language she is supposed to be speaking to him.

We caught the bus back to Maria's in Żoliborz. As we went to the busstop we passed one of the many Ruch kiosks that dot the streets of Warsaw and every other town in Poland. You can buy bus tickets there, and newspapers and magazines, soap, toothpaste, cigarettes, small toys—all kinds of things you might decide you need as you are walking down the street. Nine years before when I had come back from that kayak trip, one of the first things I wanted to do, besides take a hot shower in Maria's bathroom, was to shave my legs. I had accidentally taken a dull razor blade with me on the *spływ*, and at the end of two weeks I had felt uncomfortably hirsute. We had passed another Warsaw kiosk then and I had seen razor blades in the window. I told Maria I would like to buy them, but she looked at me in horror and said, "You don't want that! They are razors for men!" I saw

223

that it would be easier to have hairy legs for another week than to explain that I really did want those razor blades for myself. Now in the summer of 1997 I noted that Gillette razors for women were displayed in kiosk windows. I wondered if Maria had noticed the changing times. In 1988 I might have managed the purchase by myself, but with Maria's help it was out of the question.

Witek's garden was a favourite place for this retired architect. The first time I had ever met him in 1988 at the Wnuks' he had brought us a bag of cherries from his garden. The garden was separate from his house or flat, like an allotment in Britain. One morning Maria suggested that we walk over to his garden to see if he was there. She made it sound as though it were just around the corner, but as we walked there—down streets, through estates of flats, through underpasses and parks—I realized that it was a matter of three or four miles. When we got there, Witek was away. His garden was one of a group arranged like town lots on residential streets. Maria took me into the area and we walked along a straight path until we came to Witek's property. There was a little summerhouse in the middle of a luxuriant patch of vegetation with numerous fruit trees and berry bushes and a picket fence around the whole garden. We found the summerhouse unlocked and brought out chairs to sit in for a while until we felt like going back. I wondered if Witek would turn up and find us, like a couple of Goldilockses eating his porridge. Then Maria decided it was time for us to find our way back through that maze of streets and shortcuts by which we had come.

Once again I thought how remarkable Maria's knowledge of Warsaw was. I had learned in 1988 that she seemed to have the whole bus and tram system in her head. She was not a native Varsovian, but she had arrived soon after the War when the place was still in ruins. She would have come to Warsaw in 1944 to take part in the Uprising as a nurse, but at the last moment her parents wouldn't allow her to go. You don't think of the

Warsaw Uprising as depending on parental consent. She had trained in first aid and was ready to go, but her parents decided that Poland's future did not depend on their 18-year-old daughter, and so she sat out those fearful days in Puławy carrying messages for the underground resistance and more or less obeying the curfew and probably getting very good at bridge.

Maria's sister-in-law, Włodek's sister, was Krystyna, yet another architect. Sometimes I had the feeling that everybody I met in Poland was an architect or a doctor. Sometimes I was sorry I wasn't an architect, too, so that we could all talk shop. Krystyna was a recent widow, and we were going to go with her to put flowers on her husband's grave. She came in her car and drove us to the cemetery, where she bought a bouquet of flowers at the gate. Then she began looking for her husband's grave, but she had forgotten where it was. We went along row after row of similar tombs, acres of black marble and concrete, side by side like beds in a crowded ward. There were large gold letters incised into the headstones with dates and porcelain photographs of the deceased. The pictures usually showed the people in a healthy prime of life and smiling and made for an eerie juxtaposition with the sombre black marble slab in this city of the dead. Finally, after wandering the narrow streets and alleys, Krystyna found the right grave and placed her flowers on it. She had also brought a votive candle in a lidded red glass jar like the one I had once wanted Maria to buy for our tent. Now she knelt and said some prayers here in this place of stone slabs where her husband's remains lay, to be remembered with a candle and a bouquet of August flowers.

It was Krystyna who was going to take Maria and me to the airport the next day. On the way there I looked through my carry-on bag and for a moment couldn't find my light silk jacket. I had no sooner mentioned it than I found it, but Maria had concluded that I had left it in the flat and told Krystyna to turn around at once. I was sitting in the front seat and explained that I had found it and there was no need to turn around. For several minutes Maria continued to shout excitedly that we must turn back and I continued to tell her that I had the jacket, look, here it was, this is the jacket! "Maria!" I said sharply, "will you listen! This. is. the. jacket. right. here. I have not lost it. It is not back in the flat. This is *it*!" I was sorry to speak so severely to her, because it was disrespectful, but sometimes her habit of not paying attention to what I was saying was irritating. Eventually she listened, but I was sorry we had had this lack of harmony in front of her sister-in-law and as I was about to leave the country.

When we got to the airport Maria stayed with me until I went through passport control, but Krystyna had to leave. Okęcie had changed all out of recognition since I had first seen it in 1988. In those days it was a scruffy little third-world sort of airport with a tiresome emphasis on how much money you had and in what currencies and where and how you were going to change it. It was like a run-down bus station but with a luggage carousel. Anybody in a uniform or behind a desk was evidently required to be gruff and abrupt and unsmiling on pain of being demoted to floor-scrubber. Now the airport had been entirely rebuilt. It was high-ceilinged and airy, with lots of cylindrical steel beams and glass. There were bright ads for airlines, cigarettes, and luxury items. Shops sold souvenirs and amber jewellery and were fairly relaxed about your personal financial circumstances.

Maria looked around and said, "I am not used to places like this." Perhaps the prospect of being in such a strange place had made her nervous on the way here and had caused her to be slightly hysterical about my silk jacket. She told me that it was an old Russian custom to sit quietly at the beginning of a trip to compose oneself, and that she would like us to do that now. We sat quietly together on some chrome seats and composed ourselves. She was right. This was a better way to part company than shouting about the whereabouts of a jacket.

Maria was 71 that summer, but she looked much as she had when I had first met her 17 years before. As there happened to be 18 years between our ages, it meant that I was then, at 53, almost the same age she had been when we first met on the Warsaw-Wrocław train. In some ways her life would always be a mystery to me—and perhaps mine to her. We had always tried to explain ourselves to each other and share both our similarities and dissimilarities. I remembered that her father was a Russian-born architect who had studied in St. Petersburg and said that he had lived in three different cities, as it changed to Petersburg and Leningrad, without actually moving house. Her parents had lived through the Russian Revolution, and when he designed their house in Puławy he had specially included a wall safe to hold the candles, matches, and salt that would be needed in case of another civil disturbance. In that house she and her older sister Janina and their parents had endured the curfews by settling down to hands of bridge. Young Maria, running errands for the underground resistance, had once narrowly missed being mown down by a Stuka, which had left a row of bullet holes across the front of the house. But still, as she told me when we visited the Czartoryski Palace in Puławy, one day during the War she and her school friend, Misia, had danced in the snow on the avenue through the park out of sheer girlish exuberance. I could almost see those schoolgirls dancing (did they waltz? was it more of a foxtrot? maybe a polka?), and it was a vivid image for me, like the family bridge games when the world was collapsing outside.

And then there was the plan, which her parents had squelched, to go to Warsaw to help with the Uprising. She pursued her serious education in the highly secret underground education system. Teachers or pupils could be punished by death, but a secret administration persisted in running a sophisticated network of underground schools and universities all over Poland. Maria and her friends had studied literature and mathematics by hiding their school books under their clothing and going to take tea with various elderly gentlemen in the town who were secret teachers. Outwardly, she was taking a course in tailoring because only practical, vocational studies were officially allowed.

After the war she had been able to study architecture, although she really wanted to be a journalist. She met another young architect, Włodzimierz Wnuk. He borrowed a book from her and somehow in the course of his returning it they fell in love. They married and had two children. It seems to me that whatever honest pursuit one undertook in Poland in those early years after the War and even up until 1989 took courage. She favoured Solidarity when it started and did some things that would not have been approved of by the government. Once she hid a box of contraband leaflets for a neighbour but didn't mention it to anyone else in her family. "One thing I learned during the War," she told me, "was not to tell anyone what I was doing. Sometimes it was better that no one knew."

Now she was a widow and a grandmother in an old country that was trying to begin again, and she too was beginning again. She had gone back to her old ambition to be a journalist. Now journalism was a more honourable profession that it had been in Poland for a long time. I said good-bye to Maria before going through the barrier that divides the sheep who are travelling from the goats who are staying at home. I was always sad to leave her. I gave her a good hug to last until the next time we met.

Chapter Sixteen

The Place of Wild Strawberries

Małgorzata phoned me one day in the following summer with startling news. Andrzej was going to retire from the BBC, and they had been looking for another place to live outside London—a cheaper place but still within striking distance of the attractions of the capital. But now there had been a slight change of plans. They were moving back to Poland! "What?" I exclaimed—I and everyone else to whom they announced their new plan. "Back" to a place they hadn't lived in for 27 years! Back to what? They had left their home in Warsaw under a cloud in 1970. They were more or less deported and deprived of their passports. Now Polish ex-citizens were being offered their Polish citizenship back by the new government. In order to own property one had to be a Polish citizen, and so Andrzej had applied to retrieve the citizenship he had been robbed of all those years ago, and now he was busy buying a house.

They had visited Poland in the spring of 1998 and seen a country house they immediately loved. Unfortunately, this house proved to be entirely unsuitable after all, because it was too dilapidated and riddled with dry rot to be repaired. But the idea of going to Poland to live in retirement had taken hold, and soon some friends of theirs had found another similar house, also in the country, also spacious and with several acres around it and a view of the Wisła. What more could one want? Well, a different country altogether perhaps, suggested several of their friends in London and Sweden. But Małgorzata and Andrzej remained enthusiastic. The friends in Poland who had found it for them were now engaging local workmen to make substantial alterations and install modern plumbing and wiring.

I was seriously dismayed, because I considered Małgorzata one of my dearest friends and I liked having her at the other end of a local phone line. We didn't actually see each other very often, but we were in touch almost every day. When either of us got bored with whatever we were writing or translating, we phoned the other to complain, ask advice, and generally have a change of pace. And *now*, I moaned to her, *now* what was I going to do? Now who was I going to phone at odd moments on a whim? Who was I going to have at hand to ask any question that occurred to me about either Poland or Sweden? How were we going to translate anything else with this enormous distance between us? Neither of us had e-mail at the time.

"Never mind," she said breezily. "You can always come and visit. It's a big house. You can have a room of your own in it. There's an orchard. You can come and sit under a tree and read a book!" That sounded very appealing. I could go and visit and lounge about in their orchard. But it was 900 miles away, across a large chunk of Europe. Their bit of north London, up in the northwest practically in Harrow, had seemed far away at the distant reaches of the Jubilee Line, but *Poland* was on the other side of Germany!

Now practically from one day to the next their future plans had changed radically and they were preparing to sell their flat, pack up, and move in October. The house was nearing completion and their agents on the ground were overseeing the work. There might be a few more things to do after they got there, but they would move in anyway and the work could continue around them. One day Małgorzata drew a sketch of the floorplan for me on a napkin in a restaurant. "This is the downstairs. We're going to have three bathrooms. Here is the kitchen and a hallway, the living room, and there's a room here and here, and this one has an en-suite bathroom with under-floor heating. I hope we can persuade my mother to come and live with us, and that can be her room. Then upstairs..." and she was sketching another rectangular area... "we're having this wall taken out, and this will be our study, and here is another bedroom. So you see there is plenty of room. We can have guests to stay." We soon hatched a plan that has worked well ever since. I would send them any books they wanted from London and then I would visit them periodically and the finances would more or less work out even. As time has gone on, each of us thinks we are getting a bargain.

October arrived. The Koraszewskis sent all their household effects to Poland via a shipping company and then went off to London City Airport with some hand luggage to catch a flight to Rotterdam, where they bought a small car and continued on their way to their new home in the country town of Dobrzyń nad Wisła, west-northwest of Warsaw. One of the things they were carrying with them was the name of a dog. Not the dog, just the name. They were going to acquire a dog at some time in the future and his name was going to be Darwin.

The new house in Dobrzyń nad Wisła where Małgorzata and Andrzej moved in October 1998. The house was red brick but the following year they added white siding.

Letters arrived from Dobrzyń. The household goods hadn't come yet, and so they were camping out in their new house, which still needed some work. The workmen hired by their unofficial agents were incompetent and were doing the work badly, so they had fired them and found some others. There was plenty of work to do, but I could come at Christmas if I liked.

They didn't have to ask me twice. I went there at Christmas 1998 and stayed for three weeks. I was given the big downstairs bedroom with the attached bathroom. They were still exploring their new property, and I was happy to join them in their discoveries. The large foursquare brick house was reached by a long straight drive between onion fields that belonged to the house but were being rented by a local farmer. The property

231

extended beyond the house to a sharp declivity and then a more level stretch down to the bank of the Wisła, or Vistula, River. It was a long slope wooded with saplings and bushes and general undergrowth, so that we had to hack a path to the river. On these excursions, Andrzej went in front with a sort of machete in his hand.

The house had been built in 1949 and was set in an enclosure that contained a small orchard, but it was hard to tell in December what kind of trees they were. There was another older orchard outside the enclosure, with a lot of broken limbs and piles of old branches. Near the house was a large barn-like outbuilding that contained the garage in the central section and other sections with separate doors for storage or livestock. One part had apparently been a pigsty but was now full of old pieces of wood, from sawn planks to tree branches. Gradually Małgorzata and Andrzej were pulling apart these heaps of rubbish and burning them in their two fireplaces or putting them into plastic sacks for refuse collection.

They told me more about the situation they had found when they had first arrived at their new home. "We spent the first week picking up vodka bottles," Małgorzata said.

"We found about sixty empty bottles in and around the house," Andrzej added.

"No, it was more like a hundred," Małgorzata corrected him. "Workmen came and did everything wrong, then we had to find new workmen to put those things right. But the second team of workmen often destroyed something, and still other workmen had to come and repair it. The underfloor heating in the downstairs bathroom has been ruined for good by the man who installed the tub."

On a later visit when most of the work had been done Małgorzata stood in the living room and waved her hand at the rest of the house and said, "Everything you see has cost us double or triple what it should have. Everything has had to be done at least twice." On that first visit I bought Andrzej a stud and cable detector, because the electrician had strung the wires

232

about in such a haphazard way that hanging a picture was to risk electrocution. A ventilation duct in the bathroom turned out to be only a few inches deep—it was only a little grating set into the wall over the shower but with nothing behind it. It turned out that the loft insulation in the attic had been left in big round bales and never laid on the floor. Finally after much trial and error they assembled a team of competent workmen, but there had been many, many false starts.

It was like *Mr. Blandings Builds His Dream House*, but much less funny. The pattern was that something, perhaps the water pump, would fail to work and a plumber would be called to repair it. The process would take all day and require a few trips to distant specialist shops. The plumber and his mate would work diligently on the pump and related apparatus. They would screw and unscrew things; they would attach one thing to another; they would stand back and look at it; they would connect switches and bark instructions to each other. After long hours spent addressing the problem, the workmen would assure Małgorzata that *now* it would work. *Now* they had got to the bottom of the problem, and now at last it was in working order! But more than likely the mechanism would still fail to function. Małgorzata called it "heroic incompetence".

Once when we were standing in the utility room where the washing machine and the central heating boiler were, Małgorzata pointed to the exhaust duct for the gas-fired central heating. "You see that duct? It should go outside, of course, but it leads directly into the kitchen."

"What!" I said, horrified. "But you could be poisoned with carbon monoxide!"

"Yes, but don't worry, it doesn't work."

Małgorzata and Andrzej Koraszewski at their kitchen table in their new house in Dobrzyń nad Wisła in 1998.

When they had first arrived there had been a mouse problem. Mice were in the pantry and the basement. Soon they put down poison for the mice, but then a neighbour, hearing of their infestation, gave them a young cat to catch the mice. She had been in a litter of a stray cat in the town and was still scrawny at four or five months. By the time I saw her a few weeks later she was a beautiful, glossy-coated, lively cat who pounced on everything that even looked as though it might move. She was a sociable brown tabby with golden eyes and a patch of white around her mouth and chin. When Andrzej had been asked what to call her, he had immediately suggested—for no reason he could ever later remember—the Swedish name, Pia. There was still no Darwin to match his pre-selected name, but they now had a tabby cat named Pia.

Pia looked like a very promising mouser, but the problem was that the mice had already been poisoned, and if Pia ate them she might be poisoned, too. For this reason, the cat had to be kept away from the mice at all costs. When Małgorzata and Andrzej went to the cellar to clear out the rubbish that had accumulated there, Pia had to be restrained from following them and investigating the interesting mouse odours that wafted up to her. Before long we were used to having a cat that had to be protected from mice, and it became almost normal.

As we explored the area around the house and on the slope down to the Vistula, we found odd structures: an old well and the foundations of something that had probably been used by the Germans during the War. There had apparently been an encampment about here, some sort of fortification on the river.

234

That winter of '98-'99 was one of the hardest on record locally and the temperatures dipped into the minus numbers Fahrenheit and reached -27 Celsius. Most things were covered with snow. The river was frozen and we walked out on it and a bit upriver. Local men would sometimes go out to the deeper part and try to fish through the ice, but on some days they must have had to bore down a foot or more to reach the water.

We didn't stay out for very long at a time, but every day we would cut up some wood from the old broken-down orchard and bring it back to the house in a wheelbarrow. There were baskets by the fireplaces to hold the wood, and we had fires every day to augment the central heating. It was cosy in the house by the fire when there was a blizzard raging outside on a grey afternoon that imperceptibly turned into an early evening.

One day when it wasn't snowing I offered to help Małgorzata investigate a midden at the side of the barn/garage. She wanted to know what exactly was in it: whether it was organic waste or household junk or what. It turned out to be old broken furniture and dishes and miscellaneous rubbish. As we poked around we found a white dinner plate that was a bit scratched, but not broken. As we looked at it and turned it over we noticed a swastika on the underside of it. A souvenir of the German occupation! It was creepy to realize that this Nazi plate had held food 54 years before when some iron-crossed duelling-scarred SS officer might have eaten from it. Małgorzata had first thought it might be usable as something to put under a plant pot, but then on reflection she realized that she really didn't want it in her house. I also realized that I didn't want it in my house, either, but I offered to take it away and give it to the Imperial War Museum.

Later, back in London, I phoned the Imperial War Museum and spoke to a curator. I described my plate and explained where I had found it. He recognized my description of the mark on the bottom—it was made by a certain ceramics works in Munich in 1942—but he had to decline my offer. I wasn't trying to sell the object, it was understood that it was just a public-spirited gift; however, he couldn't be sure of its authenticity.

"But I found it in a rubbish heap in Poland," I said. "It would hardly be a forgery." But a museum curator can't be too careful. Apparently you never know who's out there manufacturing phony Nazi dinner plates. Of course it does have to be authenticated, but I didn't see how anyone could authenticate it without at least looking at it, and as many things in museums were found far from where they originated, I wondered how they could discount my plate. I was sure that it was entirely authentic, and I still didn't want it around the house. Nor did I want to contact some private collector of Nazi memorabilia, of whom there are no doubt many. I still have the wretched thing.

When I had arrived at their house in mid-December Małgorzata had shown me the translation work we were going to do. We had agreed to do some more of Jan Twardowski's poems because a Polish editor had contacted us about a bilingual volume. The editor hadn't told us which poems she wanted, but we decided to go ahead anyway and do the ones we thought were best. Or rather, the ones Małgorzata thought were best, because I had no opinion one way or the other about the Polish texts, which I still couldn't read. We adapted our usual *modus operandi* to the new house. We set up shop in the living room on the dining table with all our dictionaries and scrap paper. Pia was intrigued and undertook to keep the scrap paper in line and kill a pen or two if need be.

We worked diligently on the poems, poring over the texts and discussing every line. We sipped coffee and tea and peeled oranges and apples. I would suggest various renderings of some line and Małgorzata would ponder their accuracy. We talked about register and verb tenses. We talked about Polish customs and sayings. There were puns and obscure references. I learned, indelibly, the Polish word for "kingfisher": *zimorodek*. When Małgorzata started to prepare a meal, I took a draft of a poem with me to the kitchen so that I could ask her some questions while she mixed the ingredients of the dish of the day. She was using a Swedish cookbook and muttering in Swedish under her breath from time to time as I read my English versions of Twardowski's poems, and then she would pause to explain some point in Polish grammar to me. This scene has stayed with me: the cookbook and the mixing bowl and Małgorzata commuting among the three languages at the kitchen table.

By New Year's Eve we had finished the whole sheaf of 50 poems and all that remained of the work was for me to take it home and mull over a few little details. We decided to celebrate the New Year with a proper little party for the three of us. We had a light *kolacja* and then a further spread around midnight with pickled herrings and some other delicacies. Andrzej got out a tape they had had since the 1960s, when it had been smuggled into Poland by a student friend of theirs. And what was this hot property that had to be smuggled into Poland? It was a tape of Tom Lehrer's songs, satirical comments on the scene in the United States in about 1964 or 1965. I remembered several of them, but Małgorzata and Andrzej knew them all by heart.

"But," I said, a bit slow on the uptake, "why did they have to be smuggled? What was objectionable about them? After all, the satire is all directed at the United States. You'd think the Polish authorities might like something that made fun of the American government or society."

"That's just the point," Małgorzata told me. "Lehrer was free to make fun of it! It was that freedom that was so exciting to us and so feared by the authorities here." We went on listening to the tape, and I tried to think how it would have sounded 30 years before in Poland, and I remembered how we had taken it for granted that Lehrer could sing unfettered about "National Brotherhood Week" and "Poisoning Pigeons in the Park".

Małgorzata had also once told me about the arrival of cowboy movies in Poland after the thaw of 1956. I had loved cowboy movies as a child. Roy Rogers and his magnificent palomino, Trigger, were the idols of every American child of my generation. I had grown up assuming—if I thought about it at all—that people in other countries wouldn't be interested in our entertainment because they would have their own. It had come as a great surprise to me years later when I discovered that Roy Rogers and all the rest of the cowboy pantheon were as entertaining to Europeans as they were to us. Małgorzata told me that only people over 16 or 18 were allowed to watch Western films when she was a girl, but she had seen them when she was only 13.

"I always looked older than I was," she said, smiling at the memory of those Westerns.

But I was outgrowing them by that age. In the late '50s when there was a fad for "adult Westerns" on prime-time television, I wasn't very interested in them any more. (The popular joke was that "adult Westerns" meant Westerns with plots over 21 years old. The plots were different, of course, and relied less on Trigger's personality and more on inter-human relationships.) So why should Western movies, with all that harmless galloping around on desert locations and all those stylized gun fights, be available only to people over 16? As usual, I couldn't see what would have been remarkable about them to a Polish audience in the '50s, except for the exotic locations.

"So what could have been objectionable about them?" I asked Małgorzata.

"Oh, plenty!" she replied. "Those people were self-governing. They punished criminals and there was a sense of right and wrong, with the bad people being put in jail at the end. The sheriff and his men went after the thieves or bank robbers, and justice was done. But one of the most interesting things was to see how those people lived 100 years ago in the USA. We had been told that the poverty in the USA was indescribable, really dreadful, but here were these frontier people living better than people in the present-day Polish countryside!"

I tried to think what kind of mod cons she had seen in those frontier cabins with their kerosene lamps and hitching rails. I must have looked baffled.

"They had pumps, for one thing, and not just wells and buckets for their water. And even more than that, just the sense of *freedom*! Those people could decide where to go! They could stay in the city or they could get in a wagon and go wherever they wanted! The choice was theirs! That was such a breath of fresh air for us!"

Małgorzata hadn't watched Roy Rogers in the 50s, I learned, but the more cerebral Westerns like *Stagecoach* and *High Noon*. She had never heard of Trigger, nor probably of Gene Autry and his songs around the campfire. We had been watching entirely different movies, in more ways than one.

As we sipped our wine by the fire waiting for a time signal on the radio, they told me more about their lives as students in the '60s, which bore little resemblance to my life as a student in the '60s. They were involved in some underground student activities. (My only "underground student activity" would have been a Coke and a sandwich on the lower ground floor of the Student Union Building.) When the Soviet Union invaded Czechoslovakia in 1968 and Radio Free Europe was jammed, they listened to the broadcasts through the static anyway and gleaned the facts of the Warsaw Pact invasion and tried to alert other Poles to what was going on. They bought a children's printing set and made leaflets.

"But you couldn't hand them out on the street, could you? How did you distribute them?" I asked.

"No," answered Małgorzata, "that would have been much too dangerous. We left them in public toilets and places like that. We were running a considerable risk."

Once she had been called in for a little chat with the secret police. They wanted to know about a certain clandestine meeting that had taken place, but she had maintained that it was only a birthday party. They wanted information about some of the other people at this meeting, but she said she didn't know all the other guests. It was just an ordinary birthday party.

"And was it a birthday party?" I asked.

"Of course not."

"Weren't you frightened?"

"Yes, I was frightened! But the secret police weren't as bad in the 1960s as they had been in the 1950s and during the Stalinist times. They were still bad, but you weren't likely to be summarily shot."

"After 1956," said Andrzej, "after Krushchev came to power in the Soviet Union, there were some things they just couldn't do any more. They knew the people hated them."

Other student memories were less political. During her summer vacations Małgorzata earned money by conducting surveys for a polling organisation connected to Polish Radio. Sociology students were naturals for this work, so she would ride her bicycle to various villages around Poland.

"So were these villages within reach of Warsaw by bike?" I asked.

"Oh no, we went all over the country. It wasn't just me—there were lots of others. We took our bikes on the train, and then we would be based in some small town for several days. We would all go out in different directions during the day and then come back again in the evenings."

I asked what sort of questions they had to ask. I wondered what public opinion would have been worth in Poland in the 1960s.

"Oh," Małgorzata laughed. "It wasn't about opinion. We had to ask about their *cultural* life! We went out to very poor villages and farms and asked about their cultural interests!" She shook her head at the absurdity of it. The Polish countryside was extremely poor in those days. Another story of hers concerned a woman who lived in a hayloft in a barn with her 12 children. There was no furniture—just hay. Her children were dressed in burlap sacks.

"You must have had to apologise to them for the crazy questions you had to ask," I said.

"Yes, they were so inappropriate!"

The survey was, however, quite scientific, statistically speaking, and the young survey-takers were given specific names to contact, chosen at random from the registered residents of the district. Once Małgorzata approached a dilapidated farmhouse that was even poorer and more ramshackle than any of the others she had visited.

"The house looked as though it could fall down at any moment. There was a barn or shed that was in the same condition."

She went through a broken-down gate and was immediately confronted with a huge puddle of semi-liquid manure, which she carefully skirted around to get to the house. A man came out to meet her.

"He looked like someone from a concentration camp. He was gaunt, and his clothing—well, he was just dressed in rags."

"And you had to ask him about his cultural interests!"

"He invited me into his house..." she said, and I waited for her description of the unbelievable squalor she must have found there. "And he had the largest collection of classic music recordings I have ever seen in my life! He knew a vast amount about classical music—certainly a lot more than I did. I found out later from a neighbour of his that his farm had been unusually large and prosperous. From an early age he had loved to listen to classical music, and when he inherited the farm from his parents he began to sell things, and he spent all the money—every *grosz* he could get his hands on—for these recordings of classical music! So he just sat there all the time listening to the music!"

There were some definite perks connected with doing these surveys (besides collecting stories to dine out on forever). The peculiar system for distributing commodities under the communist system extended to books. Books that everyone wanted to read sold out quickly in Warsaw, but they were still available in small towns, where the same number of copies might have been sent regardless of the number of potential customers.

"That's how I got all the Tolkien books!" she said. "You couldn't find them in Warsaw, but I would look in the little out-of-the-way kiosks in villages, and they would have ten copies that they didn't know what to do with! I found lots of good books. I took them back for my friends in Warsaw, too."

I asked Małgorzata how they felt when they were young about travel to other countries. She told me that in their student days she and Andrzej were in the Sudeten Mountains with some friends. One of them longed to set just one foot over the border into Czechoslovakia so that he could have the illusion to going to a foreign country. He found a friendly border guard who would let him do it, and with great satisfaction he carefully placed one foot squarely in another country!

But my East German friend in the 60s, Hartmut, went on his *motorroller* to Prague and Budapest and sent me large black-and-white postcards from those places. Some travel within the East Bloc must have been possible. Perhaps the Polish and East German laws differed, and—which is even more likely—perhaps the laws changed capriciously so that what was possible in 1963 was no longer possible in 1966, but was positively encouraged in 1969, and then was strictly forbidden in 1972.

One day I came into the kitchen to find Małgorzata cutting Andrzej's hair very expertly with long tapered scissors and I asked her how long they had been cutting each other's hair. They laughed and Małgorzata explained. "When we went to Sweden we had to get used to a whole new scale of prices. Things were more expensive than they had been in Poland, but there were some bargains that would have been completely impossible in Poland. One day we noticed a special offer for a trip to Paris. It was by bus and was very cheap. Andrzej saw that the fare to Paris amounted to the price of exactly ten haircuts! Instead of having his hair cut ten times he could afford a trip from Lund to Paris! After that, haircuts seemed far too expensive to bother with, at least commercial haircuts." They both wanted their hair kept in order, and so they began to cut each other's hair.

Andrzej Koraszewski at Smultronstället.

Andrzej has a scar from where his harelip was repaired, and he once told me how that happened. When he was born in the spring of 1940 the local hospital had become an army hospital for the German Wehrmacht and the surgeons were there to patch men up after battles and to remove bullets and shrapnel from their bodies. However, one of them had been a paediatric surgeon in civilian life, and now he saw a baby who needed his skill. It must have been a welcome relief after the war wounds in adult bodies. So this Wehrmacht surgeon carefully repaired the baby's hernia, cleft palate and harelip and prescribed treatment for his hepatitis. His mother couldn't understand what the doctor said and never knew his name, but Andrzej probably owes his life to this anonymous German surgeon.

At the time his mother was living in a presbytery with a priest who told everyone that she was his sister. She already had a four-year-old daughter and now a new baby. The priest was a little uneasy about public opinion when the baby arrived, but he doted on the little girl. Meanwhile, Andrzej's father, a young army major, was escaping from the massacre at Katyń by finding a bicycle and riding out through the gates of the Soviet internment camp, confidently waving his driving license as he went as though it were an official pass. He found his wife and new son at the presbytery, and the priest found himself sheltering a family of four.

243

We sometimes talked about aspects of life in Poland, and I remembered to ask Małgorzata about my puzzlement concerning public eating place and my quest for the Marxist hamburger. Maria had already told me that everyone used to eat at home, but I wondered if Małgorzata had any insight about this.

"In 1980 we had a terrible time finding any place to eat. Didn't people ever go out to eat? What did they do to enjoy themselves?"

"You've complete missed the point," Małgorzata said briskly. From anyone else this abruptness could sound irritating, but coming from Małgorzata it is somehow endearing. "You weren't supposed to enjoy yourself. You were supposed to be making the revolution."

So no Marxist hamburger, after all. I had forgotten about the puritanism of communist theory.

In Poland trying to lead an entirely honest life is like having some quirky minority interest—like being a vegan or collecting Uruguayan postage stamps.

When they moved to Poland the Koraszewskis were temporarily without health insurance and therefore needed to pay a higher charge for prescriptions. When Małgorzata went to their new GP she explained the situation and insisted on the prescription being marked correctly. Then she went to a pharmacy to have the prescription filled. As she was walking away, she discovered that she had been charged at the lower rate after all and went back to rectify the bill. The woman behind the counter was at once on the defensive, assuming that Małgorzata was complaining about the goods or wanting a refund. When she finally realized that it was a question of underpayment rather than overpayment, she didn't know what to do. The owner of the business came out and there was a long discussion. By now a considerable queue had formed, and the consensus being voiced was that they all would have been glad to be charged too little and they would have made a quick exit before the mistake was discovered. The owner was so flabbergasted that a customer was apparently complaining about paying *too little*, that he said that such honesty should be rewarded and therefore Małgorzata should not have to pay anything extra!

She shrugged when she told me about it. "You see what you're up against if you try to do things according to the rules!"

The state health insurance paid by the self-employed is in practice a flat rate based on the average monthly wage. It is very low for the well-off but too high for people just starting in business, and so it is an incentive to join the black economy, declare no income, and remain officially unemployed, since the unemployed are covered by the state health insurance scheme.

Everywhere you look, it seems, there are obstacles to efficiency, fair play, and the smooth running of the economy. At the time of writing, there is general surprise in Britain at the number of young Poles who have come there to work. Half the waitresses in London are Polish, and the plumbers and builders are legion. Maria wrote me long ago that people shouldn't leave their country just to wait until things get better. She was no doubt right, but it is hard to blame people for getting fed up.

In many other areas it is an uphill job to deal honestly and expect the same behaviour of others. The Koraszewskis' cherry orchard made a loss in successive years because the orchard manager charged them through the nose and the wholesalers reneged on their contracts and rarely paid for the cherries until they were taken to court. Now a new man has leased the orchard. His extended family harvests the cherries and he has enough local clout that the wholesaler doesn't dare try to cheat him. His only expense is the lease of the land, he shows a healthy profit, and the Koraszewskis are no longer in the red with their cherries, as it were. For once they are getting a return on their own investment, but it is because they are now dealing with an honest person who in turn can prevent the wholesalers from being dishonest.

But there are pockets of honesty in Poland, and you value them all the more when you find them.

I had such a great time with the Koraszewskis that first winter that I made it a winter habit to go back, like a mixed-up swallow, every year. The next winter we translated some aphorisms by S.J. Lec, and I took some more of my own work to do. Many changes had happened during the year, and as we both had email now, we were in touch again much as we had been when they lived in north London. The house was now white with a layer of insulating siding and a small enclosed porch had been added. Over the door of the porch was a rustic wooden sign made by a Swedish friend that read "*Smultronstället*", which means "the place of wild strawberries", a name Małgorzata and Andrzej had given their country retreat, and is a Swedish expression meaning a place where you have everything you most desire. (This is the allusion in the title of the Bergman film, *Wild Strawberries*.) The loft of the garage had been turned into a small theatre space for children's plays. Andrzej had wanted to have the house thatched but the rafters weren't suitable, so he now turned his attention to the barn/garage and was thinking of having it thatched. The old orchard had been cleared up and the rubbish in and around the big outbuilding had disappeared.

The children's theatre gave me an idea. There is a charming little play by Lope de Rueda, *The Olives*, dating from the mid-16th century that I thought might be suitable. I had already translated it from Spanish, and when I went home I got it out and sent it to Małgorzata, who then translated it into Polish. The Polish teacher at the school was enthusiastic and the children and their parents made some costumes. I have often wondered if any of those children went on to study literature and had the chance to say, "Oh yes, Lope de Rueda. We put on a *paso* of his when I was in school in Dobrzyń." It could change somebody's stereotype of rural Poland.

A cousin of Andrzej's raised Polish sheepdogs and produced a perfect Darwin. The young Darwin had been a pale, almost white, puppy who then, Małgorzata told me, grew almost before their eyes. From one day to the next, certainly from one week to the next, he got bigger. When I finally met him he was huge but still growing. His coat had become a pale straw colour and his big soft ears were light brown. He was not a pure-bred sheepdog; his father had been an unknown interloper in the kennels. He looked to me like something between a golden retriever and a Pyrenean sheep dog. His coat was so thick that from some angles he looked a little like a sheep himself. He had turned into a great friendly hulk who adored everyone who came to the house and greeted them extravagantly with much tail-wagging and leaping about. If someone appeared to read the gas meter or install a water pump Darwin greeted him as though he were a long-lost master. Darwin would be taken out for walks without a collar and lead and would sometimes follow strangers home. The fact was, he was sweet tempered but decidedly dim witted.

"So," I said, summing up the situation, "you have a cat who has to be protected from mice and a watchdog who loves everyone and won't go outside." Małgorzata nodded.

Darwin had a doghouse but refused to use it. It was a palace of a doghouse, and to prove it, Małgorzata took me out to see it. There was a fenced-off run like a front garden at the side of the garage where the old pigsty had been. Inside was the doghouse. The whole doghouse, roof and all, was inside this shed. Inside the doghouse was a soft dog-mattress. In dog terms, the accommodation was five-star stuff. In the early winter of 1999, witless Darwin had left his sumptuous doghouse and gone and lain on the icy back step of the house until he had contracted pneumonia. The vet had come and prescribed antibiotics and a lot of indoor coddling. Darwin had loved being inside the warm house and being fed dog-delicacies and had then refused ever to leave it again for any length of time. Małgorzata took pity on him and sided with the dog when Andrzej wanted to put him back out again after he recovered from the pneumonia. Darwin, whose name had preceded him, was firmly established as a house pet, if not quite the lapdog he apparently would have preferred.

Pia, meanwhile, was clearly appalled at this enormous, unpredictable creature who was slobbering around her own house on huge yellow paws. She withdrew in horrified hauteur for a while. When they met she arched her back and hissed, but Darwin often failed to take the hint and came close and sniffed at her, wagging his tail all the time. She soon learned that he was harmless and stupid, and with some claws in his nose now and then to remind him of his place in the hierarchy, Pia was in control of the situation again.

My later annual winter visits have followed the pattern we set in the beginning. I arrive sometime in December or January and stay for about three weeks. We sometimes work on a translation together and sometimes I use the time for some undisturbed work of my own: book reviews, a translation of Jacques Prévert, or my own poems. Two long poems I wrote about my first two visits were published by Hearing Eye under the title *Friends in the Country*. We enjoy meals together and continue discussions we started by e-mail. We go shopping at the new supermarket in Włocławek and at the Tuesday market on one side of the main square in Dobrzyń. We take walks down to the river in the snow and look at the strange orange patch where the water doesn't freeze. We think it is a hot spring, as the whole area is dotted with thermal springs.

Małgorzata and I have made a few school visits in Dobrzyń and Włocławek. We talk to the final year English classes about our translations of Jan Twardowski and give the pupils a chance to talk to a native speaker. They have been friendly, intelligent pupils and it has been a pleasure to talk to them. One class in Dobrzyń gave me a hand-made card that they had all signed, and in Włocławek Małgorzata and I were each given a long-stemmed red rose.

At the Koraszewskis' I once met Małgorzata's old university friend Inka, who had been in the Warsaw Ghetto as a child. After the last of the Jews had been rounded up and sent off to death camps in 1943, Polish workers were sent into the Ghetto to clear up the refuse left behind, and one of them found Inka, aged 4, in a sewer pipe. Her parents, about to be forced into the cattle wagons and knowing what was in store for them, had hidden their little daughter in the best place they could think of, hoping against hope that she might be found by a kind person and allowed to live. Inka had the good luck to be found by such a person. The workman took her out of the Ghetto under his coat and gave her to a children's home in Warsaw that was known to shelter Jewish children. After the War she was adopted by a non-Jewish Polish couple. It was only when she was 18 and her adoptive mother was dying that she was told the truth about her origins. After that, with the help of the Red Cross and other organisations she was able to trace her biological family and even discovered some relatives in Israel and Britain.

One day in the new millennium Inka, who was involved with an organisation called the Children of the Holocaust, contacted Małgorzata to ask if she could translate some pages to go on their internet site. Małgorzata then asked me if I would help with this project and I agreed at once. From time to time now we have something from the Children of the Holocaust to translate—a report of an annual meeting, a description of a school project they have organised, or an account of a conference. As this isn't a literary effort, we find we can do it by email.

There are usually a blizzard or two and picturesque snowdrifts. A second dog, Emma (named after the wife of Charles Darwin), put in an appearance a few years ago. She arrived one day and made a shameless play for poor Darwin, who fell for her wiles. She was a stray but suspiciously tame.

"If we had let her stay in the house, there would be nothing left of the house," Małgorzata told me by email. Emma demolished anything she could get between her jaws. Her previous owners were probably very relieved when someone else took her over, and they had kept a low profile when Małgorzata and Andrzej were trying to find out who Emma belonged to.

(Recently, however, Emma has had a complete change of personality and now lives in the house.)

It is uneventful at the Koraszewskis' country retreat, at least in the winter. In the summer it is a different story, because the trees are in fruit and the large cherry orchard where the onion fields used to be is a commercial business. But in the winter it is an idyllic if frosty place to hole up with some books and a laptop and celebrate a now long-standing friendship.

Before I fly home from Warsaw I always spend a few days with my friends there, too. They are the Mach family, Maria Wnuk and her family and Witek Dębski. Maria and Witek and I attend some sort of exhibition and sometimes we go to a concert or opera in the evening. Ania or her friend Agnieszka Kołodziejska meets me and takes me to the Mach flat, where I sleep on a convertible sofa. (There are a cat and dog there, too, who both sniff me and my clothes carefully, gleaning information about Darwin and Pia.) Latterly, it is only Ania who meets me, as Agnieszka is now living and working in London.

I stay in Warsaw with the Mach family, whom I met 17 years ago on a kayak trip, but now it is young Ania who is easiest to talk to. In the meantime she has grown up into a woman in her 20s, a graduate in English from Warsaw University. Her father Tomek sometimes makes use of her interpreting skill when we are all together, but when she is not available he manages in English and has a surprisingly large vocabulary for someone who has apparently just picked up the language. With Ula, on the other hand, I now have conversations in Spanish. She took up the language as a hobby a few years ago with a Chilean teacher and is now fluent in it.

(clockwise) Maria Wnuk, Ania Mach, Tomek Mach, Ula Mach, and Agnieszka Kołodziejska at kolacja *around the Machs' dinner table.*

Sarah and Maria after another night at the opera.

Once when I was in Warsaw before I had fallen into the habit of staying with the Machs, Ania Bentkowska, a friend from Medical Aid, had lent me the flat that she still owned in the Mokotów district. It was near a metro station and in an interesting neighbourhood. Her flat was in an old building with a courtyard on one side and a prison on the other. The flat itself seemed faintly French to me for some reason. The floorboards were in a herringbone pattern and there were high ceilings and tall windows. It was early summer and light streamed in through the trees in the courtyard.

Nearby there was a large florist shop, and one afternoon when I went to see Maria Wnuk I took her a big bouquet, knowing how much she would like it and knowing what second nature it was for Poles to take each other flowers. Somewhere among the nearby streets there must have been the dry cleaner's

251

Ania once described to me. She used to take coats and other garments there to be cleaned, but one day when she went with an armload of clothes, everything was different. For one thing, it didn't smell like a dry cleaner's, and for another thing there were no racks of cleaned clothes in plastic bags. There was no indication that it was a dry cleaner's at all, although the sign was still up and the place seemed to be open for business. About the only thing in the room was a table with a woman sitting at it reading a newspaper. Ania asked if this was a dry cleaner's, and without looking up the woman said yes; Ania asked if she could have her clothes cleaned, and the woman said no. When Ania asked for an explanation, the woman told her curtly that the business was no longer private but state run. The proprietors would be paid a salary regardless of what they actually did, so of course they were doing nothing. Ania had to go and find another dry cleaner who still cleaned clothing.

Witold Dębski, Maria Wnuk and Sarah in Maria's flat in Żoliborz.

On one of my days in Warsaw with the Machs, Maria Wnuk comes to visit, often with Witek Dębski, and they take me away for the day. Ania and I refer to this as the "kidnap plan". "Mrs. Wnuk is going to kidnap you on Sunday," she reports to me. "She has some opera tickets."

I then usually reply, with a dramatic show of alarm, "Oh, please! As long as it's not Wagner again!" And then we laugh, because she knows I am devoted to "Mrs. Wnuk", that old friend of her father's, the widow of her father's old co-worker and mentor. In fact, over the years we have gone to performances of Puccini, Rossini, and Mozart. I can't complain.

I'm grateful to Maria, and she always says I am her excuse for a cultural outing.

The first time Maria came to the Mach flat to "kidnap" me for the day, the dog, Morka, went bananas. Maria wasn't even in sight of the flat yet when the dog barked and raced around; she wanted her pack to know that she could sense a stranger on the stairway. "Unknown person in the building! Danger! *Uwaga!*" We couldn't hear ourselves think. When Maria finally appeared at the door, the dog went into further hysterics. Maria came in, calmly looked at the dog and stood still while Morka ventured near her and gave her boots a thorough sniff. I saw how at ease Maria was with this dog and thought of Fyzia of happy memory, the dog in the old photo Maria sent me when we had first begun to write to each other. Morka finally finished her sniffing and reluctantly gave up barking, content that she had done her duty. Maria then patted the dog and sat down on the sofa as though the normal way of entering a friend's flat was to be frisked by a scatty guard dog.

At the end of the theatre evening there is another familiar pattern. Maria and I and sometimes Ania or Witek are at a concert hall or opera theatre, and we wait at the door for Tomek to come and pick us up. It is usually a wild and stormy night with snowdrifts. Tomek arrives with a flourish in his Rover. Witek goes off to catch his bus home, too, but we ladies are scooped up by Tomek. Maria protests that she can easily catch a bus, but Tomek sternly orders her into his car: he will take her home and that's that, no back-talk, look at the weather! It's out of the question, get into the car at once!

You don't have to know Polish to understand what he is saying. Maria relents and thanks him and we all drive up to Żoliborz. It is dark and the streets glitter with the streetlights and the car lights and, increasingly, with neon advertising signs. There was a lot of bustle around the theatre, but late at night in the suburbs the traffic is thin. After we drop Maria off, Tomek heads back on the riverside parkway, the oddly Italianate *Wisłostrada*, and speeds back almost to the Poniatowski Bridge, where he turns toward the city. Then we are back in the bright lights of the Mach flat having a nightcap and talking about the performance, the dog barking as though she's never seen me before.

Ania Mach and Maria Wnuk on a bench in Łazienki Park in Warsaw.

Sometimes when I meet Maria in Warsaw she takes me to lunch at one of her discoveries. One hot summer day she takes me to the big town hall on the Plac Bankowy. It is a big old palatial-looking office building with numerous entrances. She takes me through a door and then through a bewildering maze of halls and stairways. Finally we come to a plain door behind which is the staff canteen. It seems that after a certain time the general public can use this place, always assuming they can find it.

She parks me at a table and then goes to examine the food supply. I think it is one of those confusing (to a foreigner) places where you pay for the food first. She gives me a rough choice, "You like pork *kotlet* or fish?" and then she deals with the details. We sit by an open window looking out over the Plac Bankowy and the tramlines and the shops on the other side of Marszałkowska Street. A refreshing breeze comes through the window and ruffles the light curtains (which are themselves plain and without ruffles). Afterwards we think about coffee and I decide to see what *kawa normalna* is. "Normal coffee" can't be too unusual, and is probably just black filter coffee or something like that.

Of course it's not. It is awful Turkish coffee, a glass with coffee grounds taking up the bottom third of it. The glass is too hot to touch and the undrinkable murky coffee has grounds drifting around in it. (When I told Małgorzata about this, she said, "I always thought *kawa normalna* was horrible stuff! I didn't know they still made it.")

Another place Maria has found is near her St. Stanisław Kostka church in Żoliborz. This is a new office building for the local council just up the street from Plac Wilsona. It, too, has a staff canteen, but in the basement. Sometimes Maria and Witek and I go there on a winter afternoon when we are on our way to her flat, which is a short tram ride farther north. As before, I sit at our table while she and Witek go and corral the cutlery, soup, and plate of pork and cabbage or whatever the specialty is. I don't know how Maria finds these places, but I think it is a little game of hers to discover these out-of-the-way and unsuspected eating establishments.

Once Maria and Witek and I were at the national theatre waiting for a concert to begin when Maria told me about a former co-worker of hers. During the War he had been held with many other men in the national theatre. They were lined up in the front row of the balcony and shot, and the bodies fell down into the stalls. Her co-worker avoided being shot by falling over into the stalls with some others before the bullet came. He lay there for several hours until the German soldiers left, and then he extricated himself from the corpses around him and crept out of the building. I looked up at the balcony, now all gilt and plush. I thought of a line of young men along the front, all keeling over into the stalls far below. "It wasn't this theatre," Maria said. "This is new. The old one was destroyed."

Maria Wnuk and Witek Dębski in a theatre where no one was shot.

255

Chapter Seventeen

Too Far From the Herd

As the 1990s went on and the new millennium got under way, I met a few new Poles and deepened my contact with the ones I already knew. The ripples continued to spread. Sometimes I was surprised at where they went.

Staszek and Mirka and their two children, Małgosia and Paweł, and the black labrador, Caesar, lived with Maria. She had converted Staszek's old room, where I had stayed on my first visits to her, into a bedsitter for herself. She had her old typewriter on a desk and around the walls were pictures she had painted on her excursions with her artist friends. But now Staszek had bought some land on the northern outskirts of Warsaw in Białołęka and they were going to build a house there. For a few years, whenever I visited Maria I would be shown a new video of the progress of the house. First it was only a lot with some scrubby bushes. Then, as it was going to be in a development with some other houses, there appeared water and sewage pipes. Then the foundations were dug and the outline of the house appeared on the ground. Later the outside walls went up and the roof went on. I was told about the plans for the interior of the house; the children's rooms, the kitchen, the patio.

Recently they have begun to spend more time out at their new house. It is summer now, and they go there for weekends and treat it as a picnic place. One Sunday afternoon in August Maria and Witek and I are taken out to Białołęka for a barbeque. We have a tour of the house, now more or less livable, and then Staszek sets up the barbeque grill on the patio. Caesar romps around in his new domain. We all sit at the table on the raised terrace, and we visitors take turns congratulating them on their new house.

Maria Wnuk and her granddaughter Małgosia Wnuk at Staszek and Mirka's new house in Białołęka.

A barbeque on the terrace at Staszek and Mirka's new house in Białołęka: Mirka, Paweł, and Staszek Wnuk, Witek Dębski, Sarah and Maria.

I am pleased for all of them: Staszek and Mirka, the children, and Maria. Maria will have her flat back to herself, but her family will drop in often. In fact, as the children's schools—and later Małgosia's college where she studies psychology—are in Warsaw and not very convenient to Białołęka, the children are going to stay with their grandmother on certain days during the week. Agnieszka and the other grandchildren also come for visits.

Sarah and Maria Wnuk, her grandson Kuba, Ania Mach and Ula Mach after seeing a performance of Tschaikowsky's Romeo and Juliet.

I often think of Maria's life from her girlhood in Pilawy, the war years, the hard postwar 50s, her marriage and children. I think of the months of her life she must have spent in queues. She and Włodek may have been architects, but under the Communist regime they could never have designed and built their own house in the suburbs. Staszek bought some ready-made blueprints and was free to have his own house built on a plot of land. Maria must take a vicarious pleasure in this, too, knowing infinitely more than I do about what has gone before and what the contrast is with her earlier life.

Just as people in this part of the world can live in two or three different countries without leaving their house, so these days they can change their street address while staying in the same house. Now the new city authorities in Warsaw—and all over Poland—are busy renaming the streets. Some, like Nowy Świat, weren't changed by the Communists, and so they remain the same, but others were renamed for Communist Party officials or People's Heroes or whatever, and now the Poles are gleefully reclaiming them. While they're at it, they are naming streets up and down the country after the Pope. Now a main thoroughfare in Warsaw is Jana Pawła II, and there is hardly a town of any size in the land without its own Jan Paweł II Street. It has become the Station Road of Poland.

One summer I had an email from Ania Mach asking me if I could put her and her university friend Agnieszka up for a few days. They wanted to come to London and they needed a cheap place to stay. I met them at Heathrow and gave them the sofa bed in my living room. After that they came a few more times, once during the following winter to do some research for their MAs at the British Library. I took them there and showed them how to apply for a reader's ticket and how to use the catalogues in the reading room.

A year or two later they were back in London, preparing to start from there on a tour of Scotland. I had to go to Glasgow myself to visit my elderly mother-in-law, so I gave them a lift there, and then, encouraged by the presence of students to lapse into a student mode myself, I gave them a tour of Glasgow University. To whet their appetite for the Highlands, I drove them along Loch Lomond, across to Arrochar, and on as far as Inveraray. After that they went off to Edinburgh and Inverness and soaked up the Scottish atmosphere by themselves. As our travel plans coincided closely, I picked them up again the next week at Luton, where they had flown from Inverness, and drove them on home.

After that when I was in Warsaw I would see both Ania and Agnieszka, and sometimes Agnieszka's father, Gwidon, if he wasn't away on a cargo ship or tanker, would meet me at the bus and take me to the Machs' flat. I met some other friends of theirs and gave a poetry reading and discussion at their English department at the University of Warsaw.

A meal after the poetry reading at the University of Warsaw: Ania Mach, Ania Fadlallah, Sarah, Renata Senktas, and Agnieszka Kołodziejska at the Tokio restaurant in Dobra St.

Ania had a job with a magazine for learners of English, and she also translated technical material for a translation agency. Agnieszka taught briefly and then worked in the editorial department of the Academy of Science on an upper floor of the Palace of Culture and Science. She had a truly stunning view out over the city, but before long she decided to swap it for a view over another city.

On one of their forays around London Agnieszka had formed the idea of coming back to get a job. Starbucks in Covent Garden seemed like a good place to start, and so she gave in her notice at the editorial department high above Warsaw and arrived in London to become one of the thousands of Polish waitresses and *baristas* in the capital. She was a conscientious worker at Starbucks and introduced me to Sumatran coffee, but before long she had found an office job at the same shipping firm her father worked for. Now it was she who had to issue papers for her father and the other ship captains to sign concerning the state of the ship and its cargo and the repairs in dry dock.

One autumn Agnieszka's parents came to visit her in London, and she asked me to go with her to the airport to meet them. I was glad to meet Agnieszka's mother and repay Gwidon for the times he had met me at the bus or airport in Warsaw. We drove down to Gatwick one afternoon in early November and collected them. I wondered if they thought that this London airport was as close to central London as Okęcie was to central Warsaw. (Okęcie, now renamed the Frederic Chopin Airport, is one of the few international airports in Europe that is inside the city limits.) As we drove on the evening motorways through Surrey and then Kent I imagined them wondering where on earth London *was*. As Agnieszka was living in Archway then, they had quite a tour of London even after we finally hit the southern suburbs.

The next day I met them again and we went to a performance of *The Messiah* at St. Martin's-in-the-Fields, eating a light meal downstairs in the crypt restaurant first. (It is good to eat before tackling the whole *Messiah*, I always think.) Although the restaurant at St. Martin's isn't particularly lugubrious, it *ought* to be. There are gravestones underfoot. Shouldn't that be a pretty lugubrious element in a *restaurant*? "Here lyeth Elizabeth ye wife of William." If you drop your fork and look down, is that what you want to see? The lighting is subdued, perhaps with even more reason than in an ordinary restaurant. However, upstairs the music was ravishing. Gwidon and Maria had apparently never heard *The Messiah* all the way through, although they were both former students at a music academy. I think I missed the details of how they became a ship captain and an economist, respectively, after their grounding in music. And how do I know them, exactly? They are the parents of a young woman whose university friend is the daughter of a co-worker of the late husband of Maria Wnuk.

And what of Magda in Wrocław? In the years after The Flood I went to see Magda Lachaut, the ace tour guide and champion of the reputation of Vratislavian restaurants. She married Nicoł, and their kitchen seemed to be papered with pictures of themselves in various foreign locations; they were generally either skiing or sitting on terraces with the Mediterranean Sea in the background. The young couple resembled each other somewhat—medium height, brown hair, an exuberant laugh. Nicoł had studied history at the local university and then decided that what he really wanted to do was to spend most of his time skiing, so he started a travel agency with escorted trips to French and Swiss ski slopes. Magda was an avid skier, too, and I would get postcards from her from the Val d'Isère and such places. They both worked hard, but they were doing a job they had devised for themselves. Magda also wanted to be a translator, and so she went to further classes and acquired a certificate to translate official documents from English to Polish, but she really hankered to do literary translations. I gave her what feeble advice I could. She helped organise multinational conferences in Wrocław and did some interpreting between French and Polish or English and Polish as the occasion demanded.

I sometimes combined my trips to Warsaw with a side trip to Wrocław. I would arrive at Okęcie airport and get a return ticket for Wrocław, dated for the last few days of my stay in Poland. When my Varsovians delivered me back to the airport I then took a domestic flight to Wrocław for a long weekend, coming back to Warsaw in time for my flight to London. Nicoł would meet me at the airport when Magda was working. He was becoming a rising young entrepreneur. In fact, there was an article about him in a national news magazine about new innovative businessmen in Poland. They had a flat near the centre of the city within walking distance of the impressive town hall square and the castle-like train station where we had rushed on that morning in 1997 before the floodwaters came. it was the same station where, in 1980, I had last seen young Mariusz with his father.

Magda Lachaut on the town hall square in Wrocław in front of one of the excellent cafés of the city.

One evening the three of us went to the restaurant in the town hall, but there was no resemblance at all to the bleak canteen of 1980 where Alastair and I tried to find something palatable. Now there were two or three very upmarket restaurants. We went to one with a medieval theme. The Gothic arches of the town hall cellar were decorated with heraldic banners, but there was none of the phoney "serving wench" tat of "medieval" restaurants in Britain. This excursion was another of Magda's demonstrations to me that Wrocław was simply heaving with first-rate restaurants.

It is only a matter of time before the rest of the world discovers Wrocław as a new tourist destination. Every time I go there I am struck by some interesting new thing I hadn't noticed before. One year I suddenly noticed all the *art nouveau* architecture. I had seen the distinctive continental *Jugendstil* architecture in Helsinki and had somehow got sensitised to it, so that when I saw it the next time I was in Wrocław, it leapt out at me. The big town-hall square is a delight. I always like to go there just to look at all the old Flemish (as they seem to me) façades. Besides the town hall in the middle of the square, there is a little clump of narrow streets and small shops there, too. Sometimes when we need to arrange a meeting place, I lobby for The Griffin on the square.

The University is a venerable institution, and I always think of Brahms and his "Academic Festival Overture", which he wrote for it when it was the University of Breslau and Poland didn't exist on the map. Magda took me to an exhibition about the history of Wrocław at the University. Up on the top floor of the old, rather rococo, building on the Odra there were panels with pictures of the city at different times in history. I was intrigued by the Breslau phase, when the city, then as now, was the capital of Lower Silesia. It was a fashionable German city up until the end of the War, when Poland was forcibly moved west as the agreement at Yalta sliced off a wide strip of the country in the east and added another strip in the west and Silesia and Pomerania became Polish again.

Sarah and Magda Lachaut at one of the fine restaurants in Wrocław.

Magda drops me off at the Panorama Rakławicka, one of the sights of Wrocław. It was finished in 1894 to be exhibited in Lviv (the new name for Lvov). After the War the Soviets allowed Poland to have some of the art treasures in Lviv, and in 1946 it was taken in a rolled-up form and stored in various places and restored by various artists, and eventually displayed when a special building was built for it in Wrocław. These "panoramas" used to be popular entertainment in the 19th century, and I have seen one other in The Hague, the Panorama Mesdag. There are very few of them left nowadays, and the Panorama Racławicka is the only one in Poland. At the Panorama Racławicka you enter through a ticket office and bookshop. Every hour or so a new group is allowed into the main chamber. You go up a flight of steps and come out on a circular viewing platform.

This platform is in the centre of a rotunda covered by an immense painted canvas realistically depicting in 360 degrees the Battle of Racławice in 1794. Led by Tadeusz Kościuszko, Polish armies fight Czarist Russian forces. In the end the Poles were defeated, but it was a heroic defeat that has gone down in Polish history as a glorious event. Now on the canvas armies converge, banners flutter in the breeze, Tadeusz Kościuszko bestrides his horse; men drag canons, fire muskets, and brandish sabres. A detachment of peasants, invited to the battle by Kościuszko, march with their scythes and attack the Russian position. Dead horses and soldiers sprawl about. At one side we see some terrified peasants at their tumble-down shack, caught in the middle of the battle. This battle was fought in what is now Ukraine but was then the Galician region of Poland. The Panorama catches a moment when the Polish forces seem to be winning and the Russians are in retreat. The battle was fought in early April, but the earth seems very dry and the bare spiky trees emphasize the desolation of the landscape. Is somebody going to plant a crop here in this field, clearing away the bodies and the chunks of metal? Looking at the Battle of Racławice, I think no wonder their descendants went to Pittsburgh.

One evening Magda and I go to visit a university friend of hers, Monika, who is a child psychologist. Her husband is out of town on business, so it is only the three of us. Monika's small son Michał is playing in an adjoining room and has eaten earlier. We three have *kolacja* in the kitchen and then adjourn to the living room for coffee and more conversation. It's nice to see Magda and her old friend together, and I am glad to meet Monika. They both lived at home while going to the local university, and many of their classmates must also be fellow Wrocław-ites. I never had that experience myself, and I wonder what it must be like. I always went away from home to study, and my classmates were from everywhere. I never had this sense of overlapping communities after high school.

Magda and Monika tell me about someone they know. He was a child of 6 or 7 at the time of Stalin's death in 1953. At school it had been impressed upon the children that Stalin was more important even than their own fathers; that Stalin was their "first daddy" and the other one was a poor second. The boy and all his classmates were devastated on that day in March 1953 when they were told by a grieving teacher that their "first daddy" had died. The boy went home crying uncontrollably. At home his parents and some friends were having an anniversary get-together. The boy came in and told them the dreadful news: that Stalin, his first daddy, had died. Suddenly the party erupted and all the grown-ups were shrieking with joy. The child was shocked and indignant and threatened to tell his teacher about their unseemly behaviour. The child's innocent indignation could have meant death or deportation for his parents, so before the next day dawned they had found a different school for the boy.

Michał comes in to speak to his mother and present me with a small gift. He is a reserved but self-possessed boy of about 10. He has a seashell he found at the beach, and he wants to give it to me. I am really touched by the boy's thoughtfulness and generosity, and I thank him sincerely. In a moment he leaves again to continue playing in his room next door. Before long it is his bedtime, and his mother tells him that if we are making too much noise, he can sleep in his parents' bedroom at the other end of the hall. But Michał says something softly that seems to be negative, and both Magda and Monika chuckle indulgently. Then Magda says to me, "He said that he doesn't want to sleep in the other room because it's too far from the herd."

I have visited Magda in both summer and winter. I have scuffed along the snowy streets in heavy boots and I've resisted the heat in sandals. We are in frequent touch by email. I take my responsibilities as an Honorary Aunt seriously and dispense advice, usually but not always by request. Magda takes it all in good humour. When she comes to London on family business we usually get together and end up in a London restaurant, nearly the match of the splendid ones in Wrocław.

I was at an international PEN congress in Helsinki in 1998 when the host centre invited anyone who wanted to take part to visit a local member in his or her own home and have dinner and get acquainted. I was put in a group of five other miscellaneous congress-goers to visit a certain Kristi in the suburbs. A big cab arrived to take us there, and as I got into the cab I thought I heard some familiar Polish words. I didn't know any of the others in this group or what country they might be from.

"Is that Polish I hear?" I asked.

The delegate from the Writers-in-Exile Center in New York answered me. "Yes. How did you know?"

"Well, I've heard Polish before. I have some Polish friends. In fact, I've collaborated with a Polish colleague on some translations of Jan Twardowski." Any Pole would know Twardowski's work, and I thought she would be suitably impressed, even though we hadn't published much yet.

"Where do you live?"

"London."

"Who was the Polish person you translated with?"

I thought it was extremely unlikely that she would have heard of Małgorzata, but to satisfy her—and perhaps to let her see how pointless her question was—I answered, "Małgorzata Koraszewska."

Now the Polish-American delegate broke into a huge smile. "Gosia! Our mothers were close friends and Gosia and I knew each other as children!"

This was Anna Frajlich, a poet and teacher at Columbia University. Her sister Felicja was sitting next to her, and together they exclaimed about their old friend "Gosia". I was thunderstruck. They both knew Andrzej, too, and had visited them in their home in London. How had I managed to meet friends of Małgorzata's in a taxicab in Helsinki? (And furthermore, friends who referred to Małgorzata by a diminutive. She and Andrzej both intensely dislike Polish diminutives and never use them, even to each other. The only person I know of who is allowed to call Małgorzata by a diminutive is her mother. Perhaps people who knew her as a small child can get away with it, too.)

Later Małgorzata, who is never impressed by mere coincidence, said, "Well, you're both writers, you were at a conference of writers, and you met. There's nothing so surprising about that." Still, I have met lots of writers who *don't* know Małgorzata (at least I think they don't), and how did I happen to meet her old girlhood chum in a taxi in Helsinki, when I live in London and the chum lives in New York? And how could I ever explain to Anna Frajlich the odd chain of events that had led from the train conversation of 20 years before to the present moment?

Chapter Eighteen

Bardzo Dziękuję!

Now sometimes when I am in Warsaw I remember when I was first there in that grey city with the wide streets and so little traffic. Alastair and I braved those streets on our bicycles and learned to avoid the tram lines. It was an alien place with citizens who wanted to trade their złoty for our dollars or pounds. It was ruled by a dictatorship that exported some good and medium quality stuff and left the remainder for its citizens, a dictatorship that engineered shortages so that ordinary commodities could be dispensed as favours. It is hard for a protest demonstration to form when the would-be members of it have to spend so much of their time in queues. By the time we left Poland in 1980 we felt as though we had somehow combined tourism with prison visiting.

Poland was a country on the map, a place that had given the United States many American scholars and baseball players (and, legendarily, the entire Notre Dame University football team, known as the Fighting Irish). Poland was the scene of the most shocking atrocities of World War II, and a country that remained occupied long after the War ended; it was a land that *sounded* remote. I had no connection whatsoever with it either by kinship or culture. There was no reason for me ever to have any connection with it, other than a brief bicycle tour one summer in my 30s, made because I was curious to have a look at the place. How can it be that now it and many of its inhabitants are so firmly a part of my life? How have I accumulated all these Polish friends and experiences? Why have I found myself on kayak trips on (and in) Polish rivers? Why should I be the "honorary aunt" of a Polish woman and the co-translator of the poetry of a Polish priest? How did I end up travelling across Belgium and Germany to Katowice with a

271

Polish driver and a load of medical supplies and then get behind the scenes in so many hospitals and orphanages? How does it happen that I am in Poland now at least once a year?

My Polish connection in London is not negligible either. We meet for lunch or take each other to films or lectures. Now and then there is even a reception or book launch at the Polish embassy in Portland Place. I don't see my old friends as often as I did when we met at the Medical Aid for Poland office in Earls Court on Fridays, but they are valued friends all the same. They invite me to the annual MAPF AGM and Christmas party at the Polish Community Centre in Hammersmith or the Polish Church in Ealing and I go, happy to meet old friends and eat poppy-seed *makowiec* and hear them sing Christmas carols I still don't know the words to. A priest blesses the *opłatek* and we go around snapping off bits of each other's wafer and wishing each other a merry Christmas and a happy New Year. But what am I doing there, I who never had any connection whatsoever with Poland?

The answer to all these varied questions is simple. The origin was that brief encounter on a train. Maria and I often speak of it. We were in the same compartment on the train to Wrocław that August and we got into a conversation. She showed me pictures of her family. But we might not have had any conversation if it had not been for Mariusz, the little boy who wanted to share all his snacks with the other passengers.

It is true that our train conversation might never have had any follow-up if I hadn't sent her our leftover money, which then weighed on her conscience, or if Hanna Mazaraki had not been visiting her and provided a convenient way to send me an amber brooch. But the real cause of the whole chain reaction was Mariusz. Maria never knew, or soon forgot, the boy's last name. He was a 12-year-old who lived in Wrocław in 1980. He would now be in his late 30s and might live anywhere. Perhaps he is still in Wrocław and now with a wife and children. Perhaps he is a teacher or an engineer or a businessman. He will remember the time he went on the train to his grandma in Warsaw when his mother or stepmother was having a baby. Although it was important to him at the time, he may have forgotten how he asked his fellow passengers to share his biscuits and snacks, how disappointed he was when the foreign woman in the corner kept refusing him, and how she finally relented and accepted an orange biscuit. There is no reason for him to remember such a detail after all these years. Neither of us would recognize the other in the street.

Years have passed since my first acquaintance with Poland. Now I can not only pronounce "Krakowskie Przedmieście" but even spell it. Thanks to my regular visits to Poland, I know the Polish for "herring", "earmuffs", "cat litter" and "wholesale". I can find my way around parts of Warsaw without a map. It's not too late to learn some Polish properly, even if wholesale herrings, earmuffs, and cat litter are not much help. I can still identify myself as a piranha if the conversation turns to fishy alter egos, which so far it never has.

I would be much poorer without the experience of My Poles. They don't all know each other. The London, Warsaw and Wrocław contingents are mostly separate, but some of them have heard of the others. Sometimes when my travel plans involve several people who don't know each other, they need to exchange messages and arrange contingency plans. Sometimes one of my Poles will mention another one familiarly, although they have never met. They are in separate spheres, but are still all My Poles. They are like the arms of the Odra in Wrocław, meeting and diverging; running parallel, detouring in opposite directions, then nearly converging again.

The pleasure and stimulation of their acquaintance have been with me for so long that they have become part of the fabric of my life. The city flats I frequent in Poland have become a whole series of second homes, and the Koraszewskis have welcomed me as a transient member of their household. I wouldn't have missed the whole experience, but I so easily might have.

Once I saw a demonstration of how a chain reaction worked. The floor of a room had been completely covered with set mousetraps, and on each little trigger where the bait goes there was a carefully balanced ping-pong ball. A man stood at the door of the room and tossed another ping-pong ball into the midst of all the mousetraps, and soon the room looked like the inside of a popcorn popper. The ping-pong balls bounced madly in all directions, setting off mousetraps and causing more and more ping-pong balls to be sprung according to some exponential progression. The prime mover was the man at the door with the extra ping-pong ball. Sometimes I think of this as a metaphor for Mariusz' role in my career with all my Poles. If I ever met Mariusz again I could only say, "Thank you, Mariusz. *Bardzo dziękuję.*"